Scamming the Scammers

Don Mullan

Paperbooks Ltd
The Old Fire Station, 140 Tabernacle Street, London, EC2A 4SD
info@legend-paperbooks.co.uk www.legendpress.co.uk

Contents © Don Mullan 2014

The right of the above author to be identified as the author of this work has been asserted in accordance with the Copyright, Designs and Patent Act 1988. British Library Cataloguing in Publication Data available.

Print ISBN 978-1-9093957-4-9
Ebook ISBN 978-1-9093957-5-6

Set in Times
Printed by Lightning Source

Cover design by Gudrun Jobst www.yotedesign.com

Don Mullan is the author of the acclaimed bestsellers, *Eyewitness Bloody Sunday* (Wolfhound Press, 1997) and *The Dublin and Monaghan Bombings* (Wolfhound Press, 2000). He has edited and authored several books including his boyhood memoir, *The Boy Who Wanted to Fly* (Legend Press, 2010), *The Prophesy of Robert Louis Stevenson* (a little book company, 2009) and *The Narrative of Frederick Douglass* (a little book company, 2011).

Mullan was co-producer and associate producer on a trilogy of award-winning movies that explore the Northern Ireland conflict: Bloody Sunday (2002); Omagh (2004) and Five Minutes of Heaven (2009).

Don is the concept developer of the Pele Peace Medal and the Desmond and Leah Tutu Peace Choir. In 1984 he attended the inauguration of President Nelson Mandela as the guest of Archbishop Desmond Tutu. In March 2009, Mullan was welcomed by the Brazilian football legend, Pelé, as the first European Ambassador to represent the Pelé Little Prince Hospital, Curitiba, Brazil. He is currently working on projects exploring the themes of Sport for Development and Peace.

Acknowledgements

I would like to thank the following for their invaluable support in the production of this book: Rebecca Woodworth, sister of the late Patricia Christine Sowens, for speaking to me about her loss and sharing with me Christine's diary; my publisher, Tom Chalmers of Legend Press and his colleagues, Lucy Chamberlain and Lauren Parsons, for their belief in the concept; my editor, Jennifer Armstrong, for her invaluable advice and assistance.

Seamus Cashman was my first publisher and who has become a wonderful friend and mentor over the years. It is my privilege to dedicate this book to Seamus.

During lunch in New York a few years ago, Ruth Vitale, former co-president of Paramount Classic and the current CEO at The Film Collective, Los Angeles, laughed heartily when I told her about my Lazar Scam. She encouraged me to continue with my scamming odyssey and has remained interested. I owe much to Ruth's encouragement for the completion of this book and I am happy to also dedicate this book to her. I would also like to thank her colleagues, Michael Barlow, Alan Greenspan and Robyn Morrison, for their interest and encouragement.

I must also acknowledge interest shown by Alexandra Parent and her sister Mary.

Finally I would like to thank my family and friends for their patience and kindness during my many hours of silence and absence during the books creation.

To the memory of
Patricia Christine Sowens
whose beautiful and productive life is one of many
destroyed by a 419 Scam

To my first publisher
friend and mentor
Seamus Cashman

and to Ruth Vitale
whose warmth, encouragement and kindness
contributed to this books creation

"If we climb high enough, we will reach a height from which tragedy ceases to look tragic."
Irvin D. Yalom, *When Nietzsche Wept*

Contents

Introduction

At the heart of this book are four sets of email correspondence. Each began with an unsolicited email that I received and recognised as an Internet scam. Each scam was modelled on what is known as the Nigerian 419 advance-fee fraud, named after the article of the Nigerian Criminal Code that deals with obtaining property by false pretences, or cheating.

Such emails have been turning up in my inbox for at least a decade and my response is almost always to hit the delete button. I say 'almost always' because the arrival of a particular email on 25 April 2007 caught my attention. It was identical to one sent to me the previous day, but a change of code in the subject line, from 'lqumz' to 'lusutpblz', caused me to pause. What did it mean? Was it some sort of reference system to enable the scammer to track different lists of emails?

I began to think about the methods scammers might use to hook and then reel in their victims. Many questions invaded my mind. Why do scammers do what they do? Is it a lucrative industry with a chain of command, or is there more to it? Am I correct in assuming that a scammer would not be able to manipulate me? What money/information would this particular scammer try to obtain? Could I create a plausible scenario to waste this scammer's time for as long as possible? How would he or she react to being messed about? Wanting the scammer to know what it feels like to be on the wrong end of a frustrating scam, I decided to reply.

The exchanges reproduced here demonstrate how amoral the scammers are and their indifference to the consequences of their actions and the lives they can and do ruin. They reveal various tactics and strategies used to convince their victims that they are trustworthy. I began to recognise these patterns and summarise my findings later in the book. The scammers deal in lies. I countered with fiction. As well as engaging with various scammers, I also examined reports of notorious cases and read interviews. These are discussed and offer fascinating insights into this shameful and depraved industry. We should all be part of the fight to prevent Internet scams and protect vulnerable people and I end the book by looking at some of the steps we can take.

First, however, I invite you to join me in the fantasy worlds of the saintly Nod and Catherine Nallum and their associates, Bart Ahern, Biggles and Fr Jonathan Ross; of Pastor Patricio, Supreme Head of the Church of Serendipity, and his Parisian friends, Michael and Minnie Moose; of downtrodden Karol Joseph Wojtyla Breen and his playful partner, Annie Denver; and of the 3rd Marquess of Miserly-Scholes of Stoke-on-Trent and his PA/lover, Lady Sarah Macbeth. Please remember that these are fictional characters whose attitudes and opinions sometimes differ quite significantly from my own!

In the first scam I have included initial commemtary to help the reader understand my thinking as each email was received. However, after a short time the commentary ceases so that the reader can encounter the exchange without interruption.

Lazar Scam

24 April 2007
From: l.vukadinovic@gawab.com
To: ABCD@efg.com
Sent: Tuesday, April 25, 2007 1:16 AM
Subject: From Lazar   lusutpblz

VERY IMPORTANT AND URGENT REQUEST
Please I will be honored if you can respond to this great request, I know it's not easy, but by the will of God you can do something, my name Lazar, I am 61years old, born in Belgrade, I have been successful in business this past years, married but divorced, now I am living with my adopted daughter Angela, couple of months back I was diagnosed with Leukemia, and the doctors said, the virus have eating deep into my system, the sad news is that I was told that I have only two months to live, dying is not what I am scared of, because at 60 I have lived my life, I am only concern about my 16years old girl, what will become of her after I am gone, I am writing this letter of trust to you, based on my ignorant of who you are, but I believe if you are in my shoes, someone will show compassion on you, but I pray God will not put you in this situation, I am not soliciting for financial aid, what seeking, is a new life for my daughter in the hands of a responsible and honest individual or family, if you are have receive this message, please respond as soon as possible, to save a young girls future, do not worry about what it will cost to take care of this girl, I have over five million dollars in a private account, this money will be kept in your trust for investment, and the income generated will be used for her feeding, education and other material things, you will be rewarded greatly for this kindness. Please if you can help in this regards, please write to me as soon as you can, or just a word of prayer and comfort will help me, until I hear from you.

Sincerely
Lazar

Does anybody fall for such emails? Would a concerned father really offer his daughter to a complete stranger via the Internet? Maybe greed trumps common sense when someone sees 'over five million dollars' in an email. But what happens when the scammer gets a bite? To find out, I created a new email account, reversed my name and started typing.

25 April 2007
From: ABCD@efg.com
To: l.vukadinovic@gawab.com
Sent: Wednesday, April 25, 2007 11:00 AM
Subject: Re: From Lazar lusutpblz

Dear Lazar
You are in my prayers. What must I do to help you?
Nod Nallum

26 April 2007
From: l.vukadinovich@yahoo.com.au
To: ABCD@efg.com
Sent: Thursday, April 26, 2007 9:10 AM
Subject: Thank you for the prayers

Dear Nod Nallum,
Your prayers is what i need most, if God can turn my situation around, i will be very glad to take care of my daughter, i have not lived a better life, my life is full of sad stories, i was alcoholic, and a gambling addict, i was a very wealthy man, i lost everything because of heavy drinking and gambling, my wife filed for a divorce, she took everything that i have left, i was about to take my life, but was stopped by a female childhood friend, she encouraged me, that i can start all over again, i took her advice, quit drinking and gambling for good, i went into mining of precious stones, i came back on my feet again, unfortunately, lost my friend, she never witnessed my new beginning, i refused to marry again, i decided to adopt Angela, she is my Angela, and everything i live for, my heart was broken after i realized am ill and about to die, i have lived my life, i need her to start a better life, and i need you good help to make this dream come true, i need someone to take care of her dreams, make sure she is sheltered and fulfill her dreams, she is god fearing and a nice girl to relate with.
     If you can assist me in this way, i owe you a lot in this life, and God will pay

you in the life hereafter, please write a little more about yourself ok.
Take care
Lazar

What's a little emotional blackmail between friends? All the same, you would need to be a particularly trusting person to be sucked in by this fraudster. Interestingly, the sender's email address has changed to an Australian Yahoo account. I'm intrigued to find out where our correspondence will lead.

From: ABCD@efg.com
To: l.vukadinovich@yahoo.com.au
Sent: Thursday, April 26, 2007 4:55 PM
Subject: Re: Thank you for the prayers

Dear Lazar
I am a middle-aged professional man with a family of five children ranging in ages from 8 to 23. I commute between the UK and Ireland and travel extensively with my work globally. We have a wonderful home and a very happy environment. I wish you well with all your hopes. If we can be of assistance, we look forward to hearing from you.
Kind regards
Nod

27 April 2007
From: L. Vukadinovic
To: ABCD@efg.com
Sent: Friday, April 27, 2007 8:44 AM
Subject: Re: Thank you for the prayers

Dear Sir,
If you wish to help, i certainly need that help from you very soon, whatever you will do to keep Angela safe for me while i am gone, please do that and i will kindly reward you.
Lazar

From: ABCD@efg.com
To: L. Vukadinovic
Sent: Friday, April 27, 2007 9:56 AM
Subject: Re: Thank you for the prayers

Dear Lazar

I need you to give me specific instructions about what you want me to do. Once I am clear on that, I hope to offer you the kind of help you need to ensure the ongoing safety of Angela.
Kind regards
Nod

From: L. Vukadinovic
To: ABCD@efg.com
Sent: Friday, April 27, 2007 12:05 PM
Subject: needed more information

Dear Sir,
please note the following information, the doctors said my situation is critical, its my dream that she grow up to be somebody in life, and since i will not be around to see that dream come to pass, i am requesting that she find a place of comfort in a good family, what i want you to understand is that she is young, and she cannot start a better life on her own without the supervision of adult, i want you to be my trustee or beneficiary to what i am leaving behind, i mean you can be the executor to all my estates, i have some funds in the bank, the money will be put into investment, and the income will be used to care for her education and material needs, this does not include buying of illegal substances, like hard Drugs, weed of any kind, she can get any money she will need for academic materials, clothing and food, but the real capital will not be handed over to her at anytime, i dont know if you do understand what i am trying to say, please do let me know if you need further clarification ok.
I wait to hear from you soon.
Sincerely
Michael

Michael? Is this a slip-up?

From: ABCD@efg.com
To: L. Vukadinovic
Sent: Friday, April 27, 2007 2:39 PM
Subject: Re: needed more information

Michael?
I understood I was communicating with Lazar. All that you outline is reasonable. Nothing that any caring parent would not wish for their own children. We (my wife and I and our family) can meet all your requirements. Now all we need, given your urgent situation, is clear instructions regarding how we can advance the situation to ensure your wishes regarding Angela are fulfilled.

Kind regards
Nod

28 April 2007
From: Michael Smith
To: ABCD@efg.com
Sent: Saturday, April 28, 2007 9:33 AM
Subject: From Lazar's Attorney

Dear Sir,
My name is Michael Smith, this is to inform you that, my client Dr. Lazar Vukadinovic, passed away this morning, below is the last message you sent to his ID, please you can contact me for further information regarding his request, Angela his daughter is with me temporally.
Looking forward to hearing from you
Michael Smith Esq.,
Faase Chambers & Associates
[72 Edison Crescent Sunning Hills] (Address given is a private house in a residential suberb of north Johannesburg)
Tel: +27-832440955

RIP Lazar. Now to deal with the lawyer and, no doubt, his legal fees.

29 April 2007
From: ABCD@efg.com
To: Michael Smith
Sent: Sunday, April 29, 2007 12:56 PM
Subject: Re: From Lazar's Attorney

Dear Mr Smith
We are so dreadfully saddened to learn of Lazar's sudden passing. I had hoped we might become friends before he finally succumbed to his illness. Now what is important is to ensure that poor young Angela is taken care of. Tell me what we must do to advance the wishes of the late Dr Lazar Vukadinovic. I presume there are legal papers and the exchanging of bank details, etc.

Would it be possible for us to begin communicating with Angela? My daughters would especially like to get to know their future sister.

With kindest best wishes and gratitude for all that you did and continue to do to help our dear friend Lazar.
Sincerely
Nod

From: Michael Smith
To: ABCD@efg.com
Sent: Sunday, April 29, 2007 2:18 PM
Subject: Re: From Lazar's Attorney

Dear Sir,
It was a shocking news, although his death was anticipated, but I did not believe it will this soon, but there is nothing to worry about, I will make sure all that he wished will come to pass, he left a promissory note, in that note he indicated that he wanted you to take care of Angela, he promised you and your family the sum of five hundred thousand dollars, if you accept to take care of her, and you will be trustee over his estate and all pecuniary legacies, the sum of five million dollars will be kept in your trust, this money will be put into investment, and the profit withal will be used for Angela's education, material expenses, any illicit materials, like hard drugs and so on are not allowed at her disposal, she will get any money she needed for important things, but the real money will not be handed over to her at any time, if you are too old to keep her legacy, the next family member, likely your spouse will take control of the legacy.

I will draw up the legal process to be completed, so Angela can be handed over to you as her new Guardian, follow up will be setting up a trustee in your name, before all money involved will be transferred to your account, it must be one step at a time, please be informed that his funeral rights is coming up tomorrow, Angela will be with me temporally until all legal papers for her to join your family will be completed, I will personally come with her to meet with you, in order to complete her father's wishes, if there is any further information you will need, please contact me quickly.
Sincerely
Michael Smith Esq.,

I'm rich! $500,000 as a golden handshake plus $5 million in a trust fund and the only stipulation is that we don't feed Angela weed or hard drugs.

From: ABCD@efg.com
To: Michael Smith
Sent: Sunday, April 29, 2007 11:41 PM
Subject: Re: From Lazar's Attorney

Dear Sir
Thank you for informing me of this. I have access to a private jet. I have discussed this with my wife and we feel it would be appropriate for us to travel to the funeral to be with Angela during this distressing time. Please give us the

details of where and when. We are ready to travel this evening, if necessary.
Yours sincerely
Dr Nod Nallum

30 April 2007
From: Michael Smith
To: ABCD@efg.com
Sent: Monday, April 30, 2007 8:45 AM
Subject: Re: From Lazar's Attorney

Attention: Dr. Nod Nallum,
Dear Sir,
Thank you, for your recent message, I hope you are doing great today? I must confess that I am really surprise to read you last message, I thought over the contents throughout the night, I cannot find the single word to qualify your humanity, people like you are very hard to come by, and wherever Lazar is at this moment, he will forever be happy to have meet someone like you, and I must also forward my respect to your wife, she is a woman with integrity, to understand what it is for someone to lose love ones, but in all this, I regret to let you know that the funeral took place on Sunday, and I did not see your mail until this morning when I got to my office, sorry about that, but your kindness will not go unrewarded, its ok you save the high cost of flying your Jet thousands of miles from Britain to Africa, I guess it can be used for other important things, what do you think?

I have prepared to start the necessary paper work to have all this estate and pecuniary legacy put in your trust, and it good to let you know, that there are some legal cost the paper work will cost, below you will find the necessary legal work to be done.

Administrative Work:
1. Letter of Administration: USD$50.00
2. Affidavit of Claim: USD$150.75
3. Transfer of Title Deed: USD$275.85
4. Copy of your ID required (passport of D/License)
Once it have been agreed that you are to take care charge of Lazars legacy, a court written confirmation must be obtained, it is in form of a Certificate called "Grant Probate" this is a proof to the authorities and the rest of the world that the deceased man's estate and all pecuniary legacy is vested on you, below this, is the information on how to apply for the "Grant"

Application for a Grant:
A. form 38 (white application form)   USD$20.00

B. form 44 (blue form for capital tax calculations)   USD$790.00
C. form 37B (yellow form for listing real property)   USD$115.75
D. form 40 (yellow form for listing stock & Shares)   USD$75.45
Total Cost: USD$1,477.85 not Incl. Vat & Disbursements

As soon as all this paper works are put in place, we are ready to make the final move, to bring the young girl over to you, and the entire pecuniary legacy keep in your trust, then we know the next step forward.
I wait to get your confirmation on these procedures.
Sincerely
Michael Smith Esq.,

I'll set aside the fact that he thought all night about an email that he then claimed he didn't see until the next morning, because it looks like we are finally getting down to business. Lazar has been conveniently laid to rest and, of course, various legal fees must now be paid to advance the process.

From: ABCD@efg.com
To: Michael Smith
Sent: Monday, April 30, 2007 2:45 PM
Subject: Re: From Lazar's Attorney

Dear Mr Smith
We are saddened that we were unable to be with Angela for the interment of her closest guardian. Please let Angela know that we were very near to her during this past weekend.

I have your accounts to hand. Please advise me how I should transfer this money to you so that all necessary paperwork can be completed.

Also, we are close friends with a South African Government Minister who is also a lawyer. He will be happy to recommend a legal firm to work with you to ensure that all is handled in a proper and entirely legal manner. Is it okay if I have our lawyer in South Africa contact you directly on our behalf?
Yours sincerely
Dr Nallum

From: Michael Smith
To: ABCD@efg.com
Sent: Monday, April 30, 2007 4:36 PM
Subject: Your Contact information

Dear Dr. Nod Nallum,
Thank you for your email, its good to understand that you are family with

Government official here, but i will advice that its not appropriate to complicate matters, especially where two lawyers from different firm, handling one matter, i can take care of the process, moreover Lazar trusted me with his paper work, so i will advice we work this out without any complication, there are two different ways you can have the money transfered down here to cover the work, bank to bank transfer, and the other is much easier and faster, and that is the Moneygram International Money Transfer, if you are using the Moneygram Money Transfer, please use the information given below,

Name: Michael Joseph Smith
Address: [Edison Crescent Sunning Hills]
City: Johannesburg
Country: South Africa
Tel: 0832440955

Please kindly include your contact information in your next email.
Sincerely
Michael

He's probably trying to establish who I am. I need to create an illusion that has him searching in the wrong place.

From: ABCD@efg.com
To: Michael Smith
Sent: Monday, April 30, 2007 5:49 PM
Subject: Re: Your Contact information

Dear Michael
I will have the money transferred tomorrow morning as soon as the banks open. Please send me your account details and I will have it processed immediately. This is far less complicated than an international MoneyGram transfer.

I will trust you on this dear Michael. Lazar, I sense, was a wonderful man and if he trusted you, then I do also, implicitly.

I have investments in Bloemfontein and Uitenhage, South Africa and in nearby Swaziland and Lesotho, which are considerable. Once this matter has been concluded satisfactorily and Angela is entrusted to our care, it might be that we will engage your company again. I need a good solicitor whom I can trust from afar.
With kindest regards.
Yours sincerely
Nod Nallum
President

A Book Company Depot
West Sussex
UK

1 May 2007
From: Michael Smith
To: ABCD@efg.com
Sent: Tuesday, May 01, 2007 1:24 PM
Subject: Re: Your Contact information

Dear Sir,
Thank you for your email, i will be greatful if you engage us as your legal representative here, but we will talk more about that after this legal matters are taken care off, somtimes i will like to speak to you over the phone for urgent matters, so i will be honored if you forward your telephone number to me. Today is a public holiday here in South Africa, do the banks open today in UK? anyways, find below the account information that you will use to make the transfer as soon as possible.

Bank Account Details:
Name of Bank: HSBC London
Account No: 57026622
Swift Code: MIDLGB22
Beneficiary: Mr. I Nahanna
Swift Code: RNNSZAJJ

Please send information relating to the transfer once it is done, if you are interested in Communicating with Angela, you can write to her with this email account, its for her father l.vukadinovich@yahoo.com.au.
Looking forward to hearing from you
Sincerely
Michael Smith Esq.,

I wonder if HSBC is aware that one of its accounts is used in Internet scams. I'll follow it up with the bank, but for now, here's me as a 'new' dad!

From: ABCD@efg.com
To: l.vukadinovich@yahoo.com.au
Sent: Tuesday, May 01, 2007 2:20 PM
Subject: Hello Angela from your 'new' Dad

Don Mullan

Dear Angela

Greetings from the UK where, I hope, you will come to be with us shortly. My wife and children are looking forward to welcoming you.

We are so very sorry about the loss of your father, Lazar. We had hoped to be with you for the funeral but, unfortunately, Mr Smith, your father's trusted solicitor, did not receive our email until after the burial.

Please tell me something about you, Angela, and your hopes for when you come to be with us. What music do you like? What hobbies do you enjoy? Is there anything we can get to really make you happy?

We live in Sussex, England, in a beautiful home. You will have your own bedroom and we will help you to decorate it whatever way you want.

Our five children are looking forward to your arrival amongst us. Toby (8), Samantha (13), Julian (15), Kate (18) and Trevor (23) have asked me to send you their best wishes.

Take care dear Angela. Mrs Nallum, your new mum, and I send you our kindest best wishes.

Sincerely

'Dad'

PS. I know I can never be a substitute for Lazar, but I promised him that I would be good to you and I promise you that I will be.

From: ABCD@efg.com
To: Michael Smith
Sent: Tuesday, May 01, 2007 4:50 PM
Subject: Re: Your Contact information

Dear Michael

Yes, while it is May 1st, banks in the UK are open today. My bank has contacted me about the money transfer and raised two matters:

1. The expenses you outline are not inclusive of VAT and disbursements. Please advise me what these are and add them to the bill so that I can transfer the total amount.

2. They have asked me to check that the account you gave me is correct. It is an HSBC London account and not in the name of you or your solicitor's firm.

I look forward to hearing from you.

Sincerely

Nod

PS. I have written to Angela and told her we are really looking forward to her coming to live with us. We hope to hear from her soon.

21

2 May 2007
From: Michael Smith
To: ABCD@efg.com
Sent: Wednesday, May 02, 2007 7:48 AM
Subject: Re: Your Contact information

Dear Friend,
the bank information is correct, you can make the transfer with this information, the beneficiary is a solicitor in this firm, please note that matters like this we normally use this account, we only receive our legal fees with the firm's account, if the bank transfer will be a problem for you, you can use the other transfer alternative that i gave to you, there are some taxes charge for this documents, i did not include it, because i do not have the exact figure, but we can say approximately it will be an additional USD$275.17, so we are looking at an amount of USD$1,753.02

I was visiting your website, i saw few important information about your business, but we will talk more about that later, can i reach through the contact numbers on in your website? well i hope to hear from you soon, please send reference information to me as soon as you confirm the transfer is complete.

I will be sending you a copy of the agreement of Guardianship, this is a first step to take Angela under your protection.
Sincerely
Michael J Smith Esq.,

I wonder what website he was looking at? I think my best approach is to distract him with a kick in the nuts.

From: ABCD@efg.com
To: Michael Smith
Sent: Wednesday, May 02, 2007 3:44 PM
Subject: Re: Your Contact information

Dear Michael
My bank manager has sown seeds of doubt that are disturbing me. He says it is very unusual that I would be asked to make a payment into a London account for services rendered by a solicitor's firm in South Africa. He suggests that this might be an Internet scam.

I do not want to believe it as I had grown to like Lazar before his sudden and untimely death and also because I gave a commitment to our deceased friend to look after young Angela.

Please assure me that this is an entirely bona fide arrangement. For the purpose of satisfying my financial advisers, please explain why I am being

asked to lodge money into a London account when you are in South Africa. The bank manager has encouraged me to have my own lawyer deal with you on this matter to ensure that everything is legal, particularly since it involves the transfer of guardianship of a minor to a foreigner. I trust this will be okay as we both wish to ensure that Angela's welfare is managed in an entirely appropriate manner and in accordance with the wishes of Lazar. Don't worry, I will pay for your costs as well as my solicitor's.
Yours sincerely
Dr Nallum

3 May 2007
From: Michael Smith
To: ABCD@efg.com
Sent: Thursday, May 03, 2007 9:35 AM
Subject: Message

Dear Dr. Nallum,
Scam, Scam, that is the only thing the western Countries think about Africa, they were our colonial masters, enslaved us, because they never believed in us, they never think anything good can come out of us, this is totally wrong and unacceptable, after reading your message, and what your bank said, I was totally down, what is unusual if we use a bank based in England, does that mean we are not entitle to save in a bank that is not in our own place of birth, that is total meaningless to me, the account given to you is a Renes account, and it is routed to South Africa, is quicker, you are familiar here in south Africa, you should know what I am talking about, honestly I don't understand.

I am sorry if I am sounding very insensitive; please inform your bank they should forget about transferring the funds, I am very familiar with the banks in England, I know how irresponsible they can be, I did my master degree in England, and so I am not a novice to the system there, forgive me, for what I am about to tell you, will not sound nice, I am not interested in convincing your bank in anyway, I have a wife and 4 lovely kids living in the States, my wife can also be kind to take care of Angela if it becomes too hard, please with all due respect I am not ready to disclosed Lazars classified documents to unauthorized person or solicitor, he is not stupid to have left Angela in my care, I will take care of her.
Please send my regards to your wife and kids
Take care,
Michael Smith Esq.,

'Smith' is claiming the high moral ground. He is right about the exploitation and abuse of Africa by Western countries, but should realise that his

actions are feeding Western prejudices and damaging Africa's reputation.

From: ABCD@efg.com
To: Michael Smith
Sent: Thursday, May 03, 2007 10:01 AM
Subject: Re: Message

Dear Mr Smith
I am quite taken aback by the tone and contents of your latest email. My bank manager asked legitimate questions and gave sensible advice. What is wrong with this?

You are not entitled to change the wishes of Lazar. He asked me to take care of Angela and I, in consultation with my family, agreed to do so. I fully intend to fulfil that commitment to our dead friend.

My wife and I will fly to South Africa next Wednesday. We are bringing two of our children, Kate and Julian. We would like to meet you and Angela there and we will hand over the money you have requested in cash. We will spend a week there to help you with the various legal documents necessary for the transfer of Angela to our care in the UK. This will also give Angela time to get to know us.

We will have our lawyer with us to ensure that everything is handled in an entirely proper way. In this regard I have asked my friend in the South African Government to recommend a good solicitor and also to investigate what is involved in having Angela transferred to our care.
Please advise where we shall meet. I look forward to hearing from you.
Yours sincerely
Dr Nallum

From: Michael Smith
To: ABCD@efg.com
Sent: Thursday, May 03, 2007 10:31 AM
Subject: Re: Message

Dear Sir,
I am sorry, but that will not be possible, i am his attorney, i have the right to keep the young girl, if things are not going on well, i do not intend to change lazars wish, but its my responsibility to make sure his daughter is safe, which was his first priority.
Sincerely
Michael

I think I need to soften my approach!

From: ABCD@efg.com
To: Michael Smith
Sent: Thursday, May 03, 2007 2:25 PM
Subject: Re: Message

Dear Mr Smith

I would like to resolve this amicably. I believe that my family will offer Angela a wonderfully loving and safe home. I wish to avoid any acrimonious dispute with you. What can we do to bring this to a happy conclusion for, first and foremost, Angela?

We have decided to continue with our journey to South Africa as planned. We still hope to meet you and Angela next Thursday or shortly thereafter.
Respectfully
Dr Nallum

From: L. Vukadinovic
To: ABCD@efg.com
Sent: Thursday, May 03, 2007 5:20 PM
Subject: Re: Hello Angela from your 'new' Dad

Dear Sir,

this is angela, i got your email, i was so happy to hear from you, i am still trying to recovr from my loss, but i am doing firne now, i will be very happy to meet with your family in UK, i hope i will be welcomed, but there is something i dnot understand, Mr Smith said he is having some differences with you, sir please i will be happy if you can resolve it, he is a good man, and i believe you are the same, i dont want my dads dream to go in vain, so please help me achive it, i love teddy bears, but i will love to get there before my room will be organised, i will hear from you later
Angela

4 May 2007
From: ABCD@efg.com
To: L. Vukadinovic
Sent: Friday, May 04, 2007 8:50 AM
Subject: Re: Hello Angela from your 'new' Dad

Dear Angela

My wife and I did not sleep very well last night worrying about you. The loss you have suffered is terrible. My wife cried thinking about how lonely you must be feeling and all she wanted to do was to enfold you in her arms and kiss away your tears. Please know, dear Angela, that we will try to fill the terrible void in your life with all the love we have.

We will get you the most beautiful teddy bear from Harrods in London. During the mid-term school holiday, we usually have a family vacation in New York, where we will bring you to the famous toy store FAO Schwarz. Believe me, you will have the choice there of getting a teddy to snuggle beside you in bed at night or to fill – from floor to ceiling – a full corner of your bedroom!

Angela, please understand, we are not in a dispute with Mr Smith. I know he is carrying out the wishes of your father. My wife and I, plus two of our children, will be flying to South Africa next Wednesday to meet you and him. We can take care of all the paperwork and legal requirements then and I will pay him the money he requires.

Please don't worry. These are things to concern adults only. I wish Mr Smith had not told you about this as it's not a dispute over you. It's really about making sure your father's wishes are properly handled in your very best interests. Believe me Angela, all will be well and I know you will be very happy with us.

We are so excited about meeting you. We will spend a week in South Africa and really want to get to know you. Who knows, if all the necessary paperwork can be completed on time, maybe you will be ready to fly back to the UK with us to begin your new life. Wouldn't that be wonderful?

With all good wishes and with much love and kisses from your new family.

I love you.

'Dad'

PS. If you feel comfortable calling me 'Dad', I'd love it. 'Sir' seems a much too formal and distant title from my new daughter.

5 May 2007
From: Michael Smith
To: ABCD@efg.com
Sent: Saturday, May 05, 2007 1:54 PM
Subject: Re: Message

Dear Mr. Dr. Nallum,

How are you doing today? i want you to understand that i do not hold anything against you, neither am i saying you are a racist, something it is hard to really deal with colored people, because everything they think about you is racial, i will also want this matter to be settle amicably, because the young girl is kind of worried, and i dont appreciate that at all, we set a plan to handle this matter, before the bank interupted the process, at the first instance, i told you to have this money sent via moneygram, you resisted and decided to use bank transfer, i would have gone half way with this legal papers, Dr. Lazar have got some investment in Ghana as well, and all this must be included in the transfer of trustship, i will be travelling to Ghana to get some documents, if you want this process to be quick it will be wise you send this money via moneygram, i need to get Lazars Death Certificate, i need to present it to the authorities in Ghana, to prove his is late, and the reason to transfer his estate to you as he recommended, if it can be attained this way, it might enable Angela to fly back with your family, there are some documents she need to obtain, like travelling passport, this is my suggestion, let me know what you think.

If you agree with me, kindly let me know, so i can give you the details to use for the transferring of the money, .

Take care
Michael Smith Esq.,

Smith is nibbling again, but his email is confusing – perhaps he is attempting to mesmerise me.

From: ABCD@efg.com
To: Michael Smith
Sent: Saturday, May 05, 2007 10:52 PM
Subject: Re: Message

Dear Mr Smith
I am so glad to receive this very kind response. Both my wife and I are immensely relieved.

Since we are coming to South Africa on Wednesday, I think it will be just as quick for me to bring cash and hand it to you upon arrival. We expect to be in Johannesburg around noon. Will you and Angela have lunch with us? That would be wonderful. I am also bringing a gift for you, Mr Smith, which I'm sure you and your family will appreciate.
Sincerely
Nod

7 May 2007
From: Michael Smith
To: ABCD@efg.com
Sent: Monday, May 07, 2007 8:42 AM
Subject: important information
Attachments: Lazars Driving Licence and Passport + Bank Details

Dear Sir,
If you can delay your trip for another week, it will be fine with me, i have to be in the City of Accra Ghana tuesday evening, to present some legal documents to secure Dr. Lazar's estate and pecuniary legacy, but if you have some other

important things to do here in South Africa, you can as well come and wait for my arrival, i think this is what we have to do, since your trip is so close to date, and i cannot wait until wednesday, please let me know what your next plans are after this message, attached is a copy of Lazar's ID and bank statement in Standard Chartered Bank, High street Accra, please keep this confidential.
I will talk to you later, you never send me your contact number still.
Regards
Michael Smith Esq.,
Note: Angela will be in Durban waiting my return to South Africa.

The documents forwarded appeared to be of a stolen identity and were passed to the police in Ireland, Australia and South Africa.

From: ABCD@efg.com
To: Michael Smith
Sent: Monday, May 07, 2007 6:59 PM
Subject: Re: important information

This is wonderful news, Michael.

I've spoken with my family and our pilot, and we have decided that we will fly to Ghana first. I, for one, have always wanted to visit Ghana, primarily to see Elmina Castle, where so much trauma and tragedy was visited upon the African people, enslaved to Western inhumanity.

We will spend three nights in Ghana and then will fly on Saturday morning, 12 May, to Durban, where we hope to spend some days with dear Angela. If you have concluded your business in Accra, you will be very welcome to fly to South Africa with us.

We plan on spending Wednesday and Thursday night in the Ghanaian capital so it will be great to meet you. On Friday we will visit Elmina and its infamous castle. Where can we meet? Will you, by chance, be staying at the Labadi Beach Hotel in Accra?
Kind regards
Nod

8 May 2007
From: ABCD@efg.com
To: L. Vukadinovic
Sent: Tuesday, May 08, 2007 00:29 AM
Subject: Re: Hello Angela from your 'new' Dad

Dearest Angela
Mrs Nallum and I are so excited. Mr Smith has told us you will be in Durban

next week while he is away in Ghana. Well, we have decided to fly to Accra to meet with Mr Smith on Wednesday and on Saturday we will fly to Durban to meet you. Thank God all is coming to fruition as your dear father, Lazar, had hoped.

With love and affection and looking forward so much to meeting you next Saturday.

Always

'Mum and Dad'

From: Michael Smith
To: ABCD@efg.com
Sent: Tuesday, May 08, 2007 5:15 PM
Subject: Re: Message

Dear Sir,

I am very happy to receive your latest mail, i will like to know if it will be possible that you fly via South Africa to pick me up, so we can fly together to Accra Ghana, there we will have much time to chat over this whole matter away from job load, i believe it will be a pleasant trip together, actually i am flying with my personal clerk, to assist me while in Ghana, i will also be willing to visit the old Elmina castle with your family, if all goes well with the legal papers over there, i will be eager to fly back to Durban with your family where we can pick up Angela, please let me know what you think about this new development.

Please confirm this information as soon as possible.

Thanks in anticipation

Sincerely

Michael Smith Esq.,

Is he calling my bluff? I'll adopt the 'too late' tactic that he used with Lazar's funeral. As it happens, I wish I was in Ghana – it's freezing here!

9 May 2007
From: ABCD@efg.com
To: michael_smith163@yahoo.com
Sent: Wednesday, May 09, 2007 3:00 PM
Subject: Re: Message

Dear Michael

I am accessing my email by remote server and have just seen your message. I thought you would already be here in Ghana. Where are you? If you are still in South Africa, I can send our pilot to collect you. Your clerk will be most welcome also. If relevant, please confirm his/her name in advance so that we can register you both for the flight from South Africa to here.

We have decided to travel today to Elmina so that we have Thursday and Friday to meet you. Our plans are still to fly to Durban on Saturday to meet dear Angela.

I called home and one of our children told us it is quite cold. The heat is stifling here but the sea breeze is refreshing. I was amazed at how green Ghana is from the air as we made our approach.

Looking forward to hearing from you.

Sincerely

Nod

10 May 2007
From: Michael Smith
To: ABCD@efg.com
Sent: Thursday, May 10, 2007 10:03 AM
Subject: Urgent Response

Dear Mr. Nallum,

Its unfortunate you did not get my message earlier before you left for Ghana, i suggested it will be wise we fly together to Ghana in the Jet to save the cost for the ticket, anyways i am still in Johannesburg South Africa, i have made reservation for two, against tomorrow morning, with Interlinks travel and tour, tel: +27114873421, mobile: 0725325507 contact person: Riana, i have the reference numbers with me, FLGSCP and FLDWKD, i am suggesting if you can make the payment for the tickets. instead of flying the Jet in and out of South Africa, i believe this will save you some cost, i am really sorry for the incoveniences this might have cost you.

I am coming with my clerk, and the name to be registered is Mr. May O. Chukwuma, but if you decide to pick us with the Jet, its is ok by me, and if he is to fly, he will be landing at the OR Tambo International Airport, formally known as the Johannesburg International. i really need to talk to you, i am suggesting you call me on this number +27-781330018 or you can give me a contact number locally there in Ghana or your private number available.

I wait to hear from you shortly

Sincerely

Michael Smith

What a rogue! To make the call, I've invented a new character, Bartholomew Ahern. When Bart eventually got to speak to Riana (she was in the toilet when I first called), she said that Smith had visited the agency yesterday and booked two tickets to Ghana, via Nigeria, including a ticket for his clerk. All that is required is payment from me. Incidentally, there are

direct flights to Accra but this circuitous route means that he will arrive in Ghana after our supposed departure on Saturday!

From: ABCD@efg.com
To: michael_smith163@yahoo.com
Sent: Thursday, May 10, 2007 4:18 PM
Subject: RE: Urgent Response

Dear Mr Smith
I am sorry for the delay in replying. We were sightseeing in this most beautiful country. I was distraught by my experience at Elmina Castle. I am reeling from all the sadness and inhumanity that the castle's walls and cells contain.

I am in Ghana because you said you would be here when I first suggested that I would deliver your fee in person. Now, not only are you not here, but you are asking me to pay the airfare for you and your clerk. I find this highly inappropriate. As Lazar's legal agent, surely your fees, including expenses, are taken care of. On principle, I will not pay your airfare to Ghana.

I will be happy to see you when you arrive. Indeed, I must tell you about an extraordinary dream I had last night in which Lazar came to visit me. It was amazing. When you arrive in Ghana, I will tell you all about it.
I have your flight reservation number and will contact Riana regarding your arrival time. I will be there with my driver to collect you and Mr Chukwuma. With every good wish for now and hoping you have a very safe and pleasant journey.
Sincerely
Dr Nallum

No response. Let's try again...

11 May 2007
From: ABCD@efg.com
To: michael_smith163@yahoo.com
Sent: Friday, May 11, 2007 3:00 PM

Dear Mr Smith
I am confused but still hoping that you and Mr Chukwuma will arrive this evening at 21.45 on SA52 from Johannesburg to Accra. That flight was due to leave South Africa at 14.55. However, my PA in England, Mr Bartholomew Ahern, call Riana at Interlinks Travel and was informed that you did not collect the tickets for the flights you booked. And this is where I am particularly confused. Mr Ahern was told that you had booked the following flights:

Friday 11 May 2007: Depart Johannesburg 10.30 am on Flight No: VK 302. Arrive Lagos, Nigeria at 3.30pm

Saturday 12 May 2007: Depart Lagos 3.20pm Flight No: VK 803. Arrive Accra at 3.15pm (55 minute flight)

I also learned that you booked your return flight for 9 June. How can this be, since we had already informed you that we would be leaving here tomorrow to fly to Durban?

I hope you appreciate we have put ourselves to considerable trouble to try to help you accomplish the dying wishes of our dearly departed friend Lazar. I am sure there has been a mix-up and I am sincerely hoping that you and your colleague are currently flying to Accra. I will have my PA check my emails throughout the day to see if there is any response from you. If not, I will assume you are arriving in Accra at 21.45. I very much hope so, for my good wife and children will be deeply disappointed if you do not show up.

If you are not coming to Accra, please explain to me where and when we shall meet in South Africa as I am anxious to pass to you the cash payment I have brought to cover the cost of your legal fees. We also want to meet our adopted daughter, Angela, whom dear Lazar asked us to care for. Already we all feel a deep emotional attachment to her and are anxious to welcome her into our family.
Yours sincerely
Dr Nallum

12 May 2007
From: Michael Smith
To: ABCD@efg.com
Sent: Saturday, May 12, 2007 8:41 AM
Subject: RE: Urgent Response

Dr. Nallum,
How are you doing today? i am fine myself, there is something i do not understand in this whole matter, i have sat down with other members of this chambers to discuss this matter with them, and how our conversation have been so far, first of all, you bank have said certain things that disturbed me, after you were requested to send the money for legal purpose, i never understood the truth about that incident, secondly, i have asked you severally to give me you telephone number to speak with you, you ignored it, you said you are in Accra Ghana which i suppose you are, i asked you for a local contact number there, you ignored, i must tell you that i am not comfortable with that, and i am feeling insecured about your intentions towards Angela, you must understand

that i am not interested in your money or whatsover, what Lazar left behind for his daughter is beyond imagination, and you can confirm that, even if i have to meet with you, i need to know where you are, we cannot just communicate through email, and this is what is troubling my heart, i want you to prove your intentions legitimate, anything other than look suspecious to me.

If you care to know, Lazar gave me instructions of which i hold very strong, that i should not hand Angela over, until i am certianly sure that all that you are doing on her behalf is legitimate, forget about the money he promised you, i am not willing to keep that from you, but you must follow the procedures as they are supposed to be done.
I look forward to your quick response.
Sincerely
Michael

I need a convincing excuse to assuage my correspondent's suspicious mind.

From: ABCD@efg.com
To: michael_smith163@yahoo.com
Sent: Saturday, May 12, 2007 6:12 PM
Subject: FW: Re: Urgent Response

Dear Mr Smith
I have a good reason for avoiding calling you personally. When, eventually, we meet in person you will understand and, I hope, have sympathy for my condition. You see, I have a very bad speech impediment, which, in particularly emotional environments, gets worse. It is a source of great embarrassment and I only speak on the phone with very close friends and associates.

I worried that you would get a bad impression of me and that is why, when you said you would be coming to Ghana, I was excited, for it provided me with the opportunity to bring my wife and two of our children. My simple logic was that with them beside me, the focus would not be entirely on me, and they could help me overcome the embarrassment of trying to communicate with you through my stammer. That is also why I had my PA, Mr Ahern, call your travel agent yesterday to check about the flights – I could not make the call myself.

Other than my family and our pilot friend, Biggles, with whom we flew here, I have told absolutely no one about the nature of our business. Even my bank manager does not know the reason for the transaction you wished me to do. I understood that confidentiality was a condition of our arrangement. I did ask my wife to call you but – as you will see when you meet her – she has a very timid and gentle nature and is quite overawed at the thought of discussing Lazar's dying wishes with such a highly educated and articulate lawyer. I understand your doubts. But that is the truthful reason. Nothing else.

I went to the airport last night and waited until every passenger on flight SA52 had passed through the arrivals area. My driver held up a large sign bearing the names: Michael Smith Esq. and May O. Chukwuma Esq., but we left alone. And now, we are just back from meeting Flight VK803 from Lagos with the same result.

I am in Accra because you told me that you had business here and that was why you could not meet me in South Africa. However, I find you are not here. Now it is my turn to feel perturbed and nervous. Indeed, I am also worried about Angela's welfare.

I have not met Angela but, as you know, we have exchanged brief emails. From what Lazar told me about his daughter and the delicacy of the words she has written to me, I have no doubt that we will give her love and kindness beyond what Lazar had hoped for. You see, Mr Smith, while I do have a speech impediment, my disability has made my family very sensitive and compassionate towards the afflicted. That is why Lazar's heartfelt appeal resonated so deeply in the heart of our home.

You say your legal fees are not important, but they are very important to me. I am a man of honour and I believe, as the Holy Gospel states, 'the labourer is worthy of his hire'. That is why I brought with me your payment in cash, plus a beautiful gift worth much more than your fees. I respect your lofty profession and, but for my stutter, I believe I would have been a successful barrister. But, alas, the hand of the Lord blessed me with this affliction and I have found other ways of articulating His Truth.

With very heavy hearts we have decided not to travel to Durban. My dear wife is distraught. Doubts have descended on her mind like dark clouds before a storm. We have made a long journey to meet you. We have done everything you have asked. Now, my wife wants to return home to our other children. She thinks you have made fools of us. It distresses me to see her so upset. I know her heart has already opened to Angela and she has begun loving her, even at such a distance.

We leave at midnight tonight for the UK. I am going to the market first to buy soccer shirts for my children, who admired greatly the fighting spirit of the men who represented this vibrant country during the 2006 World Cup in Germany. Thank God we found the people of Ghana to be so warm and welcoming. Their kindness has made our pain more bearable.

I still believe you are an honourable man. A man who has Angela's best interests at heart. Mr Smith, I appeal to you, indeed I beg you, please help us to fulfil the wishes of Lazar. I have not discussed this with my wife or children, nor will I discuss it with anyone, but I am prepared to give you half the monies that Lazar instructed you to sign over to us for taking care of Angela. I am a successful businessman and Angela would be very comfortable with us even without Lazar's inheritance.

I await your response my friend. But, believe me, I fly home tonight with a very heavy heart, full of disappointment.

Yours sincerely

Nallum

PS. I must tell you about the dream I had involving Lazar. It was very vivid and his words were deeply moving.

13 May 2007
From: ABCD@efg.com
To: Michael Smith
Sent: Sunday, May 13, 2007 10:15 AM
Subject: Re: Urgent Response

Dear Mr Smith

We are back safely in the UK, thank God, but are tired after the long flight home.

Where are you my friend? Why are you so silent? Taking care of Angela is very important to us, we are determined not to let this rest until she is safely here with us and we have fulfilled the promise I made to her dying dad. Have I done something wrong? My wife is in a deep depression for she is increasingly afraid that you are a fraudster. Please help me to reassure her.

Last night something extraordinary occurred while we were flying home. I need to tell you about it. It is to do with Lazar.

With kind good wishes

Nallum

14 May 2007
From: Michael Smith
To: ABCD@efg.com
Sent: Monday, May 14, 2007 12:13 PM
Subject: Re: Urgent Response

Attention: Dr. Nallum,

Dear Sir,

I thank God that you and your family arrived home safely; I thought it will be wise if I begin this message with an apology, to you and your entire family, and I hope you will find a place in your heart to pardon me, I could not meet you in Accra Ghana due to personal reasons, as a matter of fact I was skeptical about meeting you, and this is for security reasons, I was actually in Accra before your arrival, I went to Tamale the very day you arrived in Accra, I thought I could have reached with you over the telephone in Accra so we can meet, but since I did not get the number to contact you, I was very uneasy and decided to protect myself from something I am not sure about, please send my apology to your lovely wife and kids, do not see you trip to Africa as a waste, you are committed to helping Angela, its not just an easy task, at least one day after all this is complete, you will write a story about it, and the book will not be complete without including what you experienced at the awful Elmina Castle in Cape Coast, once again I am deeply sorry for the whole miss up, after I read your message explaining why you could not speak with me over the phone, I was sorry for the actions I took, and asked God to forgive me, I did not know about your disability, and you can confirm that, there is not way I would have been embarrassed for that, let by gone be by gone now.

I have couple of your emails, and I will like to respond to all of them one after the other, the money you can along with, is not supposed to be my legal fees, I am sure I stated what that money was suppose to be used for, since my client is late, all my legal fees will be paid once all the legal papers are complete, and his legacy transferred to you as the trustee, then I will receive all my legal fee for administrating his estate, please do not promise me half of Lazars estate or pecuniary legacy, I am not a greedy man, I am contempt with what I have, if I do such a thing, I might enjoy the money, but the spirit of my client will never let me rest, do you know what is a scam? And how can you know when you are being scammed, please explain it to me In your next letter if you don't mind, this is what stated our misunderstanding at the first instance, I am ready to move on with this process, but I will like you to understand that we have to do it the way it should be done, and please if I am going astray, you can call back my attention, and I will also like you to follow my directions, if we work together, we can achieve this goal, I am an African, but I do not have black sense, I can offer to give you the five hundred thousand dollars (USD$500,000.00) Lazar offered you, and keep Angela here with my family, but as a Christian that I am, I will not hold back the wishes of a dead man, because they might come hunting you later, but that does not mean that I do not have the legal power to keep Angela, If I feel she is going to be in danger from whoever her father appoints as his trustee.

Please let me know when you are ready to move on, already I have secured some important documents from the Probate office in Ghana, as well as have a letter of Guarantee from the Standard Chartered Bank High Street, that once all the legal papers are signed and legalized, they funds will be released to whoever the trustee is, if you are ready to proceed, lets do this as men, and it should be confidential as you said, but if you do not have the trust In as Lazars attorney, then I will not be wiling to work with you at all, this is very simple and I do not mean anything wrong, the money should be sent to start the paper work first, every other thing can come later, we have to start all over again, and I hope there will be no obstacle at this time, I will be in Ghana until the 17th

of May. So you can have the money sent down here via Western Union Money transfer, I have to go for now, let me know what want to do next.
Sincerely
Michael Smith Esq.,
Notice: Please do not forget to tell me what you experienced while flying back home, about Lazar and your wife

Interesting question he raises: 'And how can you know when you are being scammed?' Perhaps it reflects his doubts in his dealings with me.

15 May 2007
From: ABCD@efg.com
To: Michael Smith
Sent: Tuesday, May 15, 2007 00:23 AM
Subject: Re: Urgent Response

Dear Mr Smith
I have just returned home after a very long day of travelling by car to attend the funeral of a dear friend who passed away while I was in Ghana. I feel dreadful that I did not have the opportunity to say goodbye to him. I read your email and there is much in it that needs my full attention. My mind is too tired now so I will respond tomorrow or Wednesday.
Kind regards
Dr Nallum

16 May 2007
From: Michael Smith
To: ABCD@efg.com
Sent: Wednesday, May 16, 2007 12:41 PM
Subject: Re: Urgent Response

Dear Dr. Nallum,
I am really sorry to hear about your loss, please accept my sympathy, i need to hear from you, regarding my last email, what need to be done next, there the need that we proceed quickly, that is if you are willing to proceed, if not, i need to know the next step forward to secure Lazars estate, and to keep Angela in a safe place.
Take care
Michael

He's chasing the money. Sadly, however, Nod isn't feeling well at all. The challenge will be to make it sound authentic.

From: Catherine Nallum
To: michael_smith163@yahoo.com
Sent: Wednesday, May 16, 2007 4:09 PM
Subject: Dr. Nallum

Dear Mr Smith

I am Catherine Nallum, the wife of Dr Nod Nallum who has been communicating with you about Angela. We were disappointed that we could not meet you in Ghana or Angela in South Africa. We hope and pray that this will happen soon. My husband has been unwell since our return from Ghana and seems to have developed a particularly bad flu and headache. He has asked me to write and request your patience.

Please tell Angela that we look forward to welcoming her to our beautiful home. She will love it, I know, for Nod is a very loving father. Nod may have told you that we have five children in all. I have two from my previous marriage: Trevor and Catherine, and Nod and I have three of our own: Julian, Samantha and Tobias. Nod and I met in Switzerland seventeen years ago in the beautiful winter of 1990; in truth, thus began the summer of my life. I had been divorced for six months, after a very abusive marriage, and Nod became my angel. He made Trevor and Catherine his own and has shown no favouritism, even after we had our own three children. So I know that when Angela arrives, she will be given the same love and kindness. Please pass on our kisses to dear Angela and tell her we love her very much. Would it be okay for me to write to her?

We feel so privileged that dearly departed Lazar considered us worthy to assume the welfare of Angela. We became convinced of this during our flight back to the UK from Ghana. It was a very spiritual experience. Have no doubt that when my husband is well he will conclude whatever business is necessary to have Angela with us.
Yours respectfully
Mrs Catherine Nallum

17 May 2007
From: L. Vukadinovic
To: ABCD@efg.com
Sent: Thursday, May 17, 2007 9:29 AM
Subject: Re: Hello Angela from your 'new' Dad

Hi Dad
its been a long time i heard from you, is everything ok,i thought i will be meeting you in Durban as promised, i dont have much time to spend at the cafe, so its kind of hard to write to you everyday, i hope i have not been forgeting, i need to hear from you soon.

Thanks
Angela

Looks like he's not sure about me and has decided to fish for information using 'Angela'.

From: Catherine Nallum
To: l.vukadinovich@yahoo.com.au
Sent: Thursday, May 17, 2007 8:35 PM
Subject: Hello from Mum

Dearest Angela

I have tears in my eyes writing this note to you. Tears for two reasons. The first is because I am, at last, communicating with you. I was deeply disappointed when Mr Smith failed to meet us in Ghana. We had hoped to fly with him to Durban to meet you. It was such an unfortunate mix-up. I wish we had planned it better. Angela, how we long to bring you to our home in England and to share with you all the love we can. Oh my dear, you will be so very welcome.

The second reason is that your new dad is in hospital. Since returning from Ghana, your dad has not been himself. On Monday he travelled to the funeral of a friend. It was too far for him to drive and he was exhausted afterwards. The next morning he had a high temperature and blinding headache and stayed in bed. I insisted on getting the GP last night and immediately the doctor had him admitted to hospital. After monitoring his condition and failing to bring down his temperature, they fear he has contracted an aggressive viral infection while in Ghana. Today, he was transferred to a tropical clinic in London. I am very worried but I am sure he will be okay.

Angela, Dr Nallum loves you very much. It is so typical of him the way he responded to your father's appeal for help. Together we decided that we should offer you our home. We cannot wait until you get here. Please say a prayer for your new dad to make a speedy recovery so that we can complete all the necessary details that Mr Smith requires.

All your brothers and sisters send their love.
With lots of kisses and hugs
Catherine

18 May 2007
From: Michael Smith
To: ABCD@efg.com
Sent: Friday, May 18, 2007 11:53 AM
Subject: Re: Urgent Response

Dear Dr. Nallum,
I hope everything is alright with you, i have sent you couple of emails, without any response, i need to hear from you as soon as possible, to enable me work my way through the next step possible, if i do not hear from you, it clearly means something to me, and i will decide to move on with the next level.
Take care
Michael

Doesn't he realise I'm very ill? Step forward Bartholomew Ahern, faithful PA of Dr Nod. He's a bit like Smith: he can use a full stop, but doesn't care so much for capital letters.

From: ABCD@efg.com
To: Michael Smith
Sent: Friday, May 18, 2007 5:10 PM
Subject: Re: Urgent Response

Dear Mr Smith:
My name is Bartholomew Ahern, PA to dr Nallum. mrs Nallum asked me to reply to you before the close of business.
    Dr Nallum is very ill. He is in a london hospital that specialises in tropical illnesses. Mrs Nallum and the children are with him now.
Please keep dr Nallum in your prayers.
yours sincerely,
Bart Ahern

From: Michael Smith
To: ABCD@efg.com
Sent: Friday, May 18, 2007 5:47 PM
Subject: Re: Urgent Response

Dear Bartholomew,
I am very sorry to hear this news from you, actually no one told me anything about his illness, i will be joining the family in prayers until he is back home safely, nothing will happened to him, since he believes in the healing power of the lord Jesus Christ, i assure him a safe recovery back home, please do extend my regards to Mrs Nallum, she must not lose guard, because nothing is going to happen to him, please keep me informed as to what his condition is ok.
thanks in anticipation
Michael Smith Esq.,

I've a spooky feeling about what I am going to do next.

20 May 2007
From: ABCD@efg.com
To: Circulation
Sent: Sunday, May 20, 2007 4:28 PM
Subject: Dr. Norbertine OD Nallum, Requiem et Pas
Attachment: Requiem et Pas.doc

As a mark of respect to our Founder and President, this office will be closed on Monday and Tuesday, 21 and 22 May 2007. It will re-open at 9.00 a.m. on Wednesday 23 May.
Recipients:
(A): Dr Nallum's personal mailbox
(B): Family
(C): Clients and Associates
(D): General
Attachment: Requiem et Pas Notice

Requiem et Pas
Dr N.O.D. Nallum (1960–2007)

It is with profound sadness that we must inform our clients and associates of the unexpected passing of our Founder and President, Dr Norbertine Onslow Desmond (Nod) Nallum, PhD, following a short illness.

Having returned from Ghana on Sunday 13 May, Dr Nallum fell ill. He was diagnosed with meningococcal meningitis and, despite the best efforts of the doctors and nurses of the Queen Victoria Infirmary and the Royal Tropical Clinic, he passed away at 10.23 this morning, Sunday 20 May. He was surrounded by his loving wife, Catherine, and their five children, Trevor, Kate, Julian, Samantha and Tobias. His brothers, William and Winston, and sister, Elizabeth Regina, were also present.

Until last evening, despite obvious physical discomfort, Dr Nallum was lucid and serene and made his peace with God. As a devout Roman Catholic, he received the sacraments of the sick and reconciliation from his close friend and spiritual director, Rev. Fr Jonathan Ross, SJ.

Dr Nallum will be cremated tomorrow, 21 May 2007, following a private ceremony and, in accordance with his will, which, remarkably, he amended the evening before his passing, his ashes will be flown to the monastic island of Iona, off the west coast of Scotland, for interment at sunset. Dr and Mrs Nallum have, since their marriage in 1991, made an annual pilgrimage to Iona, founded in 563 AD by the Celtic missionary, St Columba.

The family have requested that no cards or floral tributes be sent. Instead, they have asked that donations in kind be forwarded to Dr Nallum's favourite charity, Oxfam.

Dr Nallum, who was known for his great kindness, compassion and fairness, will be sadly missed by all. May he Rest in Peace.

> *A friend to share the lonesome times*
> *A handshake and a sip of wine*
> *So say it loud and let it ring*
> *We are all a part of everything*
> *The future, present and the past*
> *Fly on proud bird*
> *You're free at last.*

Charles Daniels

Is it tempting fate to invent one's death? Once I reminded myself that Nod is a fictional character operating in a fantasy world of lies and subterfuge, I began to relax and enjoy the process. What does Nod stand for, I thought, if not Don reversed? And what would Jonathan Ross be like as a Jesuit priest? I hoped it would make the scammers feel part of Nod's inner circle. I also wondered if they had any conscience. Would they feel even a little responsible for Nod's untimely death?

From: ABCD@efg.com
To: Michael Smith
Sent: Sunday, May 20, 2007 4:40 PM
Subject: Re: Urgent Response

Dear Mr Smith
Sadly, dr nallum succumbed after a short illness. We are devastated and in shock. Please reassure angela that all is well. before his passing he made provision for her in his will with the full agreement of the family. It is a measure of the kind of man he was. Please continue to keep the family in your prayers.
best wishes
Bart Ahern

21 May 2007
From: ABCD@efg.com
To: Circulation
Sent: Monday, May 21, 2007 9:14 PM
Subject: Fr. Jonathan's Homily at dr Nallum's funeral mass

Dear friends,
    At this moment, some 500 miles north, on the scottish island of iona, the nallum family will be gathering to commit dr nallum's ashes to the wilderness

of that holy place as the sun bows below the horizon.

This morning i was privileged to attend the funeral mass presided over by dr nallum's friend, fr Jonathan ross. i asked fr ross to forward me a copy of his moving homily and I am sending it on to you all now so that we can feel close to the family at this time. It is a beautiful tribute to such a very special man by one of his dearest friends.

Fr ross's homily, 'Song of hope', proved to be a great source of comfort and support to all present at the funeral. I hope you too will find it equally moving.

Thank you to everyone who has sent words of comfort. I will reply over the coming days. we all must try to begin to pick up the pieces.

It is hard to believe that we will never again see nod's warm and inviting smile.

sincerely

Bart

Attachment: Fr Jonathan Ross's Funeral Homily

The attached eulogy was almost eight pages long and full of anecdotes and quotations. It took me four hours to write it! A bit much perhaps, but Nod had become a part of me. As this whole fiction began with an email from Lazar (who then 'died' and later 'reappeared' to the Nallums in a vision), it seemed appropriate to write the eulogy around the gospel story of Lazarus. My aim was to support information already imparted in emails so that the scammers might be impressed by the consistency of various sources. Here are a few extracts:

Today, we stand before the human remains of our brother Norbertine. The body, the envelope of the spirit, is dead. In truth, however, he is already unbound and, through the passion, death and resurrection of Our Lord Jesus Christ, the angels have already responded to the command of Jesus: 'Let him go' (John 11:44). And let us have no doubt about the freedom of our brother Norbertine.

At his request, this is a private and very intimate ceremony, attended by those whom he loved most profoundly. All of us gathered in this beautiful oratory, where he and Catherine were married in 1991 and where their three youngest children were christened, know that the goodness and generosity of such a beautiful man was but an expression of God's love to the world.

To Catherine, he was a loving husband. To Trevor, Kate, Julian, Samantha and Toby, he was a dedicated father. To William, Winston and Elizabeth Regina, he was a caring brother. To Bartholomew and Jessica, he was a loyal boss. To you all, including Dan Dore, his pilot chum whom he affectionately nicknamed Biggles, and Andrew Harding of the British Stammering Society, and myself, he was a loyal friend. [. . .]

His charitable contributions were enormous, as I know from personal experience. But for Nod, I might not be here today. In 2001 I was diagnosed with prostate cancer and Nod arranged for Biggles to fly me to New York for emergency treatment. The list of his generous acts is too long to recite now. [. . .]

Though tragic and sad, it is perhaps not surprising that it was Africa, a continent he deeply loved and cherished, that ultimately claimed his life. [. . .]

Now, back to my newly discovered feminine side. . .

24 May 2007
From: Catherine Nallum
To: l.vukadinovich@yahoo.com.au
Sent: Thursday, May 24, 2007 1:35 PM
Subject: Fwd: Hello from Mum

Dearest Angela,
I hope Mr Smith has gently informed you of the heart-breaking news that your adopted father passed away suddenly after a short illness. I am in a trance with grief.

Before he died he made me promise that I would take care of you in accordance with the commitment he had made to your father, Lazar. He even bequeathed to you a legacy, in keeping with all our children. Such was Nod. It was one of the last things he did, for a few short hours later he fell asleep and never woke up again.

Angela, now that the love of my life has gone, I need your love all the more and want to reassure you that you are very welcome among us. All my children feel the same way. I can write no more today but I'll contact your father's lawyer, Mr Smith, in the next few days.

Thank you for your love.
Always
'Mum'

Still no response. I hope Nod hasn't died in vain!

25 May 2007
From: ABCD@efg.com
To: Michael Smith
Sent: Friday, May 25, 2007 11:18 AM
Subject: Re: Urgent Response

Dear Mr Smith
I have just had a short meeting with mrs nallum. She asked me to enquire if angela has received her emails. She would dearly love to hear from her. Could

you check? Her personal address is: catherinenallum@yahoo.co.uk It would mean a lot to her during these very difficult days.

We are still struggling to come to terms with the loss of dr nallum. I am trying to pick up the pieces within the company and to help his good wife cope. sincerely,
Bartholomew Ahern

From: Michael Smith
To: ABCD@efg.com
Sent: Friday, May 25, 2007 11:35 AM
Subject: Re: Urgent Response

Please have Mrs Nallum call me on this number +27832440955 i need to talk to her about certain issue.
Thanks
Michael Smith Esq.,

From: ABCD@efg.com
To: Michael Smith
Sent: Friday, May 25, 2007 2:56 PM
Subject: Re: Urgent Response

Dear Mr Smith
Mrs nallum is in mourning. I asked her if she wished to call you and she simply does not have the heart at present. Perhaps in a week or two i can ask her again.

I note a coldness in your response. Given our recent experience and the warm correspondence we exchanged it seems unusually heartless. Is there a problem? Perhaps i can help. Just note i am not entirely familiar with all the matters you and the nallums have been discussing but i can try to help.

Thank you again for your prayers. I assure you that mrs nallum was most grateful. I assure you too, any assistance you feel i can give you, please do not hesitate to ask.
best wishes,
Bart

From: l.vukadinovich@yahoo.com.au
To: Catherine Nallum
Sent: Friday, May 25, 2007 3:09 PM
Subject: Fwd: Hello from Mum

Dearest Mom,
I am very sad to read your message, i am just wondering why i am losing loved

ones around me, it was my dad, and now my new father, why all this happening to me? i cannot write anymore, because my hands are shaking, please, please, can you send me a photo of you and the family, at least i need some kind of picture to look upon, to know who my new parent and family will be, i will be very happy to get that, please do not be hartbroken, god knows the best.
please write me soon with the photo, god bless you
Angela

27 May 2007
From: l.vukadinovich@yahoo.com.au
To: Catherine Nallum
Sent: Monday, May 28, 2007 00:59 AM
Subject: Fwd: Hello from Mum

Dear Mom,
I have not heard from you again, i hope everything is ok, and the family, please send me the photo i asked in my last email before this, i will be waiting to hear from you soon
Angela

Despite the sent date and time, the above message arrived during the afternoon of Sunday 27 May. The time difference suggests that, as the email address indicates, it may have originated in Australia.

From: Catherine Nallum
To: l.vukadinovich@yahoo.com.au
Sent: Sunday, May 27, 2007 11:36 PM
Subject: Re: Fwd: Hello from Mum
Attachment: Family Photo

Dearest Angela
It was so nice to return and find your two emails. Trevor took me away for a weekend to our house that overlooks the Cliffs of Dover. Kate kindly took the other children to stay with friends. I was so looking forward to the break and for some long walks along the cliffs where your dad and I often went. The weather, however, was dreadful.

There was a terrible emptiness in the house. In our bedroom the windows open onto a balcony with views over the English Channel. Nod's telescope looked so forlorn. It was not unusual for me to wake up in the morning to see him gazing out onto one of the busiest shipping lanes in the world, watching ships and tankers crossing from France and other European destinations to the UK or making their way to and from the Atlantic Ocean. The rain was so heavy at times today I could not even see to the edge of the cliffs. The dark clouds matched my mood.

Angela, dear child, you ask questions that I cannot answer. I am as much at a loss as you and I understand your pain and sense of abandonment. We both have an enormous hole in our hearts. That is why we must try now to love one another. Before he died, your new dad made me promise to take care of you. And he made me promise him that you would be treated as an equal with the rest of our children. The only comfort I can send you dear Angela is that you had two wonderful fathers, who have ensured that you will never want for anything in life. With the legacy that Lazar left you and the legacy that Nod left you, you are a very wealthy young woman. Materialism, I know, is no substitute for the more important things in life, but it will give you security. And when you come here, dear child, I will teach you how to manage your inheritances.

I'm attaching a picture as requested. It was taken during a family gathering in the spring of last year. We are all together. Kate and I are very alike. I was chuffed one day when two Jehovah's Witnesses rang the doorbell and when I opened it they asked, 'Is your mum at home?' When Kate joined me they were incredulous that we were mother and daughter. We had a great laugh telling that story.

The following people are in the picture:

Back row: Your Uncle William (with glasses) and Aunt Rita; your Uncle Winston (with yellow top) and Aunt Leah; your Aunt Elizabeth Regina (with mauve top) and her daughter, Elizabeth Mary, who is holding her daughter, Zoe; then Elizabeth Mary's husband, Albert, and her father, your Uncle Zack.

Middle row: My father, John; your dad (I'm sitting directly in front of him with the lemon top); my mother, Teresa. Then come your brothers and sisters: Samantha and Trevor and

Front row: Kate, Julian and Toby (nicknamed 'Bruiser'). Toby is a real rascal.

We are a very happy family, Angela, and I know we will do everything we can to make you happy too. Come soon, for the love we share will help to fill the void.

With kisses and warm affectionate hugs
Mom

I searched extensively for a photograph that might match all the details I had previously given to 'Lazar'. I found one on the Internet when I Googled 'Family Pictures'. I have no idea who this family is. The photograph sent was harvested from the internet of a family gathering. We are unable to reproduce it here without permission as the identity of the family is unknown.

28 May 2007
From: l.vukadinovich@yahoo.com.au
To: Catherine Nallum
Sent: Monday, May 28, 2007 8:05 AM
Subject: thanks Mom

Dearesrt mom
am happy to hear from you, the picture is very nice to look at, soory if my
question boardesr you, its just that i was just thinking about the whole incident
that have befalling me this past months, anyways thank you so much for the
photo, i will send you mine soon, dear mom, please when will all this legal
papers complete so i can be with the family? i am really eager to come to
england as soon as possible, i am lonly and bored here, looking at the photo i
can imagine myself in the picture of another family gathering in 2007

There ios something in my heart that i wanted to ask from youi, its a little
favor, and i need it so much, i need some girls stuff that i cannot ask from Mr;
smith, like a Pad for my period circle, underwears and others, i am wondering
if you can send me a little gift so i can buy this things for myself, i need this
things urgently, but if its going to be a burden for you, you can foget about it ok

if its in your heart to do it, i will leyt you know to get it send to me, i hope
i will hear froim you soon, i will send you a photo of myself soon, may God
bless you and your famuly, and my dads gentle soul rest in peace
from Angela

**I hadn't anticipated getting involved in an exchange on 'girls stuff', but
I'm always ready for new challenges!**

From: Catherine Nallum
To: l.vukadinovich@yahoo.com.au
Sent: Monday, May 28, 2007 12:47 PM
Subject: Re: thanks Mom

Dearest Angela,
Your emails are like a sunburst in my heart. The weather here is still cloudy,
with rain threatening, and the temperature for this time of year is unusually
cold. How I wish I could enjoy the warm sunshine of South Africa. One day,
please God, we will return there together for a holiday.

Today is a bank holiday in Britain and everything is closed. But tomorrow
I will speak to the solicitor who helped your father to amend his will for you.
I will ask her to write to the solicitor my husband was communicating with in
South Africa before he died.

Of course, I will help you dear Angela. It is a mother's pleasure. Our

Samantha made me laugh one day during dinner with friends at a hotel. Your dad was complaining of stomach cramps and Samantha turned to me and whispered, 'Welcome to OUR world – once a month!' I laughed so much I had to share it with everyone at the table. Your poor dad laughed too, despite his discomfort.

Just send me your address and I will get something off to you immediately, dear daughter. And never be afraid to speak to me in confidence about anything. Please consider me, truly, as your mother.

Tell me, does Mr Smith have access to this email address or can we share 'women's talk' here privately? If I know you are the only person reading these emails, then I can be more open and, I hope, you might feel at ease to be more open with me.

I am glad you liked the photograph. That was such a wonderful family gathering. I look forward to getting your picture too. I can imagine how beautiful you are.

With love and deep affection always
Mom

From: Catherine Nallum
To: ABCD@efg.com
Sent: Monday, May 28, 2007 1:16 PM
Subject: Ms Mansfield

Dear Bart,
Thank you for all your kindness and help at this difficult time.

Please email Ms Mansfield with the address of Angela's solicitor in Africa. Angela was enquiring about the legal papers as she is anxious to come to England as soon as possible. Please ask Ms Mansfield to move matters along quickly.

Biggles will fly me to South Africa to meet Angela in a few weeks' time. I would like you to come with me Bart as I would feel very vulnerable on my own. Thank you again for everything you have done to ease our burden and pain.

Always
Catherine

Sending messages between my different aliases did make me wonder if I'd become too obsessed with this project. After all, my plan was to waste the scammer's time, not my own. But having come this far I wanted to see how long I could frustrate the scammers before they started ignoring/deleting my emails.

29 May 2007
From: ABCD@efg.com

To: seoflondonchambers@yahoo.co.uk
Cc: Michael Smith
Sent: Tuesday, May 29, 2007 10:05 AM
Subject: Fw: Ms Mansfield

Dear Ms Mansfield,
Below is an email i received this morning from mrs Catherine Nallum. I should
be grateful if you would advance the process of dr nallum's amended will and
also the issues pertaining to the legal adoption of the south african teenager,
angela, whom dr nallum was anxious to assume care of. The solicitor dr nallum
had been dealing with in south africa is mr Michael Smith. His email address
is: michael_smith163@yahoo.com

According to Mrs nallum the beneficiary is 16. Mrs nallum is not sure if
the teenager assumed the name of her father upon adoption. If yes, then her
name is Angela Vukadinovich. Sadly, her adopted father died on 28 April 2007,
less than a month before dr Nallum's death. It is our understanding that the
solicitor, mr smith, is angela's sole guardian with responsibility for executing
the will of her father, Lazar Vukadinovich.

Please try to move things along quickly as mrs nallum is anxious to bring
angela to england as soon as possible. As you know, mrs nallum is a very gentle
person. I should be personally grateful, therefore, if you would ensure that she
is fully briefed and represented.
yours sincerely,
Bartholomew Ahern
PA Mrs Catherine Nallum

----- Original Message -----
Dear Bart,
Thank you for all your kindness and help...

From: Catherine Nallum
To: l.vukadinovich@yahoo.com.au
Sent: Tuesday, May 29, 2007 10:17 AM
Subject: Re: thanks Mom

Dearest Angela
I have been awaiting your reply to my last email. I am anxious to send you
some pocket money so that you can buy the personal items you need. Also, I
am working on getting everything ready for your arrival here. I've asked my
assistant to put pressure on our solicitor to get all the paperwork done. I just
want to reassure you that I am doing my best.

Please write soon. The light of your existence eases the sad and painful

darkness of our hearts during this time of great loss. We all love you very much Angela. All the children have asked me to send you their affection and kisses. We cannot wait to have you with us.
Always
Mom

From: Michelle Mansfield
To: michael_smith163@yahoo.com ; ABCD@efg.com
Sent: Tuesday, May 29, 2007 11:40 AM
Subject: Codicil

Dear Mr Smith
I act on behalf of the estate of the late Mr Norbertine O.D. Nallum.

Shortly before his death on 20 May 2007, Mr Nallum completed a Codicil and made provision for a minor whom, I understand, is under your temporary guardianship. The Codicil was witnessed by his wife, Catherine. It is their understanding that the minor's name is Ms Angela Vukadinovich, the adopted daughter of Mr Lazar Vukadinovich, who passed away on 28 April 2007. Mr Nallum informed us that he gave Mr Vukadinovich an undertaking that he would assume responsibility for the wellbeing of Angela and the purpose of the Codicil is to fulfil that promise, following his demise.

To advance the process and carry out the wishes of the deceased and his widow, I would be grateful if you would provide me with the following information:

1. Full name of the minor.
2. Date of birth of the minor.
3. Confirmation that you are her current legal guardian.

For the purposes of Probate I will also require proof of identity of both you and the minor to satisfy HM Revenue and Customs. Scanned copies of these will be acceptable for the time being. However, given the large bequest that Mr Nallum has left to the minor in your care, it will be imperative for us eventually to have original documents, in which case it may be necessary for me to travel to South Africa or have you deliver same to the UK.

As this office will close from 4 June to 2 July 2007, please attend to this matter urgently so that I can complete the initial paperwork prior to the holidays.
Yours respectfully,
Michelle Mansfield, LL.B

From: l.vukadinovich@yahoo.com.au
To: Catherine Nallum

Sent: Tuesday, May 29, 2007 8:08 PM
Subject: Re: thanks Mom

Dear Mom
I am happy to hear from you so quick, I want to ask, if you know about the moneygram international money transfer, it si much quicker and safer to send money, I will be using a friends address for the money, because I do not have my id yet, if you know about it, I will give you the address information in the nest mail. If you do send the pocket money, just let me know who much that was sent, so I can go for it. I am so blessed to have a mom like you, I have never known one before, i owe all my life to my dad, I never know who my mom was, there was a time I felt very rejected why a woman will abandone her only child, well to god be all the glory I ended up in a safe heaven.
Anyways god bless you dealy, with love an kindness.
Angela

30 May 2007
From: Michelle Mansfield
To: michael_smith163@yahoo.com ; ABCD@efg.com
Sent: Wednesday, May 30, 2007 1:03 PM
Subject: Codicil to the Will of the late Dr. Norbertine OD Nallum

Dear Sir,
RE: Codicil to the Will of the late Dr Norbertine O.D. Nallum
I would be grateful if you would kindly acknowledge receipt of my correspondence of yesterday concerning the above. Your attention to the three questions posed will enable me to ensure that the process is progressed with due diligence in the interests of our clients. A speedy response will be greatly appreciated as we close for summer holidays on Friday next.
Yours sincerely,
Michelle Mansfield, LL.B

From: Michael Smith
To: ABCD@efg.com
Sent: Wednesday, May 30, 2007 2:55 PM
Subject: Re: Fw: Ms Mansfield

Dear Mr. Bartholomew,
How are you doing today? I got a forwarded message from you yesterday; I have been trying to understand what exactly is going on, first of all who is Ms Mansfield, and what connection has she with my client daughter Angela, this troubles my heart, secondly I am not still in a doubt that Mr. Nallum passed

away, I never had the chance to speak with him over the telephone, not even his wife or you his PA, all this is creating doubt in my heart, I will be happy to hear from you or Mrs. Nallum, to clarify this whole situation.

Please if I can get a kind of proof that Dr. Nallum who I barely knew really passed away, it will settle a lot of worries in my mind, for security reason, I am seizing all correspondence regarding this matter with you, until I get the picture of who I am dealing with, I am sorry for any inconveniences this might have cause you, I am trying to keep my client on a safe side.
Looking forward to hearing you soon
Sincerely
Michael

From: ABCD@efg.com
To: Michael Smith
Sent: Wednesday, May 30, 2007 5:56 PM
Subject: Re: Fw: Ms Mansfield

Dear Mr Smith
I am well thank you. I hope you are too.

I understand your caution and your desire to protect young angela. However, i informed you on 18 May that dr nallum was very ill. You immediately replied, promising to pray for his recovery. After that i heard nothing from you until today, not even an expression of condolence. You seem to doubt that dr nallum has passed away. This implication is both distressing and in bad taste. After all, it was because of you that he made the trip to ghana. And it was in ghana that he contracted the fatal virus that killed him.

To answer your questions. Ms mansfield is mrs nallum's solicitor. She was called to dr nallum's deathbed so that he could amend his will to include the young girl you have in your care. quite frankly, i am staggered by the generosity of dr nallum. It would take me a lifetime to earn that amount. In the interests of your client, please show this wonderful family the respect they deserve.

An application for a death certificate his been made to the superintendent registrar of west sussex county council and is expected within 21 working days. As soon as this has been released i will ask ms mansfield to send you a copy.

Mrs nallum remains deeply distressed by her bereavement. With her permission i will be more than happy to telephone you sir. Please can you confirm that the number i should call is: +27832440955.
respectfully yours,
Bartholomew Ahern

From: Catherine Nallum
To: l.vukadinovich@yahoo.com.au

Sent: Wednesday, May 30, 2007 8:10 PM
Subject: Re: thanks Mom

Dearest Angela,
I am sorry for the delay in replying. I was away visiting my parents today.

I've never used the moneygram transfer you mention but please send me the details and I will do my best.

I was so sad to read about your abandonment by your mother. How cruel. It makes Lazar's love all the more beautiful. And, please God, I hope that dear Nod was another anointing of your life by God. That is why I am so anxious to help you.

My solicitor has written to Mr Smith to advance the process of your adoption and to ensure that the legacy that Nod bequeathed to you before he died is enacted. I am very anxious to make you secure Angela and to have you here. I know from experience that sometimes solicitors need to be pushed to do their work. It might also be worthwhile reminding Mr Smith that he needs to assist the process so that we can get you home with us.

Take care for now, dear Angela. Send me the details I need to transfer the money and I will do it as soon as I can. Meantime, keep well and stay brave. You are a beautiful person. Thank you for coming into our lives.
With all the love and affection I have,
Mom

31 May 2007
From: Michael_smith163@yahoo.com
To: Michelle Mansfield
Sent: Thursday, May 31, 2007 6:05 AM
Subject: Codicil to the Will of the late Dr. Norbertine OD Nallum

Dear Madam,
I am sorry i cannot find your previous email, i may have deleted that message unknowingly, i will appreciate it if you can forward that email to me again, so i can kind give answers to your questions.
Thanks in anticipation
Sincerely
Michael

From: Michelle Mansfield
To: michael_smith163@yahoo.com ; ABCD@efg.com
Sent: Thursday, May 31, 2007 9:51 AM
Subject: Codicil to the Will of the late Dr. Norbertine OD Nallum

Dear Sir
I attach a copy of the letter you have requested. I should be grateful for an immediate response as I am due to go on holiday tomorrow.
Yours sincerely
Michelle Mansfield, LL.B
Attachment: Copy of letter

From: Michael Smith
To: ABCD@efg.com
Sent: Thursday, May 31, 2007 1:34 PM
Subject: Re: Fw: Ms Mansfield

Dear Bert,
thank you for the message, i do not mean any harm to the widow, i do not see the reason why you will be angry with me, for now showing up in Accra Ghana, i do not want to go back to that incident, but i cannot just appear before someone i have not met before, looking at the situation of things, i do not have any information of where you people where, the hotel you were loadging at, all i was asked is where can we meet, i requested for a contact number in Ghana to reach you people, i never got any response to that, at least if Dr. Nallum cannot speak because of his disability, his wife or his PA would have done that, no word from any of you, i find it bizzare you know, if you were in my position you will surely do the same thing, anyways its all past and gone now, i am sorry for all that, i will wait to get a call from you, and look forward to see the death certificate.
    Concerning the whole affair now, when exactly are we starting the process of getting the legal paperwork and bringing the young girl to England? i believe that is Mrs. Nallum top priority.
Looking forward to your soon response.
Sincerely
Michael

From: ABCD@efg.com
To: Michael Smith
Sent: Thursday, May 31, 2007 8:26 PM
Subject: Re: Fw: Ms Mansfield

Dear Mr Smith
I have just spoken to mrs Nallum. You are right, arranging for angela to come to england is her top priority and she has asked me to help make this happen.
    I am not fully up to speed on all the communications you and her late husband exchanged. It will take me a few days to review the emails. Furthermore, i must

travel to the Mediterranean on saturday for 10 days but i will be checking my email when I can.

I should be grateful if you could fully brief me on what precisely needs to be done to advance the formal adoption process of angela. Mrs nallum has asked me to travel with her to south africa in three weeks and should there be anything we can do then, or before, please advise me.

I assure you that as soon as dr nallum's death certificate arrives i will forward you a copy. In this regard i would be most grateful if you would forward a copy of mr lazar's death certificate to me.

I do not understand your clear paranoia. But i intend to call you tomorrow, with mrs nallum's sanction. I shall call you tomorrow between 10 and 11 am GMT. Or is there another time that is more appropriate for you?

Meantime mrs nallum would be most grateful if you could forward the required information to her solicitor ms mansfield, so that she can advance angela's legacy through the probate system.
yours sincerely,
Bartholomew Ahern

From: "Angela Vukadinovich" <admin209@rslrs12.rslrs12-server.com>
To: Catherine Nallum
Sent: Thursday, May 31, 2007 9:27 PM
Subject: You have a new eCard from Angela Vukadinovich

DO NOT REPLY TO THIS MESSAGE. THIS IS AN AUTOMATIC NOTIFICATION.
Mom, you have a free eCard card waiting for you from Angela Vukadinovich!
To view your eCard, click (or copy and paste) this link . . .
[01 Image3 teddy bear ecard]

From: l.vukadinovich@yahoo.com.au
To: Catherine Nallum
Sent: Thursday, May 31, 2007 11:31 PM
Subject: Re: thanks Mom

Dear Mom
i hope you got my card, iits just a piece of my love for to you, and thank you for message you sent, they make me so strong each day, this is my private email, Mr. smith dont have access to it, so i am ok to chat with you here, its safe and secret, my period starts on saturday, i will be happy if i can get those stuff before then, below you will find the address you will use for the moneygram ok, thank you so very mucch mom.
From you baby girl Angela

From: Catherine Nallum
To: l.vukadinovich@yahoo.com.au
Sent: Thursday, May 31, 2007 11:55 PM
Subject: Re: thanks Mom

Dearest Angela,

It is always a joy to find you here. And, today, the joy was increased by your beautiful teddy bear card and message. It is so cute. Thank you, you are so very special. I know already that you and I will get very close.

I could not find an address for where the moneygram is to be sent. Perhaps you forgot to attach it? Can you send it to me? I want to make sure you have all your little comforts before your period begins.

I am glad to know that this email is safe. There is so much I would love to share with you and even some questions I'd love to ask. When he was dying, your dad asked me to promise him that I would not remain a widow for the rest of my life. I cannot contemplate the thought of starting a relationship now, but the thought of loneliness in old age frightens me. That is why I am looking forward to having you with us. I want to be surrounded by loving people. Tell me, Angela, how do you think my children will react if I begin dating someone in a few months? Would you be offended? There is someone I have in mind, but I need, for decency, to allow some time to pass.

I love you dear child and feel so very privileged to have you as a confidante. Always, and with affection
Mom

1 June 2007

It's 11.20 a.m. and time to pick up the phone and find out what 'Michael Smith' has to say to 'Bartholomew Ahern'!

Smith: Hello.
Ahern: Hello. Can I speak to Michael Smith please?
Smith: Yes. Who am I speaking with please?
Ahern: This is Bartholomew Ahern. I am calling you from England.
Smith: Oh! Hello Mr Bartholomew. How are you, sir?
Ahern: I am very well, thank you. Very nice to speak with you.
Smith: It's a pleasure.
Ahern: As you know, I've taken over because of the passing of Dr Nallum. So, I'm not entirely up to speed with everything that's been happening but there are some questions I need to approach with you but maybe you also could inform me how I should proceed with this so that we can arrange for little Angela to come and live in the Nallum house.

Smith: Yeah. Okay. Actually . . . Angela's care . . . I am so sorry to hear about the sudden death of Dr Nallum and I also send my condolences to his wife.

Ahern: Thank you.

Smith: For the good intentions they have for this young girl. You know how complicated these things are.

Ahern: Yes.

Smith: But, nevertheless, there is always a solution for the problem.

Ahern: Sure.

Smith: So, before he passed away we were on the process of getting some forms to apply for, for Dr Nallum to take over possession of Dr Lazar's estate. That's where the process was at.

Ahern: Okay.

Smith: So I don't know when we will be ready to proceed with the takeover, but we can start somewhere [garbled]

Ahern: I'm very sorry, Mr Smith. The line is very bad. I'm finding it difficult to hear you properly. Could I call you back to see if I can get a better line?

Smith: [garbled] Okay, call me right back.

Ahern: Just give me a moment and hopefully we will have a better line.

Smith: Okay. Go ahead.

Ahern: Hello. Mr Smith?

Smith: Yeah.

Ahern: Oh yes. That sounds much better. There's not as much static or noise in the background. So, sorry, you were saying what needs to be done.

Smith: We are in the process of getting the forms for the Grant Certificate completed.

Ahern: Yes.

Smith: The Grant Certificate in the case of Dr Nallum or Mrs Catherine Nallum are given the authority to take over Lazar's estate.

Ahern: Yes.

Smith: And to keep Angela under their custody.

Ahern: Yes.

Smith: That was the process before the sudden incident.

Ahern: Yes.

Smith: And I actually did a list of the forms to be applied for, which will cost about a $1,770.

Ahern: Okay.

Smith: Which I understand Dr Nallum came to Ghana with.

Ahern: Yes, that's correct.

Smith: But we were not able to meet each other.

Ahern: Yes, yes, that was quite unfortunate actually. Okay, I don't seem to have all of the communications. Could you please send me an email with those

details and I'll try and expedite that as quickly as possible?
Smith: [silence]
Ahern: Hello?
Smith: Come again.
Ahern: Could you write to me again with those details? And precisely what it is you need me to do and I'll try to expedite this as quickly as possible.
Smith: I think that will not be a problem.
Ahern: Okay. Thank you. Thank you. And we can move it along because I know that Mrs Nallum has exchanged some emails with Angela and is quite anxious to have the little girl come to her family. It will be wonderful.
Smith: Yeah, okay. Is that a contact number where I can also reach you?
Ahern: Yes, you have a number there do you? Or do you want a number do you?
Smith: Do you have a personal number where I can reach you?
Ahern: Yes, of course. You can call the following number: zero, zero, four, four –
Smith: If you can send me a short email with it.
Ahern: Oh yes, I will do that.
Smith: Well actually, when I send you that information, on your response you can add your telephone number.
Ahern: I will be very happy to do that. Yes, I will be very happy to do that. That won't be a problem, at all. Now, just some things . . . Mrs Nallum's solicitor sent me a copy of an email she sent to you. I know she's anxious to progress the Probate . . . As you know, Dr Nallum amended his will to benefit young Angela and . . . I don't know all of these things because they are to do with lawyers but I know the Probate process needs to be put in motion so she needs Angela's full name, her date of birth and confirmation from you that you are the current legal guardian. And then just some proof of identity, just a formality that is required for the Inland Revenue. I'm sure you won't have any problem in doing that either.
Smith: Okay. Did you send that by email?
Ahern: I have a copy she sent to our system of the letter she sent to you. And she sent you a copy again yesterday. I think you wrote to her asking her to send it again and I know that she did that.
Smith: Yes.
Ahern: She's about to leave on holiday, so she's really anxious to expedite this just to keep Mrs Nallum happy. So if you could deal with that we would be most appreciative.
Smith: What actually needs to be done on their side?
Ahern: I just think she needs you to confirm Angela's full name. I know there was confusion as she was adopted by Lazar, was it, Vukadinovich?
Smith: Yeah.

Ahern: So we don't know, does she have Vukadinovich or does she have her original name? And then, the date of birth of the little girl and then, just for you to confirm that you are currently the legal guardian. It's just some formality, I think. And then, proof of identity will be required at some point when this goes to the Inland Revenue. That's all. But I think if she had those three pieces of information to begin with, at least that would keep Mrs Nallum happy, you know? Because the process can get under way.

Smith: [pause] Okay.

Ahern: Okay.

Smith: That will not be a problem.

Ahern: If you could do that before close of business today, I assure you, sir, we would be most grateful.

Smith: Okay. So, how is Mrs Nallum? How is she doing at the moment?

Ahern: Well, you can imagine. She is very shocked. We all are very shocked because this happened so suddenly. And Dr Nallum was just a lovely person. He was a lovely human being. Very friendly. Beautiful smile. And in his own way he had a great sense of humour. We loved to work with him and then, suddenly, within a week, he's gone! So, she's finding it difficult and so are the children, particularly their youngest boy. He's very traumatised by it. But life will go on and they will find a way of coping. But she's a wonderful woman, Catherine.

Smith: Yes.

Ahern: But I will pass on your kind regards and condolences and I am sure she will be glad to hear that Mr Smith. Thank you very much.

Smith: Okay, no problem. Okay, I will do what I have to do. I will send you an email in this regards. So we can take it from there.

Ahern: That would be great. Okay, thank you so mu–

Smith: Where are you calling [garbled].

Ahern: Pardon?

Smith: Where are you calling from at the moment?

Ahern: Well I am still in Sussex at the moment. But I am due to leave tomorrow morning. I'm going on holidays to Malta. Have you heard of it? It's in the Mediterranean. I am going there for ten days.

Smith: Yes, I know.

Ahern: But don't worry I will be checking my emails.

Smith: Will you not be on the telephone when you are in Malta?

Ahern: Well you may be able to get me, yes. I can give you a number. That won't be a problem, if you need to contact me.

Smith: We can keep in touch by email.

Ahern: Yes, absolutely.

Smith: You know, with this kind of issue you don't just rush into it.

Ahern: Of course.

Smith: You understand? We have to take one thing at a time because [garbled]

Ahern: Yes.

Smith: So that's why I am trying to be protective. You know?

Ahern: Of course.

Smith: I need to know all that is going on and who is the family she wants to be with.

Ahern: Of course.

Smith: And I can finally say, 'Okay, it is done. You can go.'

Ahern: Yes.

Smith: Actually, I will personally want to bring her myself to England.

Ahern: Yes.

Smith: Yeah, I think that would be a good thing to do. To see in person where she is going to be.

Ahern: Yes, I think that was the logic originally behind Dr Nallum and Mrs Nallum and two of their children going out to Ghana. I think they wanted to meet you and, maybe, meet Angela, so that you would form a positive opinion of them.

Smith: Yeah.

Ahern: I think it's very important that you, as her guardian, are satisfied that she is being taken care of in a good home. And I can assure you, it's a wonderful home.

Smith: You know, as her father's [garbled] it is my responsibility to make sure she is safe. I did exchange emails with Dr Nallum [and told him] that I could keep Angela until she is eighteen, that wouldn't be a problem.

Ahern: Right.

Smith: I didn't have the right to change her father's wish.

Ahern: Yes.

Smith: You understand that?

Ahern: No. No, I'm just getting to know this as you know. I need you to be patient with me and to help me, so that I can do everything properly. Because, obviously, I want to please Mrs Nallum also.

Smith: [pause] Okay. That won't be a problem.

Ahern: Okay. Thank you very much. Thank you very much, Mr Smith.

Smith: You are welcome, sir.

Ahern: We will be in contact. I will expect your email and then I will reply. And hopefully we can do that before I leave tomorrow for Malta.

Smith: Okay.

Ahern: Okay. Thank you very much. Lovely to talk to you, sir.

Smith: And when you go, you do have a safe trip, eh?

Ahern: Thank you very much. Yes, I'm looking forward to doing some fishing and swimming and all those wonderful things we do on holidays.

Smith: Yeah.

Ahern: So it will be nice. Okay, thank you very much.
Smith: [garbled] You are welcome.
Ahern: Take care and God bless you.
Smith: All right. God bless you.
Ahern: Bye bye. God bless. [Hangs up the phone and giggles.]

From: michael_smith163@yahoo.com
To: Michelle Mansfield; ABCD@efg.com
Sent: Friday, June 1, 2007 6:51 AM
Subject: Re: Codicil to the Will of the late Dr. Norbertine OD Nallum

Dear Michelle,
Thank you for the email, presently the young girl is under my guardianship, with the help of my mother, her full name is Angela hlubi Vukadinovich, at this time, i cannot send you a copy of her ID, because it is still in process at the Home Affairs, as soon as it is ready you will have a copy of it, i am planing on coming to the UK personally to meet with the Nallum family, i believe it will be the best time for us to meet and discuss whatever that is left, concerning the probate matters.
I have to go for now, hope to hear from you soon
Sincerely
Michael Smith Esq.,

From: Michael Smith
To: ABCD@efg.com
Sent: Friday, June 01, 2007 3:05 PM
Subject: Re: Fw: Ms Mansfield

Hello Bert,
it was nice speaking with you this afternoon, although line was not that better, i picked some vital information that i needed from you, i must say that you sound more like an American, rather than a british, anyways i have just sent a mail to Mrs. Michelle, i will prefer that i deal with either you or her, i do not find it ok, to send information both ways, if its ok with Mrs. Nallum to deal with her solicitor personally, that will be fine, but if all correspondence must be between you and I, then we will stick to that, i hope you understand my point. below is the details of the process sent to Dr. Nallum.
Attention: Dr. Nod Nallum . . .
Total Cost: USD$1,753.02 Incl. Vat & Disbursements . . .

Sincerely
Michael Smith Esq.,

From: Michelle Mansfield
To: michael_smith163@yahoo.com ; ABCD@efg.com
Sent: Friday, June 1, 2007 3:06 PM
Subject: Re: Codicil to the Will of the late Dr. Norbertine OD Nallum

Dear Sir
I am most grateful to you. I will, in due course, need proof of identity of both
you and Angela hlubi Vukadinovich. However, I urgently need her date of birth
for the purpose of completing the initial stages of the Probate process. If this is
not supplied, HM Revenue and Customs will not proceed. Please send me her
date of birth immediately. I need to assure Mrs Nallum that this stage has been
completed before I leave on holiday.
Yours sincerely
Michelle Mansfield, LL.B

From: Michelle Mansfield
To: ABCD@efg.com; michael_smith163@yahoo.com
Sent: Friday, June 1, 2007 8:04 PM
Subject: Re: Codicil to the Will of the late Dr. Norbertine OD Nallum

Dear Mr Ahern
I regret to inform you that I am unable to file the Probate documents as I am
missing the DOB of Angela Vukadinovich. HM Revenue and Customs are very
strict on details such as this, especially since Dr Nallum's Codicil is in respect
of a minor.
    Despite a further request this afternoon to Mr Smith in South Africa, I still
do not know the young girl's DOB. Regrettably, I must leave the office now.
Please offer my apologies to Mrs Nallum. I will endeavour to advance the
process as quickly as possible upon my return in early July.
Yours respectfully
Michelle Mansfield, LL.B

From: l.vukadinovich@yahoo.com.au
To: Catherine Nallum
Sent: Friday, June 1, 2007 11:34 PM
Subject: Re: thanks Mom

Dear Mom
i am happy you love the card, it came from my heart to you, sorry i forgot
to address, this is my friend i can get the money through her, the name and
address you will find below.

Name: Point Nsovo Hlatshwayo
72 edison crescent Sunning hills (Same address given by Smith, located in a quiet residential suberb of Johannesburg)
Johannesburg South Africa.

I am really getting through the pains in my heart, i feel i have a real mother, i have never had a motherly love since i was born, i am just feeling it, whoever my mother was that abandoned me in the street to die of cold did not succeed, god had a different plans for my, thank you Dear Mom for being there for me, my the gentle soul of my lovely dads rest in the heart of the lord Amen.

Mom please send me the referense as soon as you have the money sent through ok, thanking u in andvance
your Angel

2 June 2007
From: Catherine Nallum
To: l.vukadinovich@yahoo.com.au
Sent: Saturday, June 02, 2007 00:37 AM
Subject: Re: thanks Mom

Dearest Angela
Thank you so much for your lovely email. I am always so delighted to hear from you. It is just appalling how you were abandoned as a baby. It is inconceivable how someone as beautiful and intelligent as you could be so rejected. I will pray for your birth mum and dad, that God will forgive them.

Thank you for the address through which I will forward you the money. I have been so busy today for something unexpected has happened. Your dad's personal assistant, Mr Ahern (Bart), whom I have been relying on greatly since his death, has persuaded me to take a break with him on the Mediterranean island of Malta. We have a friend who is a pilot. Nod nicknamed him 'Biggles' after some comic character from his childhood. Biggles is coming too and we will all fly together. My three youngest children are coming with us. I'm glad to be getting away to the sunshine as May was quite a dull and cold month with much that I want to forget. It was a last-minute decision but that has made it all the more exciting.

As soon as I get to Malta tomorrow I will send you the moneygram. I just did not have time to do it today. We will be there in the early afternoon.

One other thing Angela. I am quite upset by Mr Smith. My solicitor requested three simple pieces of information from him, but he failed to send your date of birth and, as a consequence, the whole matter has been delayed by a month. I've told Mr Ahern that he is not to communicate with Mr Smith until I am ready. I do not suffer fools easily.

You need to know, dear child, that your English dad left you a very generous legacy: £2 million sterling. This will be placed in a trust fund until you are 21 years of age. Coupled with what Lazar left you, it is a fantastic start in life and you deserve it. I will instruct you how to manage it wisely so that you will have no cares or worries in the future. I cannot believe how negligent Mr Smith has been. I am really furious with him. Such a simple matter and he could not get it right.

Forgive me dear child for writing to you in this way. I think the only way we are going to get you safely to England is if I go to South Africa and sit on Mr Smith until he does the work.

Take care dearest child. How beautiful that you dropped the 'a' in your name for, to me, you are an angel. I will email you tomorrow and let you know I have transferred the money. Goodnight little one. Sleep softly, enfolded by angels of your own.
Always and with loving affection
Mom

From: michael_smith163@yahoo.com ;
To: Michelle Mansfield
Sent: Saturday, June 2, 2007 00:47 AM
Subject: Re: Codicil to the Will of the late Dr. Norbertine OD Nallum

Angela Vukadinovich: date of birth August 15th 1993
I am sure the probate process can wait until her ID is available, i dont know how your system works over there, let me know the procedures.
thanks
Michael

6 June 2007
From: Catherine Nallum
To: l.vukadinovich@yahoo.com.au
Sent: Wednesday, June 06, 2007 5:01 PM
Subject: Re: thanks Mom

Dear Angela
I feel so guilty about my silence but let me explain. I came to Malta at short notice, as you know. However, I didn't realise we were going to the smaller Maltese island of Gozo. It is very remote and it doesn't have a moneygram facility or an Internet café. I've been lucky in that a visitor to the hotel has a laptop with satellite phone connection and he has kindly allowed me to send this email to you.

I need to confirm that the address you sent me is okay to send cash to. I have South African money from my last visit to your homeland. Please let me know as quickly as possible if it is okay for me to send it to you at the address you have given.

I send you much love and affection. I wish you were here with us. The islands of Malta have amazing history. Most of the great civilisations at one time or another occupied the islands and left their mark upon the landscape and character of these truly beautiful people. Did you know that St Luke wrote about the friendliness of the Maltese people in the Acts of the Apostles?
Love to my little angel.
Always
Mum

7 June 2007
From: l.vukadinovich@yahoo.com.au
To: Catherine Nallum
Sent: Thursday, June 7, 2007 10:11 PM
Subject: Re: thanks Mom

Dear Catherine
if you cannot get the money through to me, its ok i will be fine, am not just enjouying my life this few days, i do not know if monye can be sent through postal address, i will wait for Gods time to manifest in my life, thanks for your care and love
Angela

9 June 2007
From: Catherine Nallum
To: l.vukadinovich@yahoo.com.au
Sent: Saturday, June 09, 2007 6:17 PM
Subject: Re: thanks Mom

Dearest Angela,
'Catherine' sounds so formal from my future daughter. I love it when you call me Mom.

I send money all the time through the ordinary post. It's never been a problem. So, is the address you have given okay for me to send it to you? I leave Malta on Tuesday. It will be easier to communicate after this. I hope I can bring you to Malta one day. The blue seas and the generous hours of sunshine have me looking like a bronzed goddess.
I love you dearest daughter.
Always
Mom

13 June 2007
From: Catherine Nallum
To: l.vukadinovich@yahoo.com.au
Sent: Wednesday, June 13, 2007 1:24 AM
Subject: Re: thanks Mom

Dearest Angela
We are back home after a wonderful 10 days on the Maltese island of Gozo.
I'm so sorry that communications were erratic.

This morning I went to the post office in Valletta, Malta and posted 20 fifty rand notes and 25 twintig rand notes to you. That is 1,500 rand in cash. I sent it to the following address: Miss Angela Vukadinovic, c/o Point Nsovo Hlatshwayo, 72 Edison Crescent Sunning Hills, Johannesburg, Republic of South Africa. Please let me know when it arrives. It is in a padded envelope and enclosed inside a small paper giftbox.

Good night dearest Angela. Soon we will formalise your adoption and arrange your journey to England. Please, I beg you, put pressure on Smith to do the work Lazar paid him to do. Oh how I detest lawyers! It's the only profession in the world where, even if they lose through incompetence, their unfortunate clients still have to pay.
Be safe my dear.
Always
Mom

From: l.vukadinovich@yahoo.com.au
To: Catherine Nallum
Sent: Wednesday, June 13, 2007 6:00 PM
Subject: Re: thanks Mom

Mom
i thought i could hear from you before you post the money, i am really tired of my life, i feel i dont know my left to my right this time around, everything is going just bad, i called my friend who leaves at the address i gave to you, and he said to me that they have moved from that address. so what will i do now, i will i know if the money arrives safely, probably someone else has moved to that residence, and probably will take the money that you said you put in the evelope, mom this is not safe at all, you should have just sent me this money to the moneygram, am not happy with everything around me, my father never treated me this way, i was a happy girl when daddy was alive, now i am not, all that i was promised seems to be going down, how i wish the hands of time can turn around, if i get the money fine, but if i dont its ok, i will be just fine, may be i should just kill myself, life means nothing to me

anymore.

    thank god for bring you back home safely, take care and God be wit you
Amen
Angela

From: Catherine Nallum
To: l.vukadinovich@yahoo.com.au
Sent: Wednesday, June 13, 2007 10:38 PM
Subject: Re: thanks Mom

Oh my dear, you sound so depressed and I am frightened that you are now mentioning suicide. How terrible. I thought I was being kind in sending you the 1,500 rand. I loved all these notes: the elephants on the 20 rand notes and the dignified gaze of the lion on the 50 rand notes. Can you not go to the address you gave me and tell the people to look out for the package? You don't have to tell them what is in it. Maybe Mr Smith could go and explain to the new residents that a packet for you is coming from Malta? It's about time he began to earn his fee. But for him we would have had you here now in our home.

    Do not despair my child. Remember, you are a very rich girl and, by the time you become a young woman, you will be secure for life.

    Thank God I didn't send the moneygram to that address you gave me, since your friend had already moved. How unfortunate. Should I send it to the office of Mr Smith and he can pass it to you? I wouldn't blame you if you don't trust him. What a mess he has created. I am sure Lazar would have sacked him for incompetence if he was still alive.

    I want to ask you a favour, dear Angela, in strictest confidence. I will pay all costs involved. Could you quietly go to another solicitor in South Africa and explain your situation and ask him or her to look into it? You would have to explain that their advice is being sought in confidence and that their fees will be paid by me. I just need to know that your adoption by me is carried out entirely legally. Mr Smith need never know you did this. It will be our little secret. Shall we do it?

    Take care, dear Angela, and please do not despair. Never talk to me again about ending your life. It frightens me. You are very close to achieving new and wonderful dreams. Believe! On our way back from Ghana we had a very spiritual experience on board our flight. I can't wait to tell you about it. It is why I am so confident that all will be well! I love you Angela. So do your new brothers and sisters. Wait and see. The best is yet to come.
Always, and with deep affection
Mom

15 June 2007

From: l.vukadinovich@yahoo.com.au
To: Catherine Nallum
Sent: Friday, June 15, 2007 9:53 PM
Subject: Re: thanks Mom

Dear Mom
i went to the address and i met this lady, but she said the owner of the house is not around, that i should come at weekend to check if the letter is there, i had a very bad day today, there is stupid boy in my hood, she always insult me by telling me that i dont know my real parents, that my father is white and i am black, this is really breaking my heart, i really want to leave this place for good, i ask Mr smith what is holding my trip to the UK, he said that dad was supposed to send some money to buy some forms that will be used for the process, and he has not receive it yet, he said he is waiting for you to finish mourning dad, so you can have the money sent to him, is this correct, please let me know, if he gets the money still doesn not do what he has to do, i will then look for another lawyer as you ask me, lets give him the chance.

I hope i can get hold of the money as they said, i really need it to take care of my personal need, mom please try and speed up the process, i am getting frustrated here, i thank you in advance, and may god bless your family.
Yours daughter Angela

From: Catherine Nallum
To: l.vukadinovich@yahoo.com.au
Sent: Friday, June 15, 2007 4:06 PM
Subject: Re: thanks Mom

Dearest Angela
I, too, am frustrated by the process and have a broken heart because of it. Mr Smith is not telling you the whole truth. He informed your father that he would be in Ghana and your father brought me and two of our children there to meet him. We had the money to give to Mr Smith. We waited and waited and he never showed up. And it was in Ghana that your dear father contracted the illness from which he died. So, my dear, I have a lot of anger in my heart towards Mr Smith and that is why I do not trust him. Furthermore, all he needed to do to advance the large and generous legacy your dad bequeathed to you was to send your date of birth to my solicitor in England. He couldn't even do this. I am really worried for you my child.

What are the forms Mr Smith is talking about? Can you check and let me know? Ask Mr Smith if it is possible for me to see the forms before he files them. That would be very helpful. He could scan them and send them to me.

Don't worry my dear child. All will be well and soon you will be with us in

England and away from all those horrible and racist bullies. You deserve better and I am determined to fulfil the wishes of your father and my dearly departed husband.

Please check again to see if the money I sent from Malta has arrived. It must surely arrive safely. Your dear fathers, Lazar and Nod, will take care of it.
Always and with affection
Mom

16 June 2007
From: l.vukadinovich@yahoo.com.au
To: Catherine Nallum
Sent: Saturday, June 16, 2007 8:45 AM
Subject: Re: thanks Mom

Dear Mom
i justr came from the address again, and the man i met told me that letters do not come to that address, so there is no letter from malta, this means nothing there, i am really exhusted it was a lond distance and cost much to go there, my dad always send money via moneygram and not by post, well i will speak to smith about what you said, take care mom, i am realy tired, i must go now
Angela

From: Catherine Nallum
To: l.vukadinovich@yahoo.com.au
Sent: Saturday, June 16, 2007 6:05 PM
Subject: Re: thanks Mom

Dearest Angela
I am confused. If it is a genuine address, how can letters not come to it? If you were able to find it twice, then surely the postman can do the same! To be honest, I think Mr Smith is a conman and has intercepted the money. I am really worried about you.

Here is what I want you to do. First, open an account in a bank in Johannesburg. We can send documentation to the manager to show that you have a very large legacy pending. Since you are sixteen years old, you have less than two years to reach your majority. Unless it is 21 in South Africa? Either way, we can arrange for a bridging loan of $6,000 per year. You really only need this for this year as you will, I earnestly hope, be with us in England before the end of the year. I will be happy to know that you have $500 pocket money per month to help you buy all your womanly needs. The only thing I implore you never to take, dear Angela – and it was a concern I know your father Lazar also had – is drugs. They will destroy you and you are much too beautiful for that.

Don't tell Smith about this for I am sure he will take the money from you. Tell me, do you really trust Mr Smith? Do you think he is a good man? I want to test his genuineness. He wanted Dr Nallum to send legal costs to cover various forms. That was the cash we carried to Ghana for him. To be honest, I couldn't understand this, for I would have thought Lazar would have covered all expenses. We too have legal costs in England. We must pay for the services of our solicitor and we must pay for various legal documents to be lodged to bring into effect the large legacy Nod has left you.

But Mr Smith has custody of you and we must deal with him. He also has much to lose if he continues to mess up the process of your adoption. Nod purchased an incredible gift for Mr Smith's family, which he wished to present to him in Ghana. I will give it to him if I discover he is genuine.

Bart Ahern is going write to Mr Smith and ask him to send $100 towards our legal fees. If Mr Smith does that, then we will know he is genuine. Once he proves to be honourable, he will be pushing an open door thereafter and I will feel very guilty that I doubted him. If he doesn't, however, we will have serious cause for concern.

Take care Angela. Do not despair. All will be well. Don't forget to go to the bank and tell them you wish to, with my help, set up a bridging loan. You can give the bank my details. If the bank needs me to contact them, I will.
With much love and affection dear child
Mom

18 June 2007
From: l.vukadinovich@yahoo.com.au
To: Catherine Nallum
Sent: Monday, June 18, 2007 7:47 PM
Subject: Re: thanks Mom

Mom
there is something i want to tell you today, i was speaking to mr. smith about the money you posted to that address, and he said to me that its not true, how come you post money via address, he said its a lie, that i am being fooled, he said that all that you and dad promised me are not true, he said why did you not send the money via moneygram rather than posting it, the most worring path of it is that he said that i am not going to the UK anymore, that you and the PA is playing some funny games with me, he said why is it that you have not called him on the phone ever since the communication began, i am really worried, what is the whole truth, i dont know what to beleive anymore, this is not the life i want to live at all, he said he was going to tell your PA to stop communicating with him, that i am not going to move to the UK, he said whatever thing that

dad has bequeted to me she be withdrawn, in the sence that my own dad left
more than enough for my future, please let me know what is the truth.
i wait to hear from you soonest
Angela

20 June 2007
From: Catherine Nallum
To: l.vukadinovich@yahoo.com.au
Sent: Wednesday, June 20, 2007 5:23 AM
Subject: Re: thanks Mom

Dearest Angela
Your email has made me angry. Not with you, dear child, but with Mr Smith.
How dare he accuse me and my dearly departed husband of lying to you
and him. He is the liar. Did he not tell you that he has already had a lengthy
discussion with Mr Ahern about your affairs?

For the record, I did post you 1,500 rand from Malta, and your dad has
bequeathed to you 2 million pounds sterling. It is the truth.

Angela, you have a choice to make. Do you want to come and live with me
in England or stay with Mr Smith? If you want to come to England, I will fight
that son of a bitch every inch of the way for you and will delight in travelling
to South Africa to kick his sorry ass.

You can escape the grasp of Mr Smith if you want. I can arrange to have you
rescued. Just give me the word and I will put a task force in place. I love you
dear child. God bless and protect you.
With much love and affection
Mom

From: l.vukadinovich@yahoo.com.au
To: Catherine Nallum
Sent: Wednesday, June 20, 2007 5:56 PM
Subject: Re: thanks Mom

Deare Mom
i am sorry for all this, i dont like what is happening to us at all, i have known
Mr. smith for a long time, he is my father lawyer, they never had argument for
once, he was kind to me anyway even when dad was here, i also believe in what
you said to me mom, i dont have to doubt you, but where will i stand at this
point, that is the problem i face, mom i have to beg a friend for R20 to come
to the cafe to write to you, because he does not want me to come to the cafe
anymore, i dont have the power of my own, because i dont have access to cash,
mom that money would have helped me alot, also i want to see one of my dads

female friend, she leaves in cape town, i need to tell her what is going, but i need money to travel that place, i know you have lost that R1500, mom please can you please send me a little more to cover this arrangement? i really wana come to england, not after all the love you have shown me, pleasxe mom help me achieve my fathers dream for me, i will be grateful to you,

i must go now, my time is over, i love you mom, take care and god be with us Amen
Angela

22 June 2007
From: Catherine Nallum
To: l.vukadinovich@yahoo.com.au
Sent: Friday, June 22, 2007 6:06 AM
Subject: Re: thanks Mom

Dearest Angela,
I've told you how we will sort out your affairs. We are going to set up a bridging loan for you so that you can access the funds your father here has left you. You shouldn't have to beg me or even Mr Smith for money.

Dear child, will you be safe to travel to Cape Town alone? You are so young and I am very worried for you.

Angela, there is something I need to discuss with you. It is a very serious matter. Please again assure me that Mr Smith does not have access to this email. Then I will tell you what you need to know. Take care dear little Angela. You are beautiful and I love you very much.
I love you
Mom

From: l.vukadinovich@yahoo.com.au
To: Catherine Nallum
Sent: Friday, June 22, 2007 6:44 PM
Subject: Re: thanks Mom

this mail is secure mom, i am in south africa, i just want to travel to cape town, its another city, mom, please i need little money, Mr. smith said he does not want me to go to the cafe, please anything small will be ok for me
Angela

23 June 2007
From: ABCD@efg.com
To: michael_smith163@yahoo.com
Sent: Saturday, June 23, 2007 3:39 AM

Subject: Angela

Dear Mr Smith
Mrs nallum has asked me to write to you concerning angela. She's concerned that angela may be in need of some pocket money. Confidentially, angela has written to mrs nallum requesting money and the good woman responded by posting some cash to an address that angela had sent her. Now, it appears, the postman doesn't deliver mail to this address, which seems a bit strange. Consequently, mrs nallum is reluctant to send cash, other than directly to a bank, as it appears the money she sent is lost. We are writing to request your help with two matters:

1. Mrs nallum would be grateful if you would help her set up a bank account for angela into which she can transfer money.
2. From the legacy that dr nallum has left angela, she wishes to organise a bridging loan for her, while the probate process is progressing. Mrs nallum will act as guarantor for the loan.

Your help and advice on this is greatly appreciated.
yours sincerely,
Bartholomew Ahern

From: Michael Smith
To: ABCD@efg.com
Sent: Saturday, June 23, 2007 12:37 PM
Subject: Re: Angela

Mr Bartholomew
thank you for your message, i will be very brief, i simply do not understand what exactly is going on, you need not to tell me about Angela's pocket money, she gets whatever she wants, good food and other material stuff, i was so amazed that Mrs. Nallum posted money to the young girl, instead of using the normal moneygram transfer agents, i simply did not believe that, i clearly told Angela that she has been fooled, and i am sticking by my word, she claimed that her husband bequeted two million pounds to the young girl, but cannot send her a little gift that she asked for, i simply do not believe what is going on, and i am about to find out, i will terminate all email correspondence with you and Mrs. Nallum, i asked her to call me, you said she is still mourning her husband, but she could travel in and out of England, visiting other country for vacation, it seems she does not trust me, i dont understand why she will ask for an account to be set up for Angela so she can wire money to her, this does not make sense to me, i am her fathers lawyer, and i am her to protect her interest, if she is

sincere and what to send money to her, she can do that through me, or send it to her via moneygram, moreover she does not have an ID book yet, so she cannot open an account, i remember you said you are his PA, and you requested that i send to you the forms needed to start the process, i did, and you did not respond to that effect, and she accused me for the delay, if i do not get the funds for the forms before friday next week, i will terminate all correspondence with both you and Mrs. Nallum, this is how it stands now.

I have to know what her intentions are, before we can proceed further, ever since i took over to administer my client estate, no legal documents have been signed in this regards, and you want me to still believe you guys have the clear intensions to assist this young girl, i doubt it, and i will continue to do so until you guys can clear prove your intensions.
I look forward to hearing from you soon
Sincerely
Michael

From: albc@eircom.net
To: catherinenallum@yahoo.co.uk
Cc: michael_smith163@yahoo.com
Sent: Saturday, June 23, 2007 3:42 PM
Subject: FW: Re: Angela

Dear catherine,
I do not know how to respond to this email from mr smith. I should be obliged if you would consider responding as you think appropriate.
kindest regards,
Bart

From: Michael Smith
To: albc@eircom.net
Sent: Saturday, June 23, 2007 4:13 PM
Subject: Re: FW: Re: Angela

Mr. Bart
I dont appreciate you forwarding emails you sent to Mrs Nallum to me, i do not see the need for that, whatever you want to discuss with her should be private ok,
Thanks
Michael

24 June 2007
From: Catherine Nallum
To: l.vukadinovich@yahoo.com.au

Sent: Sunday, June 24, 2007 6:54 AM
Subject: Re: thanks Mom

Dearest Angela
I am relieved that this email is secure.
By Wednesday I will be ready to fly to South Africa. I need you to be alert to my emails over the next few days for they will contain very important information that you MUST NOT discuss with Mr Smith. Trust me on this my dear child. I am making arrangements to bring you to England.

I will tell you things in the next 48 hours that will convince you of the truth of what I write. They involve a dream that Nod had before he died, an encounter we all had while flying back from Ghana and an apparition I had from Nod yesterday. It all makes sense to me now. Don't be frightened that I should tell you this, dear child. But yes, Nod came to me and told me that he has searched the 'beyond' for Lazar, your father, and cannot find him. But he did find someone who is related to Lazar and who has told us the whole story. He also told me that Mr Smith is an impostor and that you are in grave danger.

Angela, I have spoken with a high official of the Episcopal Church of South Africa and by Wednesday next I hope to be with you at Bishopscourt, Cape Town. I will write to you on Monday with instructions for your movements. I cannot be more specific at present as I am awaiting confirmation that my task force is in place. Trust me on this. I have your best interests at heart.

I must write to Mr Smith and he will not like what I have to say. No doubt he will try to convince you that we are insincere and making a fool of you and him. Please, please, dear child, close your ears to him. He is not an honourable man.

Keep focused on the joy of knowing that you will soon be in England, you will never want again and you will be able to invite your friends to come and stay with you for a holiday.

Take care my dearest Angela. I love you very much. Soon, very soon, we will be together.
Always
Mom

From: Catherine Nallum
To: michael_smith163@yahoo.com
Sent: Sunday, June 24, 2007 7:09 AM
Subject: Re: FW: Re: Angela

Dear Mr Smith
I have read your recent email correspondence to my PA, Bartholomew Ahern.
You will not bully me to respond in the way that you wish. I do not trust

you. Do you hear me? I DO NOT TRUST YOU.

You have been negligent in your dealings with Lazar's adopted daughter. The fact that you are threatening to break off communications with me, despite knowing that Angela is the recipient of a very substantial legacy, is a measure of who you are. Angela will never forgive you.

Angela and I do not need you. You can go to hell. Because of you, my husband is dead!

Catherine Nallum

26 June 2007
From: Catherine Nallum
To: l.vukadinovich@yahoo.com.au
Sent: Tuesday, June 26, 2007 3:38 AM
Subject: Re: thanks Mom

Dearest Angela

Thank you for maintaining silence while I have made all the necessary arrangements for your escape to freedom. I can tell you are a very intelligent young girl. Soon we will be together and I am very excited at the prospect.

I leave for South Africa in the morning. I will fly direct to Cape Town, where we will be together tomorrow at Bishopscourt. I have friends there and it is very secure. Did you know it is where Nelson Mandela spent his first night of freedom? It is there we shall meet for the first time as mother and daughter!

I have the support of a relative of a former British prime minister. This man has many associates in the mercenary world and has put together a task force for your rescue. It comprises 12 plain-clothed Special Service operatives; 4 recruits from the security staff of the Expo Centre; 4 rooftop marksmen; and a helicopter crew.

I need you to memorise the following rescue instructions. Please DO NOT print them out as I am afraid that Mr Smith may discover them. I will deal with him later when you are safe. Just trust me now my child in all that I am saying and doing. I promise you, you will never regret it.

Time and date: 12 noon, Wednesday 27 June 2007
Place: Bateleur A, Expo Centre, Corner Rand Show and Nasrec Roads, Nasrec, Johannesburg
Password: Rolihlahla
Instructions: At 10am you must call the following free telephone number: 0800 800 800. You will reach Corporate Cabs. Ask for Mr Sisulu. When he answers, say, 'I am Angela. Rolihlahla.' He will reply, 'Catherine is expecting you'. Give him specific instructions as to where he can have you picked up. Make sure that Mr Smith has no knowledge of your movements. You must

arrive at the Expo Centre no later than 11.30 am to give you time to find your way to Bateleur A. The task force will monitor your movements, for your protection. When you arrive at Bateleur A, you will find many people preparing for luncheon. You must sit on the back seat, coloured orange, immediately to the left of the entrance. At 12 noon a man in a dark suit, with wings on his lapel, will approach you. He will ask, 'Angela?' You must reply, 'Rolihlahla'. When he says, 'Catherine is expecting you', you will know you have the right contact. You must leave immediately with this gentleman. He will lead you to the helicopter pad and from there you will be flown to OR Tambo Airport, where Biggles will be waiting to fly you to Cape Town. We will meet at Bishopscourt and the Archbishop of Cape Town will celebrate a private Mass with us in thanksgiving for your rescue. During a dinner in your honour, there will be several surprises for you dearest child, including the beautiful teddy bear that Nod and I bought for you.

Angela I have so much to tell you. I am falling in love with my personal assistant, Bartholomew. He is such a lovely man. He has given me so much help regarding your rescue from the scoundrel Smith. The feeling is mutual but we must wait, for now. I think he will be your next 'dad'.

I also need to tell you about some strange events that convinced me that what is about to happen is the will of God. The first was a vivid dream that Nod had in Ghana. He told me that your father, Lazar, had come to greet him. Not much was said in the dream as the person had broken English and a strong Serbian accent. He simply smiled and said to Nod, 'Thank you for caring. All will be well. In this world truth is a fiction distorted for gain.' Nod awoke and immediately wrote down the words that had been spoken. He was very puzzled by what it meant. But now we know!

On our flight home from Ghana there was another bizarre occurrence. It should have alarmed us but, in truth, we all were calmed by a deep sense of wellbeing. As the plane began crossing the Mediterranean at Algiers, Biggles (our pilot) woke Nod to say that his instruments were acting strangely. He said the altimeter indicated that we were flying at a height above the Earth's atmosphere – an impossibility for the Gulfstream 100 jet. Suddenly the cabin filled with what appeared to be heavenly lights. They were the colours of the rainbow, but illuminated and radiant. We sensed that our aircraft had been enveloped by a mystical being and that we were flying, not on fuel, but on spirit. Then the man whom Nod had seen in his dream reappeared. He smiled and said, 'The Great "I Am" is with you and so too is your Angel.' The latter we took as a reference to you. He was gone as suddenly as he appeared. The altimeter showed we were back at 37,000 feet and approaching Barcelona. We had crossed the Mediterranean in the blink of an eye. It was then, dear Angela, that I knew that all would be well with you and that one day, very soon, you would be with Nod and me and our beautiful family.

Sadly, it has not turned out as I imagined. Nod is gone, but I know he is still with me. Last Tuesday night I was awakened by someone gently touching my right shoulder. When I opened my eyes, Nod was sitting at the edge of the bed. I sat up, my heart pounding in my breast. He smiled and said, 'Do not be afraid, it is I.' He told me how much he loved me and that he wanted me to be happy and would not be jealous should I fall in love again. He said that in the spirit world the grace of God is an open channel in which we are freed from the limitations of the human experience.

Nod then told me of his search to find your father. He could not find Lazar in the spirit world but eventually he met the man we all saw on our flight home from Ghana. This man is Lazar's twin brother and was killed during the Kosovo War in 1999. He told Nod that Lazar, your adopted father, is not dead. Lazar, he said, is alive and well in Australia. He said that Lazar knew Mr Smith, a lawyer he once employed in South Africa but later fired because he was dishonest. He said that while Lazar is aware of you, but you are not his adopted daughter!

It appears that everything Mr Smith has been writing about the death of Lazar and the legacy he left you is a sham. It is, in truth, a scam. And, Nod told me, many from the spirit world of Africa whom he has met, including former slaves from Elmina Castle, are deeply offended that Smith would use the memory of their horrendous historical suffering as a justification for such dishonest behaviour.

Mr Smith is, in fact, a low life who preys, like a vulture, on the kindness of others, drawing them into his seedy little world, trying to hoodwink them into believing that he is a caring lawyer looking after a poor little orphaned girl named Angela. And guess what? Lazar's brother also informed us that although Angela does exist, she is not an orphan, but a partner of Smith. And the glorious thing about the past two months, including the writing of this email, is knowing that it is not being written to Angela but to Mr Smith. And what a joy to know that this whole odyssey has been about scamming a scammer!

Africa is an abused continent with a harrowing history. There is much that Westerners should be ashamed of, not least the legacy of slavery. But Africa is full of vibrant people who have refused to give up. A continent of good and great human beings is emerging and they will take their rightful place in the world. What a shame that Michael Smith, aka Lazar, aka Angela, brings dishonour to his family, his country and his continent.

Nkosi sikelel' iAfrika!

Always, and forever

Dr Nod (resurrected from the dead) aka Catherine Nallum aka Bart Ahern aka Michelle Mansfield

Not surprisingly, neither Michael nor Angela responded to the above

email. However, I received another email from Smith a couple of months later, on this occasion purporting to be a diamond dealer. Below is his email and my final response.

31 August 2007
From: michael_smith163@yahoo.com
To: ABCD@efg.com
Sent: Friday, August 31, 2007 4:45 PM
Subject: Rough Diamonds   ulff

Hi
We are rough diamonds stones seller from Angola, we are capable of supplying our buyers on a monthly bases Our stones are from the mine, we are using this opportunity to advertice our product on the web, if you are interested in buying rough stones or you are a broker connected to any diamonds buyer, please respond to this email, if you are not a buyer and not interested in purchasing, please kindly ignore this message.

    Please note that we are interested in dealing with only serious buyer and not to waste time, please read our terms and conditions, if its ok for you, then we can do business

1. We dont send sample stones to any buyer
2. We dont request for any advance fee, for tickets, shipments, etc
3. Buyer must come or send germologist to inspect stones first, if satisfied with the quality and prices of the stones payment will take place in cash
4. We dont deal with the kimberly process, brinks or any security company
5. Our transactions is directly with the buyer and not a middle man
Please find below the manifest of the available stones, prices ranges between USD$100 to USD$800 per carat depending on the quality and size of the stones for contact call Michael Smith on 0027832440955
Rough Size
Between Colour Clarity Overall
7 pcs 3-5 D-H VVS-SI Makeable
9 6-8 ct D-H VVS-SI Makeable
11 9-14 ct D-H VVS-SI Makeable
12 14-17 ct D,H,K,L VVS-SI Sawable
8 18-22.5 D-H VVS-SI Makeable
4 23-25 ct D-H VVS-SI Sawable
2 27 ct D-H VVS-S2 Sawable
2 29 ct D-H,K INTER. FL Sawable
3 30-34 D-H FLAWLESS Sawable
1 32.5ct D-H VVS-SI Sawable

2 35ct D-H VVS-SI Makeable
1 36 ct D-H VVS-SI Sawable

3 September 2007
From: ABCD@efg.com
To: michael_smith163@yahoo.com
Sent: Monday, September 03, 2007 10:00 AM
Subject: Re: Rough Diamonds ulff

Hello dear friend Michael,
This is Nod (back from the dead!). How are you today? I've missed you.

Diamonds now? Wow! Fantastic! Is it okay for Biggles, Catherine, Bart, Michelle and I to fly to Angola and meet you there? I could bring the kids too. What do you think? Any chance of a discount for finding you these additional customers?

I promise you, we are serious buyers and have no intention of wasting your time. We know you are a truthful, upright, genuine and honest agent for precious stones. We are a great match.

If you want to come to England with the stones, I'd be happy to reimburse you for the airfares. That's a genuine invitation. You can trust me. Honest. You know that. After all, I AM WHO I AM!

By the way, how is Angela? Don't forget, once a month, she needs extra sensitivity. Make sure she has enough pocket money to buy what she needs.
Your friend forever,
Nod

Faustin Scam

19 August 2008
From: Faustin
To: faustin33@yahoo.cn
Sent: Tuesday, August 19, 2008 8:48 PM
Subject: Dearest One,

Dearest One,
Please i write to you with a good intention for you to help me out, I am Faustin Dogan(JR) the only son of late DR,FAUSTIN DOGAN my father was a very wealthy Cocoa merchant in Abidjan the economic capital of Ivory coast, my father was poisoned to death by his business associates on one of their outings on a business trip. My mother died when I was a baby and since then my father took me so special. Before the death of my father on JULY 2006 in a private hospital here in Abidjan he secretly called me on his bed side and told me that he has the sum of TWELVE MILLION UNITED STATE DOLLARS USD. ($12,000 000) left in fixed / suspense account in one of the prime bank here in Abidjan ,that he used my name as his only son for the next of Kin in depositing of the fund. He also explained to me that it was because of this wealth that he was poisoned by his business associates.

That I should seek for a foreign partner in a country of my choice where I will transfer this money and use it for investment purpose such as real estate management or hotel management.

I am honourably seeking your assistance in the following ways:
(1) To serve as a guardian of this fund since I am only 20years.
(2) To make arrangement for me to come over to your country to further my Education and to secure a resident permit in your country Moreover, I am willing to offer you a good percentage from the total sum as compensation for your effort/input after the successful transfer of this fund into your nominated

account overseas.

Furthermore, you will indicate your option towards assisting me as I believe that this transaction would be concluded within fourteen (14 days you signify interest to assist me).

Anticipating to hear from you soon.

Best regards,

Faustin Dogan

20 August 2008
From: ABCD
To: faustin04dogan@yahoo.com
Sent: Wednesday, August 20, 2008 00:43 AM
Subject: Re: Dearest One,

Dearest Faustin

I am a Minister and Supreme Head of the Holy Church of Serendipity. We have prayed for your delivery. We know you are the chosen one who must come amongst us. Like the choice of the Dalai Lama, you may not realise that you have been anointed but you will eventually see when you join our Church. You shall be baptised with the feathers of freedom. We await your instructions for we are responding to the call of the Great Angel of the Cosmos.

In faith

Pastor Patricio

From: faustin dogan
To: ABCD
Sent: Wednesday, August 20, 2008 2:14 PM
Subject: From Faustin/ Hope to hear from you as soon as possible.

Dearest Pastor Patricio ,

May the Lord our God Almighty bless you, I receive your mail and thank you for your willingness and your concern to help me secure this my inheritance out of this country to your nominated account where I will have access on it and invest it in a good way in your country.

I am asking for your honest and sincerity help so that you will help me without betraying me because this inheritance is the only hope I have for future and dear life. I have trusted you and believe that my trust cannot betray. And you have to understand that I don't have any access in this my inheritance money until the bank transfer the money to foreign account before I will have access on it.

Kindly send this information to enable me proceed to the bank for registration and introduction of your name officially to the bank as my late father foreign partner so that the bank will recognised you and advice us what to do to enable them transfer the money without any problem.

Below is the needed information

Your identity
Your full name
Your fax number
Your occupation.
Your house address.

I am waiting for your urgent response together with the needed information. please kindly call me on this telephone number 0022502162669

May the Almighty God bless all of us and lead us through.

Thanks and much love.

Yours truly

Faustin

21 August 2008
From: ABCD
To: faustin04dogan@yahoo.com
Sent: Thursday, August 21, 2008 1:08 AM
Subject: Re: From Faustin/ Hope to hear from you as soon as possible.

PRIVATE AND CONFIDENTIAL

Dearest Faustin

Our Church is small but we have powerful allies across the world. In every country, including Côte d'Ivoire, we have associates and members who worship the Lord God Almighty anonymously. Since we have been assured by God's Spirit that you are an anointed and chosen one, the College of Cardinals has given me permission to impart important information to you. This concerns someone in your great West African nation who can be a wonderful ally to us both. First, I need your assurance that what I am about to tell you will NEVER be divulged. We can then proceed to make everything right by way of your father's loving and very generous inheritance.

With God's Love that permeates the Cosmos.

Your brother, blessed by the eagle feathers of fraternity and hope

Pastor Patricio

From: faustin dogan
To: ABCD
Sent: Thursday, August 21, 2008 1:00 PM
Subject: From Faustin/ Hope to hear from you as soon as possible.

Dearest pastor Patricio

May the Lord our God almighty be with you, thank you so much for your concern and your willingness to secure this my inheritance in a good way. pastor you are free to ask me any thing as well as comes out from your mind.

i really understand that you are a man of God which i am very happy and with God all thing are possible in our life.

pastor i want to assure you that you can never regret helping in life and i can never let you down when ever this my inheritance be in transfer to your nominated account.

please pastor this your information is needed from the bank here for registration and introducing your name to the bank as my late father foreign partner to enable the bank recognized you and transfer the money to your account.

this your information is the only thing delaying now for the successful transfer of the money to your account

hope to hear from you as soon as possible with the needed information.

Much Love

Faustin Dogan

From: ABCD

To: faustin04dogan@yahoo.com

Sent: Thursday, August 21, 2008 7:21 PM

Subject: Re: From Faustin/ Hope to hear from you as soon as possible.

Dearest Faustin

You have made a mistake that must be rectified before we can proceed. I know it is an honest mistake but you must remedy it for the sake of the College of Cardinals. You have used a small 'p' in Pastor. In our faith this is a sign of disrespect. I must assure my congregation that you have made amends and will never offend again. Please, in your next email, write the following ten times:

I apologise profusely to Pastor Patricio and the Church of Serendipity and assure all that my mistake was honest and never intended to offend.

Also, you must write and assure me that what I am about to impart to you will be treated in strictest confidence. The information you require is already in Côte d'Ivoire. You only need to reassure me. Believe me, Faustin, together we will make this happen very quickly. The Good God has ensured that our Church of Serendipity has many influential and anonymous friends throughout the world, as well as in your beautiful country.

Always in the hands of Our Creator

Pastor Patricio

From: faustin dogan
To: ABCD
Sent: Thursday, August 21, 2008 8:53 PM
Subject: From Faustin/ Hope to hear from you as soon as possible.

Dearest Pastor Patricio
Good evening and God bless you many things, Please i am very sorry for my mistake i pologized that it will not happen again by writen small p in Pastor Patricio

Pease Pastor Patricio no body is above mistake forgive me with that mistake.

Dearest Pastor Patricio i am very happy to have someone life you because God Almighty have directed me a person who is caring and Love also honest in life.

Remain bless with God protect us.

Hope to hear from you.
Much Love
Faustin Dogan

From: ABCD
To: faustin04dogan@yahoo.com
Sent: Thursday, August 21, 2008 10:01 PM
Subject: Re: From Faustin/ Hope to hear from you as soon as possible.

Dearest Faustin
I agree with you that no one is above making a mistake. But when we do, we must make recompense and resolve never to make the same mistake again. Precept 10, Verse 21 of the Book of Serendipity states:

S/he who offends, even inadvertently, must make recompense to a measure of 10. Thus shall the flaw be absolved and the offending one shall be less likely to repeat the wayward action.

Until I can demonstrate to the College of Cardinals that you have respected the above Precept, I am unable to impart to you the important information and or introduce the trusted contact we have identified to assist you in achieving your dreams and eventually joining our community as the anointed one. You must show that you can follow instructions. So, I ask you again to repeat, ten times, the following:

I apologise profusely to Pastor Patricio and the Church of Serendipity and assure all that my mistake was honest and never intended to offend.

With the gentle love of a Dove's feather
Pastor Patricio

22 August 2008

From: faustin dogan
To: ABCD
Sent: Friday, August 22, 2008 12:35 PM
Subject: From Faustin/ Hope to hear from you as soon as possible.

Dearest Pastor Patricio
Thank you for your mail i really appreciate your mail by forgiving me and also I apologized profusely to Pastor Patricio and the Church of Serendipity and assure all that my mistake was honest and never intended to offend.
    remain bless with God Almighty
Best regards
Faustin

From: ABCD
To: faustin04dogan@yahoo.com
Sent: Friday, August 22, 2008 4:27 PM
Subject: Re: From Faustin/ Hope to hear from you as soon as possible.

Dear Faustin
Are you a stubborn boy? I need you to hear me clearly. You must respect the laws of our Holy Church if we are to assist you. I must, therefore, insist that you deliver the sentence ten times. Otherwise, I will be unable to advance our efforts to help you and, through your anointing, this wonderful Church. I am counting on you to make me proud in its purest and most humble sense. Please be rid of your pride and do what is required. Believe me, you will not be disappointed.
    With much love, flown to you on the soft feathers of a new-born goldfinch.
Your brother in Serendipity
Pastor Patricio

From: faustin dogan
To: ABCD
Sent: Friday, August 22, 2008 8:45 PM
Subject: From Faustin/ Hope to hear from you as soon as possible.

Dearest Pastor Patricio
I am reading your mail now and immediately send you this message in fact i am OK with you because from you i will know more thing in my life and with you now you are like my father so with this God Almighty continue bless you and protect us to achieve our earn
    Hope to hear from you as soon as possible.
Best regards

Faustin Dogan
23 August 2008
From: ABCD
To: faustin04dogan@yahoo.com
Sent: Saturday, August 23, 2008 00:08 AM
Subject: Re: From Faustin/ Hope to hear from you as soon as possible.

Dearest Faustin
I know you are an intelligent boy but you are ignoring me like an idiot. Let me warn you, unless you adhere to the Precepts of our great faith and do what I have instructed you, then we are at the end of the road.
With hope and blessings
Darren

['Darren' is an ancient and secret name for the God of Serendipity. Its true meaning is known only to the inner circle of Serendon – a chapel of just six cardinals. It is a title I am allowed to use but once as a sign of fatherly affection for one whom I believe is anointed in a special way. Read it, therefore, as a symbol of my affection. I hope you will respond positively so that we can get beyond this impasse. We are all depending on you to do what is required and what is right.]

From: faustin dogan
To: ABCD
Sent: Saturday, August 23, 2008 7:17 PM
Subject: From Faustin/ Hope to hear from you as soon as possible.

Dearest Pastor
Please your wish is my command i am already with you also with our great faith church immediately the bank transfer the money to your account i will follow your instructions because you are the only person i have now.

Please concerning church i have be a members of great faith church

Please Pastor you have to understand that this is weekend delay is not good please kindly forward me the required information so that by Monday morning i will go to the bank for the transfer of the money to your account.

Please my life is not good i want us to transfer this my inheritance urgent to your account by next week.
Hope to hear from you as soon as possible together in the needed info.
Best regards
Faustin

From: ABCD

To: faustin04dogan@yahoo.com
Sent: Saturday, August 23, 2008 7:41 PM
Subject: Re: From Faustin/ Hope to hear from you as soon as possible.

Dearest Faustin,
You still have not done what I need you to do. Until you apologise ten times, I am paralysed. I am happy you have communicated with me. I am not happy you are placing your inheritance and God's gift to our great Church in jeopardy. With all the humility I can muster as leader of the Church of Serendipity, I implore you to apologise, as required by the Book of Serendipity, ten times. This will, I assure you, open the floodgates of generosity and God's miracles and guiding hand. By Monday you will already be in possession of the help you require – and more.
With much love and loyalty to you my dearest anointed child of our Universal Creator.
Always, and prayerfully
Pastor Patricio

25 August 2008
From: ABCD
To: faustin04dogan@yahoo.com
Sent: Monday, August 25, 2008 9:41 AM
Subject: Fw: From Faustin/ Hope to hear from you as soon as possible.

Dear Faustin
I have returned after a very busy weekend ministering to the vibrant flock of the Church of Serendipity. I expected to find you here but, alas, nothing. I am deeply disappointed and will now call a meeting of the College of Cardinals to inform them. God's Spirit is more powerful than money and we are, therefore, quite prepared to release your offer back into the boundless Cosmos of Compassion.

We had a genuine desire to help you and had already made important contacts in your beautiful country who were prepared to assist. All the information you require is in place. We only needed you to show us your ability to be humble, gracious and obedient.

I remain hopeful but, in truth, sense that this is my last communication with you. If it is, please be assured that you will always be in the prayers of our fraternity and that the doors of the Church of Serendipity will always remain firmly open should you wish to enter.
With much love and blessings borne on angel wings
Pastor Patricio

From: faustin dogan
To: ABCD
Sent: Monday, August 25, 2008 2:06 PM
Subject: From Faustin/ Hope to hear from you as soon as possible.

Dearest Pastor
May the Lord our God Almighty be with you, many thank for your concern and your willingness to secure this my inheritance money in a good way also secure my life in God hand.

Please like i said before your wish is my command and i will follow your instructions because you life my father now

I apologized once again

1)Forgive me
2)Forgive me
3)Forgive me
4)Forgive me
5)Forgive me
6)Forgive me
7)Forgive me
8)Forgive me
9)Forgive me
10)Forgive me

I purpose to be in the bank today because the bank director have know that i want to transfer the money to your account please i am still waiting the needed info.
hope to hear from you as soon as possible.
Best regards
Faustn

From: ABCD
To: faustin04dogan@yahoo.com
Sent: Monday, August 25, 2008 8:23 PM
Subject: Re: From Faustin/ Hope to hear from you as soon as possible.

STRICTLY PRIVATE AND CONFIDENTIAL
Dear Faustin
God is testing my patience in dealing with you. I want to help you. My Church wants to help you. But I cannot determine whether you are plain stupid or simply stubborn. I hope it is the latter.

To write 'Forgive me' ten times is not what I told you needed to be written in my email of 21 August. But I will help you. Please copy the following into an email response to me:

I apologise profusely to Pastor Patricio and the Church of Serendipity and assure all that my mistake was honest and never intended to offend.
I apologise profusely to Pastor Patricio and the Church of Serendipity and assure all that my mistake was honest and never intended to offend.
I apologise profusely to Pastor Patricio and the Church of Serendipity and assure all that my mistake was honest and never intended to offend.
I apologise profusely to Pastor Patricio and the Church of Serendipity and assure all that my mistake was honest and never intended to offend.
I apologise profusely to Pastor Patricio and the Church of Serendipity and assure all that my mistake was honest and never intended to offend.
I apologise profusely to Pastor Patricio and the Church of Serendipity and assure all that my mistake was honest and never intended to offend.
I apologise profusely to Pastor Patricio and the Church of Serendipity and assure all that my mistake was honest and never intended to offend.
I apologise profusely to Pastor Patricio and the Church of Serendipity and assure all that my mistake was honest and never intended to offend.
I apologise profusely to Pastor Patricio and the Church of Serendipity and assure all that my mistake was honest and never intended to offend.
I apologise profusely to Pastor Patricio and the Church of Serendipity and assure all that my mistake was honest and never intended to offend.

This is all that was ever needed and, had you complied, we would have been well advanced regarding your request. Truly, dear child Faustin, I am exasperated, despondent and deeply annoyed.

I ask you to write to me in confidence because I am lying now to the College of Cardinals. If they knew I was doing this, they would seek to have me removed from my office as supreme Pastor. That is the extent of the risk I am taking on your behalf. Yes, you have put me at risk! Please, please, please do what is required. I am deeply angry for you have compromised my faith.
Always
Pastor Patricio

26 August 2008
From: faustin dogan
To: ABCD
Sent: Tuesday, August 26, 2008 00:29 AM
Subject: From Faustin/ Hope to hear from you as soon as possible.

Dearest Pastor
I am reading your mail now and immediately sending this massage please i want to let you know that if i can offend you as much as please forgive me but i want to tell you that i will look for another person to help me secure this my inheritance but i promise you that i will pay my Tait in your church immediately the bank transfer this money to another account
Ramon bless.
Faustin

From: ABCD
To: faustin04dogan@yahoo.com
Sent: Tuesday, August 26, 2008 5:32 AM
Subject: Re: From Faustin/ Hope to hear from you as soon as possible.

Then, Faustin, it is finished. I pray that God will forgive you for abusing so many good and naive people with your dishonest ways. As for the future, just remember that you will reap what you sow. Shame on you for being part of a scam that feeds the prejudice that has blighted your beautiful continent of Africa for too long.
Always
Pastor Patricio

27 August 2008
From: ABCD
To: holychurchofserendipity@eircom.net
Cc: faustin04dogan@yahoo.com
Sent: Wednesday, August 27, 2008 3:44 PM
Subject: Resignation of Pastor Patricio

Praised be the Holy Name of the Creator of the Cosmos.

It is with regret that I announce my resignation as Supreme Head of the Church of Serendipity. I tried to lead you to the best of my ability. However, in recent weeks, having engaged with Mr Faustin Dogan, I have done things that are against our great and holy precepts.

I acknowledge my transgressions in failing to be fully honest with the elders of the Holy Church of Serendipity. I am resolved with the help of God's Holy Grace never more to offend thee, Amen!
I acknowledge my transgressions in failing to be fully honest with the elders of the Holy Church of Serendipity. I am resolved with the help of God's Holy Grace never more to offend thee, Amen!
I acknowledge my transgressions in failing to be fully honest with the elders

of the Holy Church of Serendipity. I am resolved with the help of God's Holy Grace never more to offend thee, Amen!

I acknowledge my transgressions in failing to be fully honest with the elders of the Holy Church of Serendipity. I am resolved with the help of God's Holy Grace never more to offend thee, Amen!

I acknowledge my transgressions in failing to be fully honest with the elders of the Holy Church of Serendipity. I am resolved with the help of God's Holy Grace never more to offend thee, Amen!

I acknowledge my transgressions in failing to be fully honest with the elders of the Holy Church of Serendipity. I am resolved with the help of God's Holy Grace never more to offend thee, Amen!

I acknowledge my transgressions in failing to be fully honest with the elders of the Holy Church of Serendipity. I am resolved with the help of God's Holy Grace never more to offend thee, Amen!

I acknowledge my transgressions in failing to be fully honest with the elders of the Holy Church of Serendipity. I am resolved with the help of God's Holy Grace never more to offend thee, Amen!

I acknowledge my transgressions in failing to be fully honest with the elders of the Holy Church of Serendipity. I am resolved with the help of God's Holy Grace never more to offend thee, Amen!

I acknowledge my transgressions in failing to be fully honest with the elders of the Holy Church of Serendipity. I am resolved with the help of God's Holy Grace never more to offend thee, Amen!

It has been agreed to release the attached statement when my resignation becomes effective.

I shall now prepare for the elevation of Pastor Antonio to the Headship of our great and glorious Church.

Always in the Lord of Truth and Justice.

Your Beloved

Pastor Patricio

Press Release
Embargoed until midnight on 30 September 2008
Resignation of Pastor Patricio,
Supreme Head of the Church of Serendipity

As of midnight last night, Pastor Patricio, the Supreme Head of the Church of Serendipity, resigned from his position. Speaking on behalf of the Church, the Rev. Peter Rock, a member of the College of Cardinals, said:

'Pastor Patricio has led our Church with dedication, faithfulness and unconditional love for over eight years. His legacy will endure for generations to come. It is with sadness that we have accepted his resignation and we wish him a very fruitful ministry in St Paul's Bay, Malta, where he has been asked to serve. We wish him God's blessing in all his ministerial endeavours.'

Rev. Rock continued:

'We now look forward to a new era under the guidance of Pastor Antonio who has been a member of the College of Cardinals for over two years.'

[End.]

28 August 2008
From: faustin dogan
To: ABCD
Sent: Thursday, August 28, 2008 12:50 PM
Subject: Re: Resignation of Pastor Patricio

Dearest Pastor
I really read your last mail which i am very disappointed with you which you are calling me a scam and other thing which you may call me but i am want to let you understand that every body is not disame is like you re a Pastor while i am not a Pastor

i will still prove you that i am honest Thai t i am not a scammer or whatever you may think. i am if you really want to help me come up your mind and good spirit to help me and secure this my inheritance money to your account.
God bless
Faustin

29 August 2008
From: <ABCD@efg.com>
To: <faustin04dogan@yahoo.com>
Sent: Friday, August 29, 2008 1:47 PM
Subject: Re: Resignation of Pastor Patricio

My child
If you can help me prove to the College of Cardinals that you are, indeed, honest, then I may not have to resign on September 30th, and we can still help each other. I wait in hope.
Your Brother in the Lord
Pastor Patricio

30 August 2008
From: faustin dogan
To: ABCD@efg.com
Sent: Saturday, August 30, 2008 3:59 PM

Subject: From Faustin Dogan/Good News

Dearest Pastor Patricio,
Good day and God bless, I'm very glad to give you good news.

I went to the bank today and discussed with the bank director to find out how he can help us to transfer this money to your account in your country.

He said that, the only advice and assistance he can give to us is to use his contact and deliver the money to you in your country through diplomatic couriers Service.

He said that he will obtain diplomatic coverage through diplomatic couriers Service. The lawyer and the banker explained to me that the money will be sealed in a bank treasure trunk box and deliver the money to you in country through diplomatic couriers Service.

The lawyer and the Dr Roland Kone also confirmed that, it's the best way for us to get the money transferred out of this country because of the on going political crises in the country.

The banker told me that, if the bank transfers the money without proper arrangements, we shall loose more than 40% of the total money. So, for this reason it's better for us to follow the advice of the lawyer and the bank.

Now considering our relationship in this business and the trust & confidence we have in you, keep it very Secure and confidential for our security and that of the money.

I am urgently waiting for your response for us to proceed but meanwhile, the lawyer and the banker are making the arrangements to make sure that, everything goes legally well and successful for us.
Remain blessed
Faustin

1 September 2008
From: ABCD
To: faustin04dogan@yahoo.com
Sent: Monday, September 01, 2008 9:43 AM
Subject: Re: From Faustin Dogan/Good News

Dear Faustin
You are now my only hope. I am in your hands. Tell me precisely what I must do to ensure the money is transferred into the safekeeping of my beloved Church of Serendipity. Be assured, once this transaction has been completed successfully, you will be the anointed one of our Mission. You will be welcomed with open hearts and arms for all will be accomplished, including your salvation.
I look forward to hearing from you soon.

Always in the Lord of Serendipity
Pastor Patricio

From: faustin dogan
To: ABCD
Sent: Monday, September 01, 2008 1:25 PM
Subject: From Faustin Dogan/hope to hear from you as soon as possible

Dearest Pastor
Good day and God bless you i am always have confident in you as a man of God please i am entrusting you this my inheritance into your hand immediately the diplomat arriving to your country you now pick of the box from him and secure the money well and you now send me some money for my preparing of coming to your country and also continue a new life over there.

Please what you have to know that the diplomat did not no the content of the box please keep it very confidential for security purpose.

Please Pastor your full address in very important how you will receive the money please kindly forward your full address for me so immediately the diplomat arriving in your airport him will know your direction to hand you over the box of the money.

Hope to hear from you as soon as possible.
Best regards
Faustin Dogan

From: ABCD
To: faustin04dogan@yahoo.com
Sent: Monday, September 01, 2008 6:25 PM
Subject: Re: From Faustin Dogan/hope to hear from you as soon as possible

Okay Faustin
Transferring so much money by Diplomatic Courier is potentially illegal. I cannot put my Church at further risk. Instead, I shall travel to Paris, France, on the designated date for collection. I want the money delivered to a very close and trusted confidant, Monsieur Michael Moose. He is 80 this year, but looks deceptively younger. He is a very kind and fun-loving friend and no one will suspect someone of his age and attire to be the recipient of such a large sum of money. To make it easy for your courier to recognise him, he will be sitting in the foyer of the Sequoia Lodge wearing a black overcoat, white pants, white gloves and bib, and yellow shoes with matching bow tie. Please ensure the courier is dressed like a tourist and not a courier as this might arouse suspicion. The address is Sequoia Lodge, B.P. 100-77, Marne la Vallee, Ile-de-France, France. Tel: 01 60 30 60 30.

After shaking hands, Monsieur Moose will invite the courier to his room, where the exchange will take place. Once my friend is satisfied that all is well, he will call me and I shall come to check. You can be assured, dear Faustin, if all is in order, I will be elevated to the rank of Pope in my Church and you will be welcomed with open arms and given an exalted place as a truly anointed one of God.

I look forward to hearing from you shortly to tell me when the courier might be arriving. I am ready to leave within 24 hours.

With gratitude, much love and all praise to the God of Serendipity.
Your brother
Pastor Patricio

From: faustin dogan
To: ABCD
Sent: Monday, September 01, 2008 7:07 PM
Subject: Urgent response

Dearest Pastor,
I received your mail and want you to understand that the full information is needed so that we will proceed to the shiping company where the money is sealed and packaged in a trunk box and hand over to the company for the delivery.

Be informed that the information will be used for the air way bill so that you will know their flight shceduled and the amount of the handling charges which you will pay to the diplomat before he will release the box to you.

I want you to understand that we have trusted you and dont need any body that will betrayed us as soon as the diplomat deliver this my inheritance because this is the only hope i have in my life.

Waiting for your urgent response so that i will proceed to the company for the air way bill so that you will know the amount of the handling charges which you will keep ready before the arrival of the diplomat.

Hope to hear from you as soon as possible.
Best regaed
Faustin Dogan

From: ABCD
To: faustin04dogan@yahoo.com
Sent: Monday, September 01, 2008 8:31 PM
Subject: Re: Urgent response

Dear Faustin
All I want to do is help you get the cash out of Côte d'Ivoire so that we can live

happily ever after.

I'll level with you. Monsieur Michael Moose is sharing the room with me. We are lovers and he has lived in Paris now for fifteen years. The only other information you need is our room number. We share a penthouse known as 'Rapunzel's Romper Room'. So the courier should deliver to the following address:

Pastor Patricio D. Duckworth
c/o Monsieur Michael Moose
Rapunzel's Romper Room
Sequoia Lodge
B.P. 100-77
Marne la Vallee
Ile-de-France
France.
Tel: 01 60 30 60 30

If you require anything further, please be very clear and specific and I will reply accordingly.
Kind regards
Pastor Patricio

4 September 2008
From: ABCD
To: faustin04dogan@yahoo.com
Sent: Thursday, September 04, 2008 5:50 PM
Subject: Fw: Urgent response

My friend Faustin
Where have you gone? Did you receive my email? I am awaiting your instructions to bring our agreement to a speedy and successful conclusion. I am relying on you Faustin. We are now into September. I have just 26 days left before my resignation comes into effect. You have the power now to keep me in power. I am at your mercy.
With profound humility and affection
Pastor Patricio

5 September 2008
From: faustin dogan
To: ABCD
Sent: Friday, September 05, 2008 2:21 PM
Subject: Re: Urgent response

Dear Pastor Patricio,
Sorry for the little delay we were trying tp procure the Airway bill from the shipping compnay so that you will know the flight shedule and the amount of the handling charges to be paid to the diplomat before he can release the box.

The diplomat will call you as soon as you arrive's Paris with the consignment for the delivery to you destination, please be informed that the diplomat does not know the content of the box and please don't let him know that the box is loaded with money. the box was tagged family valuables foe security reasons and safety of the money.

Find the attached document
Waiting to hear good news from you
Thank you
Faustin Dogan

See Appendix 2 for EDCS form

From: ABCD
To: faustin dogan
Sent: Friday, September 05, 2008 3:00 PM
Subject: Re: Urgent response

Dear Faustin
My faith is restored in you. I thought you had abandoned me in my hour of need. I am very impressed. I have the Airway Bill No: 8794562135. Do I present the 6,700 euro charge upon receipt of delivery from your Diplomatic Courier in Paris? Should I present him with cash or a cheque?
Kindest regards and many blessings
Pastor Patricio

6 September 2008
From: faustin dogan
To: ABCD
Sent: Saturday, September 06, 2008 1:22 PM
Subject: Your direct number to reach the diplomat is now in france

Dear Pastor Patricio,
Please kindly send us your direct number to enable the diplomat call you and meet you to collect the handling charges to enable him clear the cosignment and delivered it to you because i got information that the diplomat is now in France.
Thanks
Yours truely
Faustin

From: faustin dogan
To: ABCD
Sent: Saturday, September 06, 2008 2:26 PM
Subject: Your direct number urgent.
Dear Pastor Patricio,
I need your urgent response because diplomat have not goten any number and need your direct contact so that he will meet with you, he promised to get a number so that you will reach him for the delivery.
Thanks
Yours truly
Faustin

From: faustin dogan
To: ABCD
Sent: Saturday, September 06, 2008 2:43 PM
Subject: The diplomat is now in france

Dear Pastor Patricio,
I want you to know that i am a litle bit worry for your delay to provide your direct line to enable you meet with the diplomat for the delivery because you know the diplomat does not know the real content of the box for safety of my inheritance.

   I want you to understand that i have treid my best and need your urgent help so that we will secure this my inheritance for the investment,i have so confidence on you and beleive that i am in save hand because i dont want my trust to betreayed when you receive the money.
Thanks
Yours truely
Faustin

From: ABCD
To: faustin04dogan@yahoo.com
Sent: Saturday, September 06, 2008 3:20 PM
Subject: Re: Your direct number urgent.

Dear Faustin
I am leaving for Paris this evening.
   Paris (Beauvais) is just 20 minutes by taxi from the hotel where I will rendezvous with the Diplomatic Courier.
   I will purchase a mobile phone upon my arrival in Paris and will send you the number immediately. Can you also let me have the telephone number of the courier so that we have back-up to ensure we meet?

I need you to tell me what will happen when I get to Paris. I have the money required by the courier and I plan for us to meet in a public place such as the hotel foyer as I am nervous. However, how will I know that all the money is in the case being handed over by the courier unless I have time to examine it?

Here is what I propose. I will take the case from the courier and I will leave him with my friend, Monsieur Moose. I shall also leave the handling fee with my friend. However, the money will not be handed over until I have had time to go to our penthouse, open the case and examine the contents. I believe this is only fair. Once I return, satisfied I hope, I will give Monsieur Moose the nod to hand over the handling charges to the courier. Is this acceptable?

Now, please let me have the courier's mobile telephone number.
Always
Pastor Patricio

From: ABCD
To: faustin04dogan@yahoo.com
Sent: Saturday, September 06, 2008 4:32 PM
Subject: Re: The diplomat is now in france

Faustin
I need to leave for the airport very soon. I need you to communicate with me immediately with a telephone number.
Pastor Patricio

From: ABCD
To: faustin04dogan@yahoo.com
Sent: Saturday, September 06, 2008 5:52 PM
Subject: Re: The diplomat is now in france

Faustin
I am about to leave for the airport with a substantial sum of money for the Diplomatic Courier. I need two pieces of information from you, otherwise I will have grave doubts about this communication and my trust in you:

1. What is the name of the courier?
2. What is the mobile number of the courier so that I can communicate with him upon my arrival in Paris?

Faustin, I am depending on you. My very future is in your hands. Please, please, please don't let me down at this late stage.
With kindest thoughts and the blessings of the great God of Serendipity
Pastor Patricio

From: faustin dogan
To: ABCD
Sent: Saturday, September 06, 2008 6:20 PM
Subject: Contact the diplomat immediately

I am happy to hear from you and want you to understand that the diplomat is geting worreid for tghe delay and bringing to my knowledge thgat he have short time in delivery the box to you in france,

For your good information the money is splited into a four different box and the diplomat does know the real content of the box as the instruction was giving to him the box was tagged as family valuable,

Dont ever complicate issue by examining the box because i know my inheritance intact in the box what you need to do is to contact the diplomat with the below number and asked him if it will possible to clear the boxes today,he is a UN diplomat,

Name of the diplomat is Edward Hanegen

This is the number of the diplomat 0033 645 321 115

Kindly call the diplomat through this number and meet him to enable him go and clear the box,
Thanks
Yours truel
Faustin

At 10.30 p.m. (Paris time) I called Mr Hanegen from my office. Prior to this I located a five-minute stream of airport background sounds on the Internet, which I played through my computer while I spoke with the 'UN Courier'. I spoke to him using a broken 'Spanish' accent and found him to be an aggressive character who, despite being on a mission to meet me, was too busy to meet me that night and actually hung up on me when he got uncomfortable with my questions. I outline the contents of our conversation in my next email to Faustin.

From: ABCD
To: faustin04dogan@yahoo.com
Sent: Saturday, September 06, 2008 10:13 PM
Subject: Re: Contact the diplomat immediately

Dear Faustin
I am at Beauvais Airport, Paris. I have just called the Diplomat, Edward Hanegen. It is an Irish or Scottish name but he sounded African. I am very confused. He said he could not help me tonight. He said he wants me to meet him tomorrow and hand over $6,700 in cash. He says he will then go to have

the baggage released and bring it to me.

Faustin, what if I hand Mr Hanegen 6,700 in cash and I never see him again? He says he travelled to Paris after collecting the consignment from you, but how do I know? When I asked, 'How do I know you don't already live in Paris?' he hung up.

I did not like Mr Hanegen. He sounded aggressive and angry and not at all in keeping with the spirit of gentleness and kindness we cultivate in the Church of Serendipity.

Mr Hanegen said he is anxious to close the deal tomorrow. So am I. But you must ensure that I have cover and protection.

I am here in Paris. I have with me the money in cash that Europa Diplomatic Courier Services require. I will hand it over, only after the consignment is delivered to me at my hotel, which they have on their airway bill. Unless Mr Hanegen comes to my hotel with the consignment, as agreed, the deal is off. I am not taking the risk. To hang up the telephone on me, as he did, is very rude. Does he not realise who I am? Does he not realise that, for now, I am the Supreme Head of the Great Church of Serendipity? How dare he do this. In my Church, he would be excommunicated for this.

What is Mr Hanegen's email address? He was to give this to me as he doesn't seem to realise the address of the hotel where I will stay tonight with my beloved Michael Moose.

I wait to hear from you, Faustin. Please do not make a fool of me. I am in Paris to help you. I am at your mercy.
Always, in the Lord God of Serendipity
Pastor Patricio

7 September 2008
From: faustin dogan
To: ABCD
Sent: Sunday, September 07, 2008 2:54 AM
Subject: Pay him the handling charge as soon as he meet you,

Dear Pastor Patricio,
I receive your mail and want you to comply with the diplomat for succesfull delivery because he is only doing his job and dont know anything concerning my inheritance dont mind the way he soundrd and only hand him over the charges to enable him clear the cosignment and hand over to nyou so that i will tell you the key code to have access to the money.

You know he arrive since morning and hope to meet you immediately,Please dont worry about the way he soundred give him the handle charges as soon as he meet you because this is the only thing you need to help out to enable him clear it and hand over to you,

I know their office here and he can run away because their company is one of the reputation company in this country and everything is well arranged and kindly undertstand that he dont know the real content and never you in any circumstances let him know the real content,

Waiting for the good news as soon as you receive the boxes give the money as soon as he meet you so that he will clear it immediately and hand over to you,

Pklease call me through this number +22566765851 so that we will discussed for more details

Thanks
Yours truely
FGaustin

From: faustin dogan
To: ABCD
Sent: Sunday, September 07, 2008 8:49 AM
Subject: Call the diplomat so that you will have access of my inheritance today

Dear Pastor Patricio,
I dont want you to look after the diplomat ggresive only comply with him as you know that he does not know the real content give him the money to enable him clear the cosignment and bring to your hotel,

He dont actualy know who you are and that why he may act like this but only mind to secure the box without delaying because delay will not be in our favour,

never ever go to the embassy to collect the consignment with the diplomat because the embassy will ask yousince you are the beneficiary to open the box which is not good.

Thanks
Yours Faustin

From: ABCD
To: faustin04dogan@yahoo.com
Sent: Sunday, September 07, 2008 9:11 AM
Subject: Re: Call the diplomat so that you will have access of my inheritance today

Dear Faustin
I had a very disturbed sleep last night. I've discovered that my 'friend' Michael Moose is married and his wife, Minnie, is now in 'our' penthouse. I am very sad about everything. Since you made contact with me, my life has been turned upside down. And now, this courier of yours, Mr Hanegen, has me truly distressed. Please let me have his email address. I don't want to communicate with him by phone as he upset me so much. I am in Paris until Tuesday so we

still have time.
Always, in the good and forgiving Lord of Serendipity
Pastor Patricio

From: ABCD
To: faustin04dogan@yahoo.com
Sent: Sunday, September 07, 2008 10:48 AM
Subject: Re: Call the diplomat so that you will have access of my inheritance today

Faustin
I need your help. What is the courier's email address? I need to finish this by Tuesday.
Pastor Patricio

From: faustin dogan
To: ABCD
Sent: Sunday, September 07, 2008 12:39 PM
Subject: reach the diplomat immediately

Dear Pastor Patricio,
Urgent because i am still worreid now you never receive the box uptill now please reach the diplomat immediately and receive my inheritance into your custody to enable us proceed for other arrangement,You know i need your urgent help to relocate to join for the investment and resetling down my life,
This the diplomat email address (hanegs@yahoo.com)
Thanks
Yours truely
Faustin

From: ABCD
To: faustin04dogan@yahoo.com
Cc: hanegs@yahoo.com
Sent: Sunday, September 07, 2008 12:47 PM
Subject: URGENT: Come to see me NOW!

EXTREMELY URGENT
Dear Mr Hanegen
I would like you to come to my hotel immediately, where I will present you with the 6,700 to secure the release of Faustin's inheritance. The address is, as stated on the airway bill, Sequoia Lodge, Marne la Vallee, Paris. Please let me know when you can come to see me.

Yours sincerely
Pastor Patricio

From: ABCD
To: hanegs@yahoo.com
Cc: faustin04dogan@yahoo.com
Sent: Sunday, September 07, 2008 4:05 PM
Subject: Fw: URGENT: Come to see me NOW!

Faustin
Where is your diplomat? I have 6,700 for him and yet he refuses to make contact. Faustin, is this a scam? Have you been betraying my goodness and faith in you? I am deeply frustrated and increasingly angry. Are you making a fool of me? I leave on Tuesday. If this is not resolved tomorrow, I never want to hear from you again. You have already done enormous damage to my life.
Pastor Patricio

From: ABCD
To: faustin04dogan@yahoo.com
Sent: Sunday, September 07, 2008 5:36 PM
Subject: Re: reach the diplomat immediately

Dear Faustin
I have great news. Your diplomatic friend, Mr Hanegen, arrived in the past fifteen minutes to my hotel. I have given him the 6,700 in cash and he has gone off to collect your consignment. We will meet at the bust of Alexandre Gustave Eiffel, which is under the left leg of the Eiffel Tower that stands closest to the River Seine, at 9 p.m. this evening. Please let me have the code so that I can open the consignment and check that all is well. I am very excited now that I have met Mr Hanegen. He is actually a very nice man.
Always, and with great affection, and renewed faith in the great God of Serendipity
Pastor Patricio

From: Edward Hanegen
To: ABCD
Sent: Sunday, September 07, 2008 5:54 PM
Subject: Re: Fw: URGENT: Come to see me NOW!

Pastor Patricio,
I am sorry for this delay, I told you yesterday that I have got some other important deliveries to make and when it dawned on me that you are still not

yet ready to commence with the arrangement/transaction I left to make two deliveries outside of France and just got into Paris because of you and saw your mails, I want you to know its no fault of Mr. Faustin and in your emails, you did not indicate any hotel address or reachable phone number and if you were very more willing to get at me urgently, you have got my direct number where you called me yesterday, you should have reached me again, however, please call me and let me have your address so we can meet this evening ASAP.
Edward Hanegen
+33 645 321 115

From: Edward Hanegen
To: ABCD
Sent: Sunday, September 07, 2008 6:08 PM
Subject: Re: Fw: reach the diplomat immediately

Dear Pastor Patricio,
I want you to understand that my involvement in this is basically to assist you and that is why I am in Paris, I need you to call me on my phone number that you have so I can have the address of where we can meet this evening.
Good day
Edward

From: ABCD
To: faustin04dogan@yahoo.com
Sent: Sunday, September 07, 2008 10:31 PM
Subject: Re: reach the diplomat immediately

Faustin
What is happening? I went to the bust of Alexandre Gustave Eiffel, as agreed, and waited and waited and waited. I even took a photograph of the lights of the Eiffel Tower to bring home as a reminder of this very special evening when I was to be part of your liberation and you were to save me as Supreme Pastor of the Church of Serendipity. But, it seems, there is no serendipity where you are concerned.

Now, unless you prove me wrong, I must return to my Church for the ultimate humiliation on 30 September, especially when they discover that I have stolen from the Church to help you! Faustin, have you been scamming me all along? Have you been pretending to be a child of God in need and appealing to the spiritual compassion that is the soul of our great Church?

Michael and Minnie are trying to console me at this moment. Hanegen is not answering his phone. Tomorrow I will call the Embassy of the Ivory Coast and pass on Hanegen's telephone number, and your details, to them, unless you assure me that there is a big mistake.

Where is my money Faustin? Are you a lying scammer? Are you cock-a-hoop tonight at the thought of having taken me for a fool? While I am devastated? This is, perhaps, the worst day of my life.
Will I ever hear from you again?
Pastor Patricio

8 September 2008
From: ABCD
To: faustin04dogan@yahoo.com
Sent: Monday, September 08, 2008 1:27 AM
Subject: Re: reach the diplomat immediately

I cannot sleep Faustin Dogan. I cannot sleep because of you! I feel horribly cheated and abused. What happens now? Does Hanegen give you 3,350 of my money? Shame on your sir, whoever you are. Eventually you will have to account before the good God of Serendipity.
Pastor Patricio

I wanted to sow seeds of doubt between Faustin and Hanegen with the above email, hoping that Faustin might believe he had been double-crossed by Hanegen. However, when my son read it he cautioned that since I was dealing with criminals, Hanegen might be shot. This was one of the few times my conscience bothered me in dealing with scammers and I decided to send a final email.

From: ABCD
To: faustin04dogan@yahoo.com
Cc: hanegs@yahoo.com
Sent: Monday, September 08, 2008 1:43 AM
Subject: Re: Dearest One,

Dear Faustin and Mr Hanegen
You thought you had hooked a fool. The truth is I had hooked you! Shame on you for what you do, preying on innocent people. I have thoroughly enjoyed scamming you scammers.

No, Hanegen didn't get any cash. But I'm glad you doubted him. I wouldn't put it past him though, if he had half a chance, to scam his own, as I suggested. Nor would I put it past you, Faustin.
All the best. Michael and Minnie Moose send your their love from Disneyland, Paris.

Always, with the affection of the great Lord of Serendipity
Pastor Patricio (who won't be resigning on 30 September because, like you, he doesn't exist in reality!)

Schranner Scam

16 August 2008
From: "Mr. Dennis Bent" <dbent2netttt@yahoo.com>
To: <undisclosed-recipients:>
Sent: Saturday, August 16, 2008 6:51 PM
Subject: Re: Urgent attention please

Mr.Dennis Bent.
Clydesdale Bank
Glasgow-Scotland
United Kingdom

I am Mr.Dennis Bent. head of Auditing, Clydesdale Bank Scotland. On Wednesday 19 April, 2000 one Mr. Andreas Schranne, German National, a property magnate, whom I was his accounting officer made a numbered time (Fixed) Deposit, valued at £6,550,000.00 (Six Million, Five Hundred and Fifty Thousand Pounds) for twelve calender months in my Bank Branch. Upon Maturity, we sent a routine notification to his forwarding address but got no reply. After a month, we sent a reminder and finally we discovered that Mr.Andreas Schranne, his wife and only daughter was aboard the AF4590 plane, which crashed Monday, 31 July, 2000 into the Hotelissimo. You can read more about the crash on visiting this site

http://news.bbc.co.uk/1/hi/world/europe/859479.stm

My investigation, proved that he died with his supposed next of kin the daughter Mrs. Andrea Eich, in the crash. The total sum,£6,550,000.00 is still in my bank and the interest is being rolled over with the principal sum at the end of each year. No one will ever come forward to claim it. Consequently, I shall present you to stand in as the next of kin to the late Mr. Andreas Schranne. Consequently, Upon acceptance of this proposal, I will give you a detailed information on how this deal would be carried out. The money will be shared in the ratio: sixty five percent (65%) for me, thirty five percent (35%) for you. I guarantee that this will be executed under legitimate arrangement that will protect you from any breach of the law as I will use my position as the Bank's head of Auditors and his accounting officer to secure approvals and guarantee the successful execution of this transaction. Please be informed that your utmost confidentiality is required. On your reply include your

(1)Private telephone/fax number.
(2)Your full name.
3)Your private email address.

Awaiting your urgent reply.
Best regards,
Mr.Dennis Bent
[03 Image1: BBC Report]

From: <ABCD>
To: <db2net@gmail.com>
Sent: Saturday, August 16, 2008 11:52 PM
Subject: Re: Urgent attention please

Hi Dennis
I would love to help you. What do I need to do? This opportunity seems too good to miss. I studied in Scotland and loved the country, including Glasgow.
Kind regards
Karol Breen

18 August 2008
From: Dennis Bent
To: ABCD
Sent: Monday, August 18, 2008 9:38 AM
Subject: Re:Re: Urgent please

Hello,
Thank you so much for your responses to my request. As you can see my contacting you was born out of inspiration after a very long and powerful prayer session that I asked for God's guidance in the choice of a foreign partner that will assist me. A person with vision that will be honest and God fearing in every regard especially at the end of the transaction.

Before I proceed I would want to let you know that my resolve to take this fund out this place is not born out of any criminal intent. Its purely ideological, because in the next few months, I'm sure other staffs will discover that Mr. Andreas Schranne is no more there to service his account and they will call on the respective Government agency which will automatically hand this money over to the corrupt Government officials. They will eventually use it for themselves. History vindicates the just.

Pleased be rest assured that 35% of the entire sum will go to you at the end of the transaction, that is why your participation is of immense importance to the successful conclusion of this transaction. Please note, the procedure for the transfer is a straight process that will not incriminate you in anyway whatsoever. You are to act as the next of kin to the deceased. You will be expected to contact the bank here and request that the fund (BRITISH POUNDS. £6,550,000.00 only) be transferred to your account. Before then I will use my position in the bank to update the deceased's bank information with your name and other information as his next of kin. You should therefore send the following information:

(1)Private telephone/fax number.
(2)Your full name.
(3)Your private email address.

Please, confirm the receipts of this message to me, as soon as you recieve it. I will like you to keep this transaction to yourself only till we succeed. Please do not discuss it or expose it with another person. To avoid monitoring our discussion through telephone I will prefer we communicate through email for the security of this transaction. If you have any question or grey areas that needs clarifications, kindly let me know. Untill I hear from you, my prayers are with you and family.
Best regards,
Mr.Dennis Bent.

From: ABCD
To: dbent2net@yahoo.co.uk
Sent: Monday, August 18, 2008 5:50 PM
Subject: Re: Re:Re: Urgent please

Dear Dennis
I understand everything you have stated. This is a dangerous undertaking and it is essential that everything is done to protect you from your bank bosses and from corrupt government officials.

You are right about not communicating by telephone. I am also wary about communicating through email. This is the email of my boss so I need to be very careful. He is unjust and a terrible bully and I would love to be in a position where I can buy him out and then sack him. That would be fantastic and, as you state, 'History vindicates the just'. What a wonderfully inspiring thought.

Can you give me your address and I will send you all the information you require? It is better that we don't do this in an open system as I know from others that the Internet and the email system is not safe.

My full name is Karol Joseph Wojtyla Breen. I was named after the great Polish Pope, John Paul II. I too am very religious and full of faith.

Rest assured that my lips are sealed and that all we discuss is locked in my heart. I can't believe that the good God has chosen me to help you. I am excited at the thought of us working together.
Much love and prayers
Karol

19 August 2008
From: Dennis Bent
To: ABCD
Sent: Tuesday, August 19, 2008 10:18 AM
Subject: Re: Re:Re: Urgent please

Hello Karol,
What is that you will mail to my address? I have noted your full name. Send your address and telephone number and bear in mind that we have to fasten up the execution of this deal.

All correspondences must be through emails as I earlier stated. If this email belongs to your boss, you should creat your own email address please, we have no time to waste.
Regards,
Mr. Dennis Bent

From: ABCD
To: dbent2net@yahoo.co.uk
Sent: Tuesday, August 19, 2008 7:39 PM
Subject: Re: Re:Re: Urgent please

Okay Dennis. I shall do this later from an Internet café. The details I wish to send are the ones you wanted – my address and telephone number. Are you in the UK? Can I call you? If you have a number it will help expedite this process. Be assured, I will contact you from a discreet place.
With trust and gratitude
Karol

20 August 2008
From: Dennis Bent
To: ABCD
Sent: Wednesday, August 20, 2008 8:51 AM
Subject: Re: Re:Re: Urgent please

Dear Karol,
Yes I am here in UK.

I stated in the last paragraph of my second mail to you that all our correspondences must be through emails to avoid monitoring our discussions. Its for the security of this deal because all calls here are being monitored since the terrorist attack here.

You should expedite action by sending the details I requested and creating your own private email today.

Finally, I would like to know more about your age, occupation and marrital status.
Regards,
Mr. Dennis Bent

From: Karol Breen <karolbreen@yahoo.co.uk>
To: dbent2net@yahoo.co.uk
Sent: Wednesday, 20 August, 2008 9:26 AM
Subject: Details

Dear Dennis
This is my new email account. I am in an Internet café on my way to work. I feel very nervous. So, let us try and do this as quickly as possible so that we can both benefit and move on to a new and better chapter in our lives.

You asked me to tell you something about myself. I am 42 years old. I am married with 2 children, a boy and a girl, aged 10 and 14. Their mother, who is alcoholic, left us six years ago for a football player. They only lasted six months and she came begging to be taken back, but I refused. We are happy together, the children and me. It is tough being a single parent and my salary is small but, thank God, we make it through from month to month. God's providential care is wonderful.

I work with a publisher in Dublin, Ireland. He is a small man in both stature and spirit. He is mean to me and the other members of staff. Always sarcastic and critical. That is why I would love for us both to help each other, so that I can be rid of him and look after my children.

I must rush now to work. Please tell me more about yourself. You seem a very kind and religious man. I hope this is the beginning of a long and good friendship.

Sincerely
Karol

From: Dennis Bent <dbent2net@yahoo.co.uk>
To: Karol Breen <karolbreen@yahoo.co.uk>
Sent: Wednesday, 20 August, 2008 12:07 PM
Subject: Re: Details

Dear Karol,
Your direct telephone number is still missing.
There is no need for you to be nervous. This is a risk free deal. I am here to perfect everything about this deal. You only needs to follow my instructions so that everything will go as planned.
Regards,
Mr. Dennis Bent

21 August 2008
From: Mr. Dennis Bent <dbent2net@yahoo.co.uk>
To: Karol Breen <karolbreen@yahoo.co.uk>
Sent: Thursday, 21 August, 2008 5:31 PM
Subject: FORM TO MY BANK.

Dear Karol,
Though it was very difficult but I thank God that I have been able to complete the updating process. Your name was successfully inserted in the central computer database as Mr. Andreas Schranner NEXT OF KIN. Fill your information and account details as shown under and forward to the bank.

Every thing will be treated officially as soon as you apply to the bank for the release of the fund to your account. Please do not give the bank any impression that you know somebody like me in the bank.. This is to avoid the bank suspecting your claim.

Please as I said earlier, keep this transaction with you (confidential) until the fund arrives in your account. I really appreciate your time and the very useful insights.

More importantly, do acquaint me with day-to-day correspondence with the bank as soon as you are in contact with them so that you don't make any mistake.

Meanwhile, stated below is the sketch of the application, which you will be forwarding to the bank... Fill it up and send immediately. Send it via email attachment.My Bank's email address is clydesdaleb@scotlandmail.com

From: Karol Breen <karolbreen@yahoo.co.uk>
To: clydesdaleb@scotlandmail.com

Sent: Thursday, 21 August, 2008 10:20 PM
Subject: Attn: Director International Remittance

International Remittance Department,
Clydesdale Bank
Glasgow, Scotland
United Kingdom
Email. clydesdaleb@scotlandmail.com
Attn: Director International Remittance
Clydesdale Bank Glasgow

Sir,
APPLICATION FOR FUND RELEASE FROM ACCOUNT No: 14-851278911. AMOUNT: £6,550,000.00 TO MY BANK ACCOUNT.
It is with respect and humility that I apply for the release of above referred fund being next of kin to the deceased Mr Andreas Schranner and confidants of the immediate beneficiary.

Mr Andreas Schranner is a customer to your bank and has a deposit of £6,550,000.00, which as the next of kin I am applying for its release to my bank account. Kindly process above fund for release to my nominated account stated below.

Name of Bank: Bank of Ireland
Address of the bank: O'Connell Street, Dublin
Ac/No: 4 5 14 14 9 19 - 2 5 14 20
Name Beneficiary's: Mr Andreas Schranner NEXT OF KIN

An expedited approval and release of this fund to my nominated account stated above shall be appreciated.
Yours sincerely,
Name: Andreas Schranner
Tel: +353 01 xxx xxx
Fax: As above
Email: karolbreen@yahoo.co.uk

From: Karol Breen <karolbreen@yahoo.co.uk>
To: dbent2net@yahoo.co.uk
Sent: Thursday, 21 August, 2008 10:27 PM
Subject: Re: FORM TO MY BANK.

Dear Dennis
I must confess to being very nervous for I am not sure if I am doing the right

thing. I am trusting you implicitly for I sense that you are a good, caring and honourable person and, in truth, I am motivated by a desire to be rid of my boss and to help my dear children. Please, please, please do not abuse the trust that I am investing in you.

As directed, I have completed the form and forwarded it to you at your bank email address. I await your further instructions. I am very worried that the police might realise that I have given a false name. I am praying very hard that all will be well. I have never broken the law in my life. I am also worried that, if I am sent to jail, my alcoholic wife will regain influence over my two beautiful children.

I trust you Dennis and I pray that we will be soon free from all worry.
Sincerely,
Karol Breen

22 August 2008
From: Mr. Dennis Bent <dbent2net@yahoo.co.uk>
To: Karol Breen <karolbreen@yahoo.co.uk>
Sent: Friday, 22 August, 2008 9:28 AM
Subject: Re: FORM TO MY BANK.

Dear Karol,
You should calm down as nothing will ever go wrong. There is nothing that will implicate you or dent your reputation as long as this deal is concerned. The bank will never suspect or punish you for anything. I have told you that this is a risk free deal so long as you follow my instructions.

Where did you give a false name? You should not give any false information please. Give your correct details more especially regarding your bank account information because any false information there could lead to misrouting of the fund. Please give your correct details.

We are handling this deal like brothers and trust should be our watch word. Your children are like my own children and we must guarantee there comfort and happiness.

Rest assured that everything is in good hands and please correct any false information you have given.
Regards,
Mr. Dennis Bent.

From: Karol Breen <karolbreen@yahoo.co.uk>
To: dbent2net@yahoo.co.uk
Sent: Friday, 22 August, 2008 10:06 AM
Subject: Re: FORM TO MY BANK.

Dear Dennis

Thank you for your reassurance about the safety and security of this deal.

On Thursday you wrote to me: 'Your name was successfully inserted in the central computer database as Mr Andreas Schranner NEXT OF KIN.' So I assumed that you had listed me as such and when I filled in the forms you had sent from the bank, that is the name I gave. Shall I go back and change this or will it be okay? I hope I haven't done anything wrong to undermine our partnership. I am very sorry if I have got it wrong.

I look forward to hearing from you soon.

God bless you dear brother.

Karol

From: Mr. Dennis Bent <dbent2net@yahoo.co.uk>
To: Karol Breen <karolbreen@yahoo.co.uk>
Sent: Friday, 22 August, 2008 11:16 AM
Subject: Re: FORM TO MY BANK.

Dear Karol,

I mean that I have fixed your name as the next of kin of Mr. Andreas Schranner. The name i put there is Karol Joseph Wojtyla Breen.

Please write to the bank and give your correct name as Karol Joseph Wojtyla Breen. Tell the bank its a mistake.

My regards to your kids.

Mr Dennis Bent

From: Karol Breen <karolbreen@yahoo.co.uk>
To: clydesdaleb@scotlandmail.com
Sent: Friday, 22 August, 2008 5:28 PM
Subject: Fw: Attn: Director International Remittance

Dear Friends

I sent an email to you last night. I am embarrassed to admit that I was quite drunk when I completed it as I was celebrating the success of Ireland's boxers at the Beijing Olympic Games and was also feeling melancholy at the memory of my dearly departed relative who has been so generous to us in death when, in truth, he had been quite a scrooge to me and my children in life. I have been stunned by his great kindness. Since I was thinking so intensely about him, I inadvertently filled in the name of my dearly departed relative, Andreas Schranner, instead of my own, on your form where you ask for: 'Name Beneficiary's' and my Name. I apologise profusely for any inconvenience I have caused you. On the form below, I have corrected my honest and silly mistake.

Please do not hesitate to contact me should you require any further information.

Yours sincerely
Karol JW Breen
Attachment: Completed form

From: Karol Breen <karolbreen@yahoo.co.uk>
To: dbent2net@yahoo.co.uk
Sent: Friday, 22 August, 2008 5:36 PM
Subject: Fw: Attn: Director International Remittance

Dear Dennis
I am very sorry for my silly mistake. I hope that my explanation regarding my mistake will not cause the bank to be suspicious. I hope they do not contact me as I am not a very convincing liar. Since you work in the bank, can I ask you to give me cover? Thank you Dennis. I hope what I have done will be sufficient.
God's Blessing
Karol

From: "MAILER-DAEMON@n8.bullet.mail.tp2.yahoo com" <MAILER-DAEMON@n8.bullet.mail.tp2.yahoo.com>
To: karolbreen@yahoo.co.uk
Sent: Friday, 22 August, 2008 5:45 PM
Subject: failure notice

Sorry, we were unable to deliver your message to the following address.
<clydesdaleb@scotlandmail.com>:
Remote host said: 550 <clydesdaleb@scotlandmail.com>: Account Deactivated [RCPT_TO]

From: Mr. Dennis Bent <dbent2net@yahoo.co.uk>
To: Karol Breen <karolbreen@yahoo.co.uk>
Sent: Friday, 22 August, 2008 7:01 PM
Subject: Re: Fw: Attn: Director International Remittance

Karol dear,
Has the bank contacted you?
   Please write to the bank so that they can correct the mistake now.
   Use clydesdale@uk2.net to write to our bank so that the director of international remittance can give his attention to the matter.
   I have told you not to creat any impression that you know somebody like me. So just write through the above email and inform the bank that its a mistake. No body is above mistake.
Regards,

Mr. Dennis Bent.

25 August 2008
From: Karol Breen <karolbreen@yahoo.co.uk>
To: clydesdale@uk2.net
Sent: Saturday, 23 August, 2008 10:41:03 AM
Subject: Attn: Director International Remittance

Dear Friends
I sent an email to you last night. I am embarrassed to admit that I was quite
drunk when I . . .
Yours sincerely
Karol JW Breen
Attachment: Completed form

From: Karol Breen <karolbreen@yahoo.co.uk>
To: dbent2net@yahoo.co.uk
Sent: Saturday, 23 August, 2008 10:57 AM
Subject: Re: Fw: Attn: Director International Remittance

Dear Dennis
Thank you for your understanding. You are a very gracious person. I will never
forget your kindness.
 So far your bank has not been in touch with me. However, I have again
sent the amended details to the new email address you sent in your last
communication.
 I have not breathed a word to anyone about you and I am so happy that I am
communicating with you now through this personal email address and not at
work. Be assured, when your bank does contact me, I will not say a word about
knowing you or the relationship we have entered into.
With gratitude always
Karol

From: Mr. Dennis Bent <dbent2net@yahoo.co.uk>
To: Karol Breen <karolbreen@yahoo.co.uk>
Sent: Saturday, 23 August, 2008 12:02 PM
Subject: Re: Fw: Attn: Director International Remittance

Karol dear,
Thanks for your email.
 I must say that I am happy you are handling your end of this deal very well.
 Perhaps my bank will contact you on Monday as today is Saturday.

Regards,
Mr Dennis Bent

From: Karol Breen <karolbreen@yahoo.co.uk>
To: dbent2net@yahoo.co.uk
Sent: Saturday, 23 August, 2008 2:38 PM
Subject: Re: Fw: Attn: Director International Remittance

Dear Dennis

Thank you for your encouragement. I am happy that you have confidence in me. I told you previously that I am not a very good liar and that is why I am a little worried about when your bank contacts me. I hope and pray I will be okay and do nothing that might jeopardise this wonderful plan of yours.

Dennis, I told you that I am separated from my wife and that is true. Beverley was a senior consultant with a PR company and I worked with her on the launch of a series of books. That was 1990 and two years later we were married. We were very happy until she met a professional footballer from Brazil at a Christmas party in 2001. I do not take much alcohol but Bev can knock back a half bottle of gin and more in an evening and hardly show the signs of it. She always looked stunning – ten years younger than her biological age – and never failed to turn me on when she wore her tight-fitting miniskirts. In a sense, that was our undoing.

I was devastated when I found out about the affair. We had a blazing row and she told me that she was in love with the young footballer. What a humiliation! The next day when I returned from work she was gone and I found the children with a neighbour. I could not fathom the coldness of her walking out on her children. Our boy, Josiah, was only 4 and our daughter, Hannah, only 8. I put it down to her heavy drinking. Only for the fact that I had to assume total responsibility for the children, I think I would have fallen apart.

She and her fancy man only lasted six months together, after which she begged me to give her a second chance. But Dennis, I simply could not trust her. Trust, once broken, is very hard to fix.

I am happy to tell you that I have fallen in love again. My girlfriend, Annie, is twelve years my junior and both my children love her to bits. I've started to think of her as my wife and feel closer to her than I ever did to Bev. She might not look so appealing in a miniskirt, but I have learned that true beauty radiates from the inside out.

Annie is the only person I have spoken to about your proposition. She is very excited. We have talked about leaving Ireland for a warmer climate. This August has been the wettest in recorded history, with many rivers bursting their banks and hundreds of homes destroyed by flooding. Once this transaction has been completed we may move to Spain or Portugal and place the children in a private boarding school. The idea of a whole new start in life with Annie fills me with hope.

I don't know why I felt the need to tell you all of this, Dennis. I just know you have brought light and magic into my life and offered me an opportunity to begin again. That is such a wonderful gift and I thank you for it. Thank you so much for being so open to partnership with me and for all your encouragement and help to date. I promise you, I shall not let you down. Dear Dennis, I look forward to sharing a wonderful and long friendship with you.

Always
Karol Breen

25 August 2008
From: Mr. Dennis Bent <dbent2net@yahoo.co.uk>
To: Karol Breen <karolbreen@yahoo.co.uk>
Sent: Monday, 25 August, 2008 9:45 AM
Subject: Re: Fw: Attn: Director International Remittance

Dear Karol,
Thanks for your mail.
It's unfortunate that Beverley treated you and your children so bad though she is now reaping what she sowed. I always believe that no evil done to man by man will go unpunished. It must be redressed, if not now certainly latter, if not by man certainly by God. The victory of evil over good can only be temporal.

God has his way of doing things. He has brought your true wife into your life now. Annie will heal the wounds Beverley inflicted on your heart.. Beverley will regret more and have more reasons to want to come back into your life when we must have concluded this transaction. You will be so rich then but it's already late for her. Thank God for he is making everything for our own goodness.

Please take good care of Josiah and Hannah. They are special gift from God. They deserved to be loved and cherished.
Regards,
Mr. Dennis Bent

From: Clydesdale Bank <clydesdale@uk2.net>
To: Karol Breen <karolbreen@yahoo.co.uk>
Sent: Monday, 25 August, 2008 3:27 PM
Subject: Re: Attn: Director International Remittance

Dear sir,
We wish to inform you that you application was received. Our board of directors has deliberated on your request and has finally approved your application.

I hereby attach our official letter with instructions on what you should do next.

You are expected to either come to our office or choose a lawyer from the lawyers we have here. If for any reason you cannot meet up with our schedule, we can give you the names of some of our attorneys so that you contract there services for legal representation.

Thanks,

Dr. Gerald Longs.

26 August 2008
From: Mr. Dennis Bent <dbent2net@yahoo.co.uk>
To: Karol Breen <karolbreen@yahoo.co.uk>
Sent: Tuesday, 26 August, 2008 8:55 AM
Subject: Re: Fw: Attn: Director International Remittance

Dear Karol,

I did not hear from you for the whole of yesterday. I hope nothing is going too wrong?

How are the children and Annie? I pray and hope that all is well with them.

I wish to know if my bank has in any way contacted you. They are supposed to have contacted you.

Please update you ASAP.

Regards,

Mr. Dennis Bent.

From: Karol Breen <karolbreen@yahoo.co.uk>
To: clydesdale@uk2.net
Sent: Tuesday, 26 August, 2008 9:50 AM
Subject: Re: Attn: Director International Remittance

Dear Dr Longs

Thank you for your kind email. This is, indeed, wonderful news. I feel deeply indebted to my deceased relative who has been so very kind and generous to me and my family.

I have tried to download the attachment you sent but I am having difficulty. Would it be possible for you to re-send it? I look forward to being in contact immediately after.

Many thanks

Karol Breen, Esq.

From: Karol Breen <karolbreen@yahoo.co.uk>
To: dbent2net@yahoo.co.uk

Sent: Tuesday, 26 August, 2008 9:59 AM
Subject: Re: Fw: Attn: Director International Remittance

Dear Dennis
My apologies. Yesterday was a bank holiday and Annie and I took the children to the zoo.

I have great news for you, Dennis. This morning I received an email from Dr Gerald Longs stating that my application had been considered and approved by the Board of Governors. He attached a letter with instructions to enable me to begin the process of drawing down the money! WOW! I am having heart palpitations at the thought of it. Thank you so much, Dennis, for your great kindness and generosity.

I had a problem opening the attachment and I have written to Dr Longs requesting that he re-send it. I will keep you informed of developments. Now I must rush to work. I cannot wait to tell my boss what to do with his grubby job. With kind regards and eternal gratitude from me, Annie and the children,
Karol

From: Mr. Dennis Bent <dbent2net@yahoo.co.uk>
To: Karol Breen <karolbreen@yahoo.co.uk>
Sent: Tuesday, 26 August, 2008 10:28 AM
Subject: Re: Fw: Attn: Director International Remittance

Dear Karol,
What a great news!
Please forward the email to me

From: Clydesdale Bank <clydesdale@uk2.net>
To: Karol Breen <karolbreen@yahoo.co.uk>
Sent: Tuesday, 26 August, 2008 10:53 AM
Subject: Re: Attn: Director International Remittance

Dear Sir,
As you requested, we hereby reattached the document.
Thanks,
Dr. Gerald Longs.
Attachment: [03 Image2: Letter]

From: Karol Breen <karolbreen@yahoo.co.uk>
To: dbent2net@yahoo.co.uk
Sent: Tuesday, 26 August, 2008 6:12:09 PM
Subject: Fw: Attn: Director International Remittance

Dear Dennis

Yes, this is truly great news. We are so excited. The bank has re-sent the attachment and I am able to open it. They have suggested the possibility of coming over on 29 August and Annie and I have decided we will do this. I am about to write to Mr Longs and tell him to expect us. We are SOOOOOO very excited. So, well done to you, Mr Bent. It seems your plan has worked and together we have pulled it off!

It is amazing how one's life can take a sudden and dramatic change for the good. It is fantastic. Thank you so much my friend. Annie sends you a very sincere and chaste hug.

Your friend

Karol

PS: If you want to give me any advice about the contents of the attached letter and how we should deal with it, please do, as we trust you implicitly.

From: Mr. Dennis Bent <dbent2net@yahoo.co.uk>
To: Karol Breen <karolbreen@yahoo.co.uk>
Sent: Tuesday, 26 August, 2008 7:41 PM
Subject: Re: Fw: Attn: Director International Remittance

Dear Karol,

It's great that the hand of God is on us.

I have gone through the mail and the official document from my bank..

Please you should not choose the option of coming to the bank to sign the documents and get other required legal documents to back up the transfer. You must not present yourself to my bank because a lot of questions will be thrown to you when you come in person. You may not get all the questions correctly and there will be no time for me to assist you with the answers since you will be here facing my professional bank colleagues. Your failure to get the answers correctly will cause rising of eye brows and even the cancellation of the approval and transfer of this fund to your account thereby jeopardizing all our efforts.

Kindly write back to Dr. Longs and tell him to give you the names of the accredited resident attorneys attached to our bank so that we can use there services. This is purely for our own good and security of this deal.

Regards,

Mr. Dennis Bent

From: Karol Breen <karolbreen@yahoo.co.uk>
To: dbent2net@yahoo.co.uk
Sent: Tuesday, 26 August, 2008 8:56 PM
Subject: Re: Fw: Attn: Director International Remittance

Dear Dennis

God's hand is truly upon us. I thank the Almighty that I checked before replying to Dr Longs' letter. I had actually come to inform him that we had booked our tickets to Glasgow for the 28th August, returning on 30th August. In my enthusiasm I had taken my eye off the ball and I could have blown all that we have worked hard to complete. Annie and the children were coming with me and I was simply going to announce to my boss tomorrow that I was taking Thursday and Friday off. I just didn't care.

Again, Dennis, thank you for your sound counsel. I shall now cancel the tickets and write a more formal letter to Dr Longs requesting, as suggested by you, the names of accredited company solicitors.

With all good wishes and immeasurable gratitude

Karol

From: Karol Breen <karolbreen@yahoo.co.uk>
To: clydesdale@uk2.net
Sent: Tuesday, 26 August, 2008 9:13 PM
Subject: Re: Attn: Director International Remittance

Dear Dr Longs,

I am writing to thank you and the Board of Directors of Clydesdale Bank, Glasgow, Scotland, for your kind and favourable consideration of my application concerning the transfer of funds from the account of my late relative, who, together with his family, perished so tragically. I am, indeed, filled with gratitude to my dear uncle for I was unaware of his filial affection for me. As you can imagine, this inheritance has come as quite a shock, but also a very pleasant surprise.

My partner and I considered coming to Glasgow to sign the final release papers but, unfortunately, at such short notice, I am unable to get time off work. I should be very grateful, therefore, if you would kindly give me the name(s) of the accredited resident attorneys attached to your bank so that I can avail of their services in the interests of judiciously concluding this matter in an orderly and proper way.

Yours respectfully

Karol Breen, Esq.

I sent Dennis Bent a copy of this and all other emails from Karol to Dr Longs.

27 August 2008
From: Mr. Dennis Bent <dbent2net@yahoo.co.uk>
To: Karol Breen <karolbreen@yahoo.co.uk>

Sent: Wednesday, 27 August, 2008 9:26 AM
Subject: Re: Fw: Attn: Director International Remittance

Dear Karol,
That's a good mail you have sent to Dr. Longs.

As soon as he send the names of the accredited resident attorneys to you, you should send them to me so that I can check there profiles here in the bank and advice you on the one to contact.

I am happy that this deal is going on very smoothly.
Regards,
Mr. Dennis Bent

From: Clydesdale Bank <clydesdale@uk2.net>
To: karolbreen@yahoo.co.uk
Sent: Wednesday, 27 August, 2008 9:54 AM
Subject: Ref: Our accredited resident attorneys.

Dear Sir,
As you requested, here are the names of two of our accredited resident attorneys:

1) Norman Fraser Email: normanfraser@lawyer.com
2) Alyson Wilson Email: ahmedesq@justice.com

You should contact any of them to render there services to you.
Thanks,
Dr. Gerald Longs.

From: Karol Breen <karolbreen@yahoo.co.uk>
To: dbent2net@yahoo.co.uk
Sent: Wednesday, 27 August, 2008 10:01 AM
Subject: Fw: Ref: Our accredited resident attorneys.

Dear Dennis
As requested, I've forwarded you a copy of the email from Dr Longs in which he gives the names of possible attorneys. Please advise me which would be most pliable in helping us to achieve a smooth and trouble-free transfer of funds.
Kind regards
Karol

From: Mr. Dennis Bent <dbent2net@yahoo.co.uk>
To: Karol Breen <karolbreen@yahoo.co.uk>
Sent: Wednesday, 27 August, 2008 12:29 PM

Subject: Re: Fw: Ref: Our accredited resident attorneys.

Dear Karol,
I have taken time and gone through the profile of these attorneys.

From all indication, Alyson Wilson will give us a better legal representation than Norman based on how many years that have been with this bank and the meritorious legal service they have rendered to this institution.

Kindly contact Alyson Wilson now and tell him that you want him to represent you in signing the fund release order of your fund in our bank and also to guide and facilitate the immediate transfer of the fund to your account. Inform me when you have received his response.
Mr. Dennis Bent.

From: Karol Breen <karolbreen@yahoo.co.uk>
To: dbent2net@yahoo.co.uk
Sent: Wednesday, 27 August, 2008 1:28 PM
Subject: Re: Fw: Ref: Our accredited resident attorneys.

Dear Dennis
I am so excited that we have got this far. It is amazing. How long do you think it will take to get the legal paperwork out of the way so that the transfer can be made?

I will write now to Alyson Wilson and forward you a copy. Poor guy. He must get lots of jokes about having a girl's name!
Kind regards my friend
Karol

From: Karol Breen <karolbreen@yahoo.co.uk>
To: ahmedesq@justice.com
Sent: Wednesday, 27 August, 2008 1:47 PM
Subject: Transfer of Inheritance

Dear Mr Wilson
I have been instructed by Dr Gerald Longs, Director, Foreign Remittance Department, Clydesdale Bank plc, Glasgow, Scotland, to write to you.

On 25 August 2008 Dr Longs wrote to me stating that the bank's directors had, in line with your allied and banking matters of 1986 section A114, subsection RT745 as amended in 1996, cleared me to receive my inheritance of £6,550,000, following the untimely death of my uncle, Andreas Schranner and his family, on Monday 31 July 2000.

Dr Longs recommended that I engage your services to sign the final fund release order and procure the papers on my behalf to enable Clydesdale Bank to finalise the documentation for the immediate release and transfer of this fund to my nominated account. I understand that the legal procedural papers must be procured by the applying next of kin or an appointed financial accredited attorney. Since I live in Ireland, I wish to appoint you to act as my attorney in this matter.

I look forward to hearing from you at your earliest convenience.
Yours respectfully
Mr Karol Breen, Esq.

All emails from Karol to Mr Wilson were copied to Dennis Bent.

From: Alyson Wilson Esq. <ahmedesq@justice.com>
To: karolbreen@yahoo.co.uk
Sent: Wednesday, 27 August, 2008 2:16 PM
Subject: Re: Transfer of Inheritance

Dear Sir
This office has received your letter and is making verifications about your claims. We shall get back to you in a short while.
Thanks,
Alyson Wilson Esq.

From: Mr. Dennis Bent <dbent2net@yahoo.co.uk>
To: Karol Breen <karolbreen@yahoo.co.uk>
Sent: Wednesday, 27 August, 2008 2:38 PM
Subject: Re: Fw: Ref: Our accredited resident attorneys.

Dear Karol,
You have written a nice letter to the solicitor.
    Kindly inform me as soon as he responds to you.
    It's the attorney that knows how fast he can get the papers but I'm sure it will not take more than 2 working days.
    My regards to Annie and tell her that I will see all of you soon.
Regards,
Mr. Dennis Bent

From: Alyson Wilson Esq. <ahmedesq@justice.com>
To: karolbreen@yahoo.co.uk
Sent: Wednesday, 27 August, 2008 4:01 PM
Subject: Re: Transfer of Inheritance

Sir,

In furtherance to your email of today, requesting for our legal services, this office wishes to inform you as follows:

(1) You should please give us your full contact particulars as to inform the office where you are contacting from.

(2) That after our preliminary investigation today 27th of August 2008 we were satisfied from the Credit Control Department of Clydesdale Bank Plc that you have a genuine claim to make from them. (Value not stated yet.)

(3) That we feel obliged to render our legal assistance to you.

(4) That in line with legal ethics, we shall require a Power of Attorney (POA) to act on your behalf. Besides the POA, we shall swear an affidavit of claims in the law court here. The POA has to be registered in the law court to give it its full legal backing.

The statutory fees involved in carrying out this assignment are listed bellow:

1. Registration of Power of Attorney === £750
2. Affidavit of claim === £500
3. Deeds and stamp duty === £300
4. Sundry expenses === £800
Total   £2350

Note that the items 1,2and 3 are statutory fees which goes to the government treasury.

You shall be paying a service charge of £8,500.00 after the successful transfer of the fund to your designated account.

You may do well to send the money covering the fees above, via western union money transfer.

You should send the control number and test question and answer via email. Upon the receipt of the fees and the draft of the POA, we shall start the registration and the swearing of the affidavit for the assignment.

Attached is the draft of the POA which you will be reproducing in your letter headed paper, duly signed, stamped and send back to us. The POA should be sent via email attachment so that we can print it out in the original colour of your letter headed paper.

Yours sincerely,

Alyson Wilson Esq.

(Attorney at law)

YOUR FULL NAMES AND ADDRESS
Ref.: POA1 POWER OF ATTORNEY
To all persons, be it known that, I ------------------------of----------------------
------------------, the undersigned grantor, do hereby make and grant a limited

Power of Attorney to Alyson Wilson, and do thereupon constitute and appoint this said individual as my lawful attorney. My attorney shall act in my name, place and stead in any way I myself could do if I were personally present, with respect to the following matters, to the extent that I am permitted by law to act through an agent. The attorney in-fact is empowered to conclude contracts for and on my behalf, to sign the release order for the release of my fund with Clydesdale Bank Plc, valued at ---------------------- ,to oversee the remittance to my account coordinates vide (Your full account coordinates as given to the bank)---
----

-- and to carry out all activities, which concern my financial activities in Scotland. My attorney in-fact hereby accepts this appointment subject to its terms and agrees to act and perform in the said capacity consistent with my best interests, as in his discretion deems advisable. This Power of attorney stands revoked as soon as the fund is remitted to my said account above.
Dated this: -------------------------------

Name: --. (Grantor) Sign: -------------------

From: Karol Breen <karolbreen@yahoo.co.uk>
To: dbent2net@yahoo.co.uk
Sent: Wednesday, 27 August, 2008 4:56 PM
Subject: Fw: Transfer of Inheritance

Dennis
I have an email from Mr Wilson. I didn't realise I would have to pay such heavy legal fees. As of yet I am not a wealthy man. Do you think it would be possible to agree with the lawyers and the bank that once the inheritance money has been released they can deduct their fees before forwarding the balance to my bank account?

I am also a little concerned about the third last sentence on the form that I must fill in, which states, 'to carry out all activities, which concern my financial activities in Scotland'. As you know, Dennis, I am in Ireland, so might that be a problem?

I also have one other serious difficulty concerning Western Union. In 1984 there was a terrible famine in the north-west of Brazil, where my younger brother was working. My father, God rest his soul, transferred £20,000 via

Western Union. The money disappeared without trace. He spent four years, indeed four increasingly obsessive years, trying to recover it, all to no avail. It broke his health and I know it contributed to his untimely passing in 1989. Before he died he made me and the rest of the family vow that we would never use this method of transfer again. We all gave him a solemn promise.

I will write now to Mr Wilson requesting that in the event of the bank not being able to deduct his legal fees before the transfer of the money that he arrange for me to pay his fees into his firm's or his personal bank account. I have an overdraft facility with my bank so it will be easier to do this anyway than having to withdraw cash to bring to Western Union.

Thank you and best wishes
Karol

From: Karol Breen <karolbreen@yahoo.co.uk>
To: ahmedesq@justice.com
Sent: Wednesday, 27 August, 2008 5:44 PM
Subject: Re: Transfer of Inheritance

Dear Mr Wilson
Many thanks for your kind services. I am most grateful to you. Attached is the completed form, granting you the Power of Attorney (POA) in this instance.

May I ask if it might be possible for you to deduct your fees before my inheritance is transferred to my account in Dublin? I would be most grateful if this were possible as I am not a man, yet, of wealthy means. If it helped, I would be happy to write to Dr Longs to seek this facility from Clydesdale Banks, given that I have such a large inheritance coming to me.

If this is not possible, I would be grateful if you would provide me with a bank account into which I can transfer the money as I am unable to avail of the services of Western Union. I am sure this will not be a problem given your association with Clydesdale Bank.

Yours respectfully
Karol Breen, Esq.
PS: Mr Wilson, for some reason I am unable to attach the form to this yahoo account. I have tried four times and the process won't go beyond scanning the document for a virus. I am, therefore, going to return now to my workplace to send it from my account there. However, please only respond to this email address. Thank you.

From: Mr. Dennis Bent <dbent2net@yahoo.co.uk>
To: Karol Breen <karolbreen@yahoo.co.uk>
Sent: Wednesday, 27 August, 2008 5:57 PM

Subject: Re: Fw: Transfer of Inheritance

Dear Karol,
I have gone through the letter. I am worried the bank may not agree to deduct this charges from the fund because it has not been transferred to your account. But thank God that he voluntarily wrote that his service charge of 8500 pounds shall not be paid now but after the transfer of the fund to your account.

I like the idea of transferring this money to him through western union money transfer. Remember that this is a deal and I want it to be concluded in a clean way without any trace.

You should get back to the attorney and please arrange and send the money to him through western union even if you will send it through another person since you took oat never to transfer money by western union. But I bet that western union money transfer is the safest way to transfer the money to him.

As for the section of the letter that talked about Scotland instead or Ireland, there is nothing to worry about. The fund is in Scotland and all what we want is for the attorney to assist and facilitate the safe transfer of the fund to your account in Ireland . That section is in order.

Finally, please arrange and get the 2350 pounds sent to the attorney so that he can get the required papers and sign off this fund to your account.
Regards,
Mr. Dennis Bent

From: Mr. Dennis Bent <dbent2net@yahoo.co.uk>
To: Karol Breen <karolbreen@yahoo.co.uk>
Sent: Wednesday, 27 August, 2008 6:26 PM
Subject: Re: Fw: Transfer of Inheritance

Dear Karol,
I'm sure you have gone through my previous letter and can reason what the point I am trying to make there. I am expecting you to heed to my advice there.. Please write to the attorney and make the payment through western union money transfer. Its very important please.
Regards,
Mr. Dennis Bent

From: Karol Breen <karolbreen@yahoo.co.uk>
To: dbent2net@yahoo.co.uk
Sent: Wednesday, 27 August, 2008 9:04 PM
Subject: Re: Fw: Transfer of Inheritance

Dear Dennis

I have not heard from the attorney, so I think it is best not to do anything for the moment. Perhaps he won't have a problem with me transferring money to his bank account. I gave a solemn oath to my father before he died which I cannot break. Whether I do it personally or get someone to do it on my behalf, it is still the transfer of my money via Western Union and that is, quite frankly, unconscionable.

My father was half-Kenyan as my grandfather, a British soldier who served in Kenya before Independence, married my beautiful Kikuyu grandmother. They brought back to England, and eventually Ireland, many African traditions and superstitions. My grandmother was the tenth daughter of her parents and was, therefore, something of an outcast. This goes back to the traditional story of Mumbi and Gikuyu [the Adam and Eve of the Kikuyu people], who also had ten daughters, the last one was an outcast because in Kikuyu tradition the number ten is considered bad luck. I tell you this simply because if I were to use Western Union I would risk the possibility of earning a terrible curse from my father's grave. I know, to your Western mind, this probably sounds crazy, but I have Africa in my bloodstream and it has a very powerful hold over me.

Dennis, believe me, I would rather forfeit the share of the £6,550,000 you will give me than risk offending the spirit world. I am sorry. But that is who I am. Annie thinks I am crazy.

Perhaps Mr Wilson will not have a difficulty with me transferring the money to his bank account. I'm dealing with a bank anyway and I've already given them my bank details for the transfer of the funds. So, I can't honestly see what the problem is.
With kind good wishes
Karol

28 August 2008
From: Mr. Dennis Bent <dbent2net@yahoo.co.uk>
To: Karol Breen <karolbreen@yahoo.co.uk>
Sent: Thursday, 28 August, 2008 10:59 AM
Subject: Re: Fw: Transfer of Inheritance

Dear Karol,
It's alright. Inform me as soon as you hear from the attorney.

If he declines to send an account to you, it means I have to get another person to do this deal with though I pray that he should send the account.
Regards,
Mr.. Dennis Bent

From: Alyson Wilson Esq. <ahmedesq@justice.com>

To: karolbreen@yahoo.co.uk
Sent: Thursday, 28 August, 2008 11:34 AM
Subject: ACCOUNT INFORMATION.

Sir,
It's absolutely not possible for me or the bank to deduct any dime from your inheritance fund.

You should transfer the money to this company's account. It's a dollar account and owned by my father in-law.

Bank of China (Hong Kong)
Address: 4-4A, Humphrey's Avenue Branch
T.S.T, Kowloon ,
Hong Kong
Swift Code: BKCHHKHHXXX.
A/C NO: 012-577-10011639
A/C NAME: POLSO AIR CARGO CO. LTD.

You should convert the £2350 to dollars which should be around 4500 dollars and pay it to this account.

Scan the payment slip and send to me as soon as you have made the payment.
Yours sincerely,
Alyson Wilson Esq.
(Attorney at law)

From: Mr. Dennis Bent <dbent2net@yahoo.co.uk>
To: Karol Breen <karolbreen@yahoo.co.uk>
Sent: Thursday, 28 August, 2008 6:56 PM
Subject: Re: Fw: Transfer of Inheritance

Dear Karol,
How is the situation like?

Have you received any response from the attorney? If he has not responded to your last letter kindly give him a reminding please.
Regards,
Mr. Dennis Bent

29 August 2008
From: Mr. Dennis Bent <dbent2net@yahoo.co.uk>
To: Karol Breen <karolbreen@yahoo.co.uk>
Sent: Friday, 29 August, 2008 10:26 AM
Subject: Re: Fw: Transfer of Inheritance

Dear Karol,
You have been silent since yesterday. I hope nothing is going too bad.
   Inform me if you have received a response from the attorney please.
Regards,
Mr. Dennis Bent

From: Karol Breen <karolbreen@yahoo.co.uk>
To: dbent2net@yahoo.co.uk
Sent: Friday, 29 August, 2008 2:32 PM
Subject: Re: Fw: Transfer of Inheritance

Dear Dennis
Yesterday I was very sick and could not come here. I am still feeling ill but
Annie was anxious to know if there was a response. I shall send you Mr
Wilson's reply. He is asking me to transfer the money to Hong Kong to his
father's account. Please tell me if it is correct to do this.
Your friend
Karol

From: Mr. Dennis Bent <dbent2net@yahoo.co.uk>
To: Karol Breen <karolbreen@yahoo.co.uk>
Sent: Friday, 29 August, 2008 3:56 PM
Subject: Re: Fw: ACCOUNT INFORMATION.

Dear Karol,
Honestly I was worried because of your silence. I am sorry to hear about your
ill health. Take your drugs and trust our good lord to restore your health.
   Since this Hong Kong account is from the attorney, you should go ahead
and make the payment.
   You should try and make the payment today and inform him as soon as you
have paid the money.
My regards to Annie and the children. Get well soon.
Mr. Dennis Bent

From: Mr. Dennis Bent <dbent2net@yahoo.co.uk>
To: Karol Breen <karolbreen@yahoo.co.uk>
Sent: Friday, 29 August, 2008 4:30 PM
Subject: Re: Fw: Transfer of Inheritance

Dear Karol,
There is not cause for you to be confused. So long as the account if from the
attorney, go ahead and make the payment.

Regards,
Mr. Dennis Bent

From: Karol Breen <karolbreen@yahoo.co.uk>
To: ahmedesq@justice.com
Sent: Friday, 29 August, 2008 8:13 PM
Subject: Re: ACCOUNT INFORMATION.

Dear Mr Wilson
I am sorry for the delay in replying. I was ill. Tomorrow I will try and get to
the bank to make the transfer but it might be Monday if I am not feeling better.
Please confirm when the money has been received in your account. Thank you
for your help with this important matter.
Regards
Karol Breen, Esq.

From: Karol Breen <karolbreen@yahoo.co.uk>
To: dbent2net@yahoo.co.uk
Sent: Friday, 29 August, 2008 8:33 PM
Subject: Fw: ACCOUNT INFORMATION.

Dear Dennis
I have written to Mr Wilson advising him that I will transfer the money
tomorrow or Monday. I am still unwell and have come here only because Annie
is putting me under a lot of pressure. I am relieved that the attorney is not
demanding I use Western Union.
Kind regards
Karol

30 August 2008
From: Mr. Dennis Bent <dbent2net@yahoo.co.uk>
To: Karol Breen <karolbreen@yahoo.co.uk>
Sent: Saturday, 30 August, 2008 10:01 AM
Subject: Re: Fw: ACCOUNT INFORMATION.

Dear Karol,
Thanks for your letter.
    Have you seen a doctor? I feel concerned that you are still not too well. It's
high time you see a doctor for proper medical attention.
    I long for this transaction to be concluded quickly for all of us are over
anxious and under pressure. We know that the conclusion will take us to
another level in life hence we cannot afford to delay. Please try your level best

to send the money to the attorney and inform me as soon as you have done so.

Most importantly, see a doctor for proper treatment please.

Send my regards to Annie and your children while I keep on praying for your quickest recovery.

Mr. Dennis Bent

From: Alyson Wilson Esq. <ahmedesq@justice.com>
To: karolbreen@yahoo.co.uk
Sent: Saturday, 30 August, 2008 10:15 AM
Subject: Re: Re: ACCOUNT INFORMATION.

Sir,

This office has received your letter.

I will inform you as soon as the money gets to the account. You should scan the payment slip and send to me as soon as you have paid in.

Yours sincerely,

Alyson Wilson Esq.

(Attorney at law)

From: Annie Denver <annie.denver@yahoo.co.uk>
To: dbent2netyahoo.co.uk
Sent: Saturday, 30 August, 2008 7:43 PM
Subject: Karol Breen's Inheritance

Dear Mr Bent

Please forgive this intrusion. I am Annie Denver, the partner of Karol Breen. I would be very grateful if you would keep this communication private, for Karol would be furious if he knew that I was writing to you without his knowledge or permission. I am very worried about him since he began corresponding with you. I cannot understand his fears and hesitancy. We had a terrible row over his refusal to transfer funds by Western Union.

He has been very sick these last couple of days and didn't get out of bed today. If he is not better by tomorrow I will get the doctor to see him. He's a very good man and I love him to bits, but he can also be very stubborn and stupid. That's why I am writing to you directly. I have decided to send the money the lawyer requires from my own account. I do not want Karol to lose this opportunity. Also, I am not bound by the promise he made to his father.

Please advise me, Mr Bent, how I can send the amount by Western Union and I will do it immediately. Also, please advise me of the amount. In your communications with Karol, don't let him know about this email. Just advise me what I must do to make our dreams come true.

From the bottom of my heart, thank you sir.

Annie

From: Mr. Dennis Bent <dbent2net@yahoo.co.uk>
To: Annie Denver <annie.denver@yahoo.co.uk>
Sent: Saturday, 30 August, 2008 9:42 PM
Subject: Re: Karol Breen's Inheritance

Annie dear,
Thanks for your letter.

My good brother Karol is a very nice man who is too proud of you. I take him like my own brother and hope to have a great relationship with your family.

First, I will advise you to get a doctor to look after Karol because he has been sick for a couple of days now. It's important that a doctor attends to him.

Alyson Wilson is my bank accredited solicitor handling this transaction for us. He must never know that you know somebody like me.. You can pay the £2350 money as the Alyson Wilson instructed in one of his letters which I have forwarded to you. After which you should contact him through ahmedesq@justice.com to give him the reverence transfer information including the MTCN number, senders name and text questions and answers.

Annie, I seriously look forward to meeting you as soon as we conclude this deal. I have heard much about you and the love you share with Karol. Its God's making.

Kindly inform me as soon as you have paid the money and sent the payment information to the solicitor.
Kind regards Annie.
Mr. Dennis Bent

31 August 2008
From: Annie Denver <annie.denver@yahoo.co.uk>
To: dbent2net@yahoo.co.uk
Sent: Sunday, 31 August, 2008 1:56 PM
Subject: Re: Transfer of Inheritance

Dear Dennis
You are most kind. Thank you for caring about dear Karol. The doctor came to see him this morning. He is not too serious. He is suffering from acute anxiety and I can only assume that it is to do with the stress of his current job (which he is very unhappy in) and also the worry about making everything okay with your offer. The doctor has given him a note to stay off work for a week and has ordered him to stay in bed for the next three days.

I've told him not to worry about this for now. While I didn't say that you and I had corresponded, I told him that I believe you are an honourable man and that you truly want to help us and will understand his inability to conclude matters immediately. I did suggest that I check his email to see if there is any correspondence from you or the solicitor but he declined. I cannot understand why he would wish to be so secretive. I am sure, however, there is nothing to worry about. If there is, won't you please tell me Dennis?

Thank you for forwarding Mr Wilson's contact details. I will contact him directly about details for the wire transfer of the funds. Don't worry, I will not breathe a word to Mr Wilson about your role in all of this. As the Good Lord advises regarding charitable work such as we are doing to help each other: 'Do not let your left hand know what your right hand is doing' (Matthew 6:3). Or, as good old Shakespeare had Falstaff say in 1 Henry IV: 'The better part of valour is discretion, in the which better part I have saved my life.' I love Shakespeare. Do you?

Take care Dennis. I cannot wait to meet you in person. We will have a fiesta of friendship. We'll get very merry that day on our fill of good wine and food. With kisses and much affection
Annie

From: Annie Denver <annie.denver@yahoo.co.uk>
To: ahmedesq@justice.com
Sent: Sunday, 31 August, 2008 2:08 PM
Subject: Karol JW Breen - Next of Kin of Andreas Schranner

Dear Mr Wilson
My name is Annie Denver. I am the partner of Karol Joseph Wojtyla Breen, next of kin of Mr Andreas Schranner.

Karol, unfortunately, has taken ill and his doctor has ordered him to stay in bed. I am anxious, however, to ensure that his affairs regarding his inheritance are taken care of. Consequently, I will pay the initial fee of £2,350 by Western Union transfer. Can you please advise me how I can do this?

Also, I understand that the remaining legal fees are £8,500. I am most anxious to surprise Karol by assisting him to bring this matter to a successful conclusion. I believe it will ensure his recovery, for his current health issues are partly due to the stress of handling this important matter. Would there be a discount if I paid the full amount in one transfer? If not, we will do it by instalments as you are suggesting.

Thank you for your assistance Mr Wilson. I look forward to hearing from you at your earliest convenience.
Yours sincerely
Annie Denver

From: Annie Denver <annie.denver@yahoo.co.uk>

To: dbent2net@yahoo.co.uk
Sent: Sunday, 31 August, 2008 2:25 PM
Subject: Fw: Karol JW Breen - Next of Kin of Andreas Schranner

Dear Dennis

I sent the email to Mr Wilson. As the beautiful Julian of Norwich wrote in the 14th century: 'And all shall be well, and all shall be well, and all manner of things shall be well in the end.' How I love this saying Dennis. It has been my salvation throughout most of my life. For indeed, in the end, all things turn to the good. I believe in this passionately. My dear Karol is living proof of it.

Again, thank you my dear friend. And thank you for all you are doing to make Karol's life a better one.
With kisses
Annie

1 September 2008
From: Alyson Wilson Esq. <ahmedesq@justice.com>
To: annie.denver@yahoo.co.uk
Sent: Monday, 1 September, 2008 9:41 AM
Subject: Re: Karol JW Breen - Next of Kin of Andreas Schranner

Dear Annie,

I told your partner to make the initial payment through western union money transfer but he opted for an account. I gave him the account details of my father in law. I can decide to tell him to pay the money to an orphanage that I am sponsoring in Africa if I so desire. His duty is to make the payment as I instructed and mine is to discharge my duty as stated in the POA he granted to me.

If you would prefer an account here, you should pay the money to:

BANK NAME: BARCLAYS BANK LONDON
SWIFT: BARCGB22 F.C.TO: LAIKI BANK SWIFT: LIKICY2N
AC, NAME: GILSON CORPORATE LTD
AC, NO: CY42 0030 0179 0000 0179 3219 2356

You can pay the fees through western union money transfer by using this information:

Receiver's name: Alyson Wilson
Address: Station Road , OBAN, ARGYLL & BUTE, Scotland , PA34 4LN
Sender's name:?????????????????
Ref. question: What is your best flower?

Ref. answer: Rose flower
MTCN:???????????

I can discount £500 for you if you would pay all the required fees now. This means that you should send the total sum of £10,350.00 for everything.

Finally, scan the payment slip and email it to me as soon as you have made the payment.
Yours sincerely,
Alyson Wilson Esq.
(Attorney at law)

From: Mr. Dennis Bent <dbent2net@yahoo.co.uk>
To: Annie Denver <annie.denver@yahoo.co.uk>
Sent: Monday, 1 September, 2008 10:24 AM
Subject: Re: Transfer of Inheritance

Annie dear,
I'm glad that my dear friend Karol is not too bad now and has seen a doctor. I am still praying for his full recovery and I trust God to do that for us.

I wonder why my dear friend would not allow you to check his email when he told me that you know about this deal.. His health is of great importance to us and he must get well first while you try your level best to push the deal forward.

Kindly inform me when the solicitor has responded to you and also try to arrange and get the fees transferred to him today so that he can start this work for us.
Kind regards,
Mr. Dennis Bent

From: Annie Denver <annie.denver@yahoo.co.uk>
To: ahmedesq@justice.com
Sent: Monday, 1 September, 2008 7:00 PM
Subject: Re: Karol JW Breen - Next of Kin of Andreas Schranner

Dear Mr Wilson
Thank you for the London account and the Western Union option. I will now endeavour to forward an initial payment towards your legal fees.
Yours respectfully
Annie Denver

From: Annie Denver <annie.denver@yahoo.co.uk>
To: dbent2net@yahoo.co.uk
Sent: Monday, 1 September, 2008 7:19 PM

Subject: Re: Transfer of Inheritance

Dear Dennis
Thank you for your concern and prayers for Karol. Last night he hardly slept. I fear it will be the end of the week before he is recovered. Please keep him in your prayers.

I received a reply from Mr Wilson today. I was not happy with the tone of his correspondence. He has given me a London bank account and also details for a Western Union transfer. I will endeavour to do this tomorrow. I hope Karol is well enough for me to leave him and get to the bank. I will forward to you a copy of my correspondence with Mr Wilson, for your review.

Thank you Dennis for all your kindness. I feel we are inching closer to concluding this phase of the project and I just hope that Karol will be very proud of me for having taken care of this matter during his illness.
With much love and many kisses
Annie

2 September 2008
From: Annie Denver <annie.denver@yahoo.co.uk>
To: dbent2net@yahoo.co.uk
Sent: Tuesday, 2 September, 2008 12:09 PM
Subject: Re: Transfer of Inheritance

Dear Dennis
Your kind words are reassuring about Karol. I will do my best to get into town today to transfer the money.

Dennis, may I be honest with you? Your letters to me have really left a deep impression, more than I can explain. I have been impressed by your great intelligence. I also have a fetish for Scottish men. One of my fantasies would be to spend a beautiful romantic evening with a Scottish man in a kilt. What might happen after that would be up to the fusion of our chemistries. Do you think, once this project has been successfully concluded, that we might do this? Obviously, it would have to be strictly confidential as Karol would be deeply hurt and it might end our relationship.

Your emails send waves of tantricity along my spine. I am still tingling at the thought of it. There is something about you, dear Dennis, that causes me to want to get to know you better and more intimately. A lot more intimately! Karol sometimes refers to me as his lioness and says my passion exhausts him! LOL.

Karol is asleep. He seems very peaceful and the cough isn't too bad today. So, I think he is well on the mend.
With much affection and many hot kisses
Annie

From: Mr. Dennis Bent <dbent2net@yahoo.co.uk>
To: Annie Denver <annie.denver@yahoo.co.uk>
Sent: Tuesday, 2 September, 2008 1:36 PM
Subject: Re: Transfer of Inheritance

Annie dear,
Thanks for your mail.
    We cannot do such a thing to Karol. It's betrayal. I appreciate your love for me and love you but like a sister.
    I am happy to hear that Karol is getting better. Thank God for that.
    Please Annie; there is no much time to waste now. You have to go and make the payment to the solicitor now please.
Regards,
Mr. Dennis Bent

3 September 2008
From: Annie Denver <annie.denver@yahoo.co.uk>
To: dbent2net@yahoo.co.uk
Sent: Wednesday, 3 September, 2008 00:13 AM
Subject: Re: Transfer of Inheritance

Dennis dear,
I feel humiliated and rejected. I will do my best.
Kind regards
Annie

From: Mr. Dennis Bent <dbent2net@yahoo.co.uk>
To: Annie Denver <annie.denver@yahoo.co.uk>
Sent: Wednesday, 3 September, 2008 9:00 AM
Subject: Re: Transfer of Inheritance

Annie dear,
I cannot reject you neither can I humiliate you. It's only that it's ungodly to do such a thing with to trusted friend and brother like Karol. Honestly I did not wish to spoil your mood. Forgive me if you felt bad about my response to you.
    How is Karol today? I believe he is ok now.
    I expected that hear that you transferred the money to the solicitor yesterday. Why are we still delaying? Please let's not talk about doing our best or going to send it today but rather send it and inform me that you have done so.
    Annie dear, you are my darling friend. I will so much cherish and respect our friendship.

Regards,
Mr. Dennis Bent

4 September 2008
From: Annie Denver <annie.denver@yahoo.co.uk>
To: dbent2net@yahoo.co.uk
Sent: Thursday, 4 September, 2008 5:39 PM
Subject: Re: Transfer of Inheritance

Dear Dennis
I have felt so terribly guilty about my indecent proposal to you. I am very sorry.
I feel absolutely dreadful that I even thought of us having 'just a bit of fun',
which was, as you so rightly point out, a terrible betrayal of my beloved Karol.

Anyway, I have good news for you. Karol is much better. I have given him lots
of good homemade soup and TLC and he has responded well to the medication.

I also have other really exciting news for you. But I am going to tease
you by not letting you know straight away as I have to find a way of getting
it scanned for Alyson. But, hear me, you must not breathe a word to Karol
about it. He knows nothing of my communications with you and the lawyer.
I really want him to be proud of me when he realises that I have taken care of
this transaction on his behalf. Believe it or not, he has not spoken to me about
this inheritance since he became sick, apart from saying this morning that he
must write to you as you must surely be wondering what is happening and he
is anxious to fulfil the agreement he has with you.

I love you purely Dennis (with or without your kilt). Thank you for being
such a saint and for admonishing me with your Godly righteousness.
Always and with affection
Annie
PS. Please forgive me for asking this question and I am not trying to be a smart
aleck: Is it true that Scottish men wear specially knitted woollen underwear
under their kilts?

From: Mr. Dennis Bent <dbent2net@yahoo.co.uk>
To: Annie Denver <annie.denver@yahoo.co.uk>
Sent: Thursday, 4 September, 2008 6:09 PM
Subject: Re: Transfer of Inheritance

Annie dear,
Thanks for your letter. I am glad to hear that Karol is much better today and
will resume work tomorrow.

I am quite busy here and cannot write much.

Inform me as soon as you are through with the solicitor.

Regards,
Mr. Dennis Bent

5 September 2008
From: Annie Denver <annie.denver@yahoo.co.uk>
To: dbent2net@yahoo.co.uk
Sent: Friday, 5 September, 2008 9:06 AM
Subject: Re: Transfer of Inheritance

Dear Dennis
You seem cold and distant. I fear that my inappropriate advances have caused a rift in our friendship. I sense that my postscript from yesterday, genuine though it was, and also sent with a hint of humour and affectionate mischief, was not appreciated by you. I realise you are a man of the highest moral integrity. Please accept my apologies. In a strange sort of way, your response to me has not only made me a better person, but has filled me with greater confidence in how you are proposing to help Karol and our future. Believe me Dennis, by the end of today, you will be very pleased and I hope my dearest Karol will be also.
Much love
Annie

From: Karol Breen <karolbreen@yahoo.co.uk>
To: dbent2net@yahoo.co.uk
Sent: Friday, 5 September, 2008 10:48 PM
Subject: Re: Fw: ACCOUNT INFORMATION.

Dear Dennis
How are you? Oh my friend, I was really sick. I don't know how to explain it, but I was really upset about the promise I had made to my father about Western Union. For some strange reason the memory of it triggered an exhaustive fever that plunged me into both a deep depression and a kind of flu with such a bad cough.

My illness meant that I couldn't go to the bank to transfer the lawyer's fees. I'll do it first thing on Monday. I am really sorry about the delay. I'll write a short letter to Mr Wilson explaining. Monday is D-Day Dennis. Let's get it done and dusted. I had a lot of time to think while in bed and now I'm ready to do all that is necessary.

Take care my dear friend.
Sincerely
Karol

From: Karol Breen <karolbreen@yahoo.co.uk>

To: ahmedesq@justice.com
Sent: Friday, 5 September, 2008 10:58 PM
Subject: Re: Re: ACCOUNT INFORMATION.

Dear Alyson
I am sorry for my delay in getting back to you. I was very sick and just couldn't get out of bed. I had hoped to get to the bank today to transfer the money but the weather was terrible with lots of roads flooded. I will now transfer the money on Monday.

What I propose to do Alyson, to minimise the possibility of raising any eyebrows, is transfer the initial fee of £2,350, as outlined in your email of 27 August, to both bank accounts in London and Hong Kong: (£1,350 to the London account and £1,000 to Hong Kong). Is this okay? As soon as I have done it I will let you know.
God Bless you my friend
Karol Breen, Esq.

6 September 2008
From: Alyson Wilson Esq. <ahmedesq@justice.com>
To: karolbreen@yahoo.co.uk
Sent: Saturday, 6 September, 2008 11:28 AM
Subject: Re: Re: Re: ACCOUNT INFORMATION.

Sir,
Thanks for your letter. Pay the £2,350 to the last account I sent to you.

BANK NAME: BARCLAYS BANK LONDON
SWIFT: BARCGB22 F.C.TO: LAIKI BANK SWIFT: LIKICY2N
AC, NAME: GILSON CORPORATE LTD
AC, NO: CY42 0030 0179 0000 0179 3219 2356

Yours sincerely,
Alyson Wilson Esq.
(Attorney at law)

From: Karol Breen <karolbreen@yahoo.co.uk>
To: ahmedesq@justice.com
Sent: Saturday, 6 September, 2008 12:24 PM
Subject: Re: Re: Re: ACCOUNT INFORMATION.

I shall do this Mr Wilson. Thank you. You are, I can see, a dedicated lawyer, working on a Saturday.

With gratitude and respect
Karol Breen, Esq.

8 September 2008
From: Mr. Dennis Bent <dbent2net@yahoo.co.uk>
To: Karol Breen <karolbreen@yahoo.co.uk>
Sent: Monday, 8 September, 2008 10:05 AM
Subject: Re: Fw: ACCOUNT INFORMATION.

Karol dear,
I thank God that you are ok now and hope to be back to your work. Please inform me as soon as you have made the payment to the attorney.
Regards,
Mr. Dennis Bent

From: Mr. Dennis Bent <dbent2net@yahoo.co.uk>
To: Annie Denver <annie.denver@yahoo.co.uk>
Sent: Monday, 8 September, 2008 10:07 AM
Subject: Re: Transfer of Inheritance

Annie dear,
Thanks for your letter. I wait to receive the joy from you.
Regards,
Mr. Dennis Bent

From: Karol Breen <karolbreen@yahoo.co.uk>
To: dbent2net@yahoo.co.uk
Sent: Monday, 8 September, 2008 12:13 PM
Subject: Re: Fw: ACCOUNT INFORMATION.

Dear Dennis
It is so good to hear from you. Thank you for your concern. The good news is that I am now on my way to the bank to make the initial payment to the attorney. I can't wait until we get this deal done Dennis. I can't wait to be able to tell my boss to shove his job where the sun don't shine. Thank you my friend. I shall write to you soon.
With much kindness and gratitude
Karol

From: Annie Denver <annie.denver@yahoo.co.uk>
To: dbent2net@yahoo.co.uk
Sent: Monday, 8 September, 2008 3:39 PM

Subject: Re: Transfer of Inheritance

Dear Dennis

And now for the joyful news. Are you ready? And talk about serendipity. I called Karol about an hour ago, only to discover that he was in the bank and ready to transfer the money. I had to tell him not to. He was confused but I told him that I would explain all over a romantic dinner this evening. I honestly hope he will be pleased.

Dennis, I was a bit mean with you last week. Because you rejected me, I decided not to tell you that I had transferred £10,000 by Western Union to Alyson. I haven't told Alyson yet either but will do straight after sending you this email. I actually did it on 2 September during a short visit to Manchester, England. I felt very excited about helping Karol but, in my naivety, I also thought it might help stimulate a kind of an affair with you. I realise now how stupid I was to think that a man of high moral standing like you would even contemplate betraying a friend whom you consider a brother. I know that Karol loves you equally Dennis. Anyway, it is done. And I am thrilled.

And yes Dennis. I do love you. I love you very much for all that you are doing to help Karol and I begin a new life together. I can't wait for us to meet and pop the champagne.

With much love, always

Annie

From: Annie Denver <annie.denver@yahoo.co.uk>
To: ahmedesq@justice.com
Sent: Monday, 8 September, 2008 3:49 PM
Subject: Karol JW Breen - Next of Kin of Andreas Schranner - Transfer of Funds

Dear Mr Wilson

I have great pleasure in informing you that I have transferred £10,000 (ten thousand pounds sterling) to you by Western Union. I did so on 2nd September so the money should be with you by now. I should be grateful if you would acknowledge receipt of this amount and proceed immediately in bringing to a successful conclusion the transfer of Mr Karol J.W. Breen's inheritance as next of kin of the late Mr Andreas Schranner.

I am hoping you will agree to giving me a total discount of £850, rather than the £500 you offered. I have not, therefore, sent you the entire balance of £10,350, as requested, as I am appealing to your humanity and compassion.

I look forward to hearing from you in due course.

Yours sincerely

Annie Denver

From: Alyson Wilson Esq. <ahmedesq@justice.com>
To: annie.denver@yahoo.co.uk
Sent: Monday, 8 September, 2008 4:30 PM
Subject: Re: Karol JW Breen - Next of Kin of Andreas Schranner - Transfer of Funds

Dear Annie,
You should scan the payment slip and send it to me. I must present the correct transfer information in order to pick up the money.
Yours sincerely,
Alyson Wilson Esq.
(Attorney at law)

From: Annie Denver <annie.denver@yahoo.co.uk>
To: dbent2net@yahoo.co.uk
Sent: Monday, 8 September, 2008 6:17 PM
Subject: Re: Transfer of Inheritance

Dear Dennis
I still haven't told Karol about what I have done. I hope he will be well pleased.
   Dennis, may I ask a naughty question? I am in such a playful mood since I feel so exhilarated over what I have done for Karol. Come on Dennis, let me see the playful side of you too. You've been so serious with me since I made my pass at you. Don't you have a sense of humour? I imagine you to be a big burly Scotsman with muscles made magnificent from consuming tons of haggis. I imagine you with an enormous hairy chest and biceps and calves as thick as a Big-leaf Maple. Ohhh! The thought of your giant maples falling out of your MacBent tartan kilt makes me weak at the knees. I imagine you with a head of flowing black locks that cascade over your shoulders like The Falls of the Clyde, at New Lanark. I'm imagining you now, a magnificent Highland Elk, standing regal upon the brow of the hill, proudly and defiantly surveying your clan-land like Mel Gibson in Braveheart. Go on, let yourself go. I promise you, you won't be disappointed and before the night is out, you and Karol will be two very happy men.
   Dennis? Do you love me? Truly love me? Do you love me enough to give me one passionate kiss when we meet? I think I'm worth at least that, after what I have done for you and Karol. I am hot Dennis. Very hot.
With love and affection
Annie

From: Annie Denver <annie.denver@yahoo.co.uk>
To: dbent2net@yahoo.co.uk

Sent: Monday, 8 September, 2008 7:33 PM
Subject: Re: Transfer of Inheritance

Oh Dennis, come on! Karol knows there is something up but I've decided not to tell him until you reply! LOL. I've had a few glasses of wine and I'm feeling very merry. It's a night to celebrate. So, to make it complete, you just have to answer my question.
I love you Dennis Bent.
Always
Annie

From: Annie Denver <annie.denver@yahoo.co.uk>
To: dbent2net@yahoo.co.uk
Sent: Monday, 8 September, 2008 9:32 PM
Subject: Re: Fw: Karol JW Breen - Next of Kin of Andreas Schranner - Transfer of Funds

Denis im pissed.............. don't you love me? 2moro is another day.......... I was feelin soo happy too
Annie

9 September 2008
From: Annie Denver <annie.denver@yahoo.co.uk>
To: ahmedesq@justice.com
Sent: Tuesday, 9 September, 2008 9:17 AM
Subject: Re: Karol JW Breen - Next of Kin of Andreas Schranner - Transfer of Funds
Attachment: Transaction 02.09 (£10K)

Dear Mr Wilson
My apologies for the delay in getting you the attached scan of the payment slip. I look forward now to the speedy conclusion of this matter on behalf of my partner, Karol J.W. Breen, next of kin of Andreas Schranner.
Yours sincerely
Annie Denver

See Appendix 3 for Transfer Slip

From: Annie Denver <annie.denver@yahoo.co.uk>
To: dbent2net@yahoo.co.uk
Sent: Tuesday, 9 September, 2008 9:24 AM
Subject: Fw: Karol JW Breen - Next of Kin of Andreas Schranner - Transfer

of Funds
Attachment: Transaction 02.09 (£10K)

Dear Mr Bent
I have sent a scanned copy of the Western Union slip to Mr Wilson (see attached).

Karol and I had a beautiful evening yesterday. Initially he did not believe me, but when I showed him the slip he was ecstatic.

I sincerely hope you are satisfied, now that I have come through.
Cordially yours
Ms Annie Denver

From: Karol Breen <karolbreen@yahoo.co.uk>
To: dbent2net@yahoo.co.uk
Sent: Tuesday, 9 September, 2008 10:02 AM
Subject: Re: Fw: ACCOUNT INFORMATION.

Dear Dennis
You were probably wondering why you hadn't heard from me yesterday since I told you I would be in touch regarding the transfer of money. To be honest, I was embarrassed. I had gone to the bank to transfer £2,350 to Mr Wilson's Barclay's Bank account when I received a call on my mobile phone from my partner, Annie. When I told her what I was doing she insisted that I not make the transfer and said she would explain all later. I was doubly embarrassed since the bank teller had already filled out the forms.

You can imagine the incredible surprise I got last night when Annie informed me what she had done. I didn't believe her until she showed me the Western Union paper. I was a bit shocked that she had paid the entire amount but we both agreed that we consider you to be a very honourable and trustworthy friend. Annie didn't break the news to me until quite late. She said she was waiting for a sign that all was okay and kept disappearing.

Eventually she came back, at about 10 o'clock, and sat me at the fireplace with another glass of wine and suddenly burst into tears. She confessed her love for me and said she wanted to prove how deep it was. She kept sobbing the words 'I'm sorry Karol' through her tears before she produced the piece of paper. It was only then that her call to me at the bank made sense. I must admit I am very blessed to have such a wonderful woman in my life. And she is a great mother to my children. They love her so much. Now we have a wonderful future to look forward to, thanks to the incredible opportunity you have given us Dennis. From the bottom of my heart THANK YOU!

I look forward to hearing from Mr Wilson soon regarding the transfer of funds. I will write to him shortly.

With gratitude and respect
Karol

From: Karol Breen <karolbreen@yahoo.co.uk>
To: ahmedesq@justice.com
Sent: Tuesday, 9 September, 2008 10:07 AM
Subject: Re: Re: Re: ACCOUNT INFORMATION.

Dear Alyson
I understand you have had dealings with my partner, Annie Denver, and that she has now transferred by Western Union the sum of £10,000 to you for the purpose of expediting my inheritance from Clydesdale Bank. I would be grateful if you could advance this matter as quickly as possible and I look forward to hearing from you, at your earliest convenience, as to the concluding steps in this matter.
Yours sincerely
Karol Breen, Esq.

From: Alyson Wilson Esq. <ahmedesq@justice.com>
To: karolbreen@yahoo.co.uk
Cc: annie.denver@yahoo.co.uk
Sent: Tuesday, 9 September, 2008 11:26 AM
Subject: Re: Re: Re: Re: ACCOUNT INFORMATION.

Sir,
I have received information from Annie that she has made the payment of £10,000 for the needed documents and my service charge. I will pick up the money as soon as I come back from the court. I will get all the documents before banking closing hour of tomorrow and will submit them to the bank same tomorrow.

    The bank should in turn arrange and transfer the fund to your nominated bank account.

    I will inform you when pick up the money.
Yours sincerely,
Alyson Wilson Esq.
(Attorney at law)

From: Mr. Dennis Bent <dbent2net@yahoo.co.uk>
To: Karol Breen <karolbreen@yahoo.co.uk>
Sent: Tuesday, 9 September, 2008 11:39 AM
Subject: Re: Fw: Re: Re: ACCOUNT INFORMATION.

Karol dear,
What a wonderful lady! Annie is so great. She has made us happier and proud.
Yes, you told me that she is all that a man would want in a wife. I am so happy
my good brother.

Hopefully the bank has to transfer the fund to your account before this week
runs out. I hope to resign my appointment with the bank as soon as the fund
hits your account. I will come to Dublin after my resignation so that we can
have a brotherly meeting before getting out of this continent.

Wow I am happy my brother and I reserve my kudos for Annie.
Regards,
Mr. Dennis Bent

From: Mr. Dennis Bent <dbent2net@yahoo.co.uk>
To: Annie Denver <annie.denver@yahoo.co.uk>
Sent: Tuesday, 9 September, 2008 11:45 AM
Subject: Re: Fw: Karol JW Breen - Next of Kin of Andreas Schranner - Transfer
of Funds

Wow Annieeeeee,
What a great lady! Annie you have made my life fulfilled. I am so happy and
I love you more. Annie I so much love you. Honestly we are building a great
relationship and I will always thank God for having partners like you and
Karol. You are too wonderful. I cannot stop loving and thanking you. We are
all blessed and my adoration goes to you without reservation.
Mr. Dennis Bent

From: Alyson Wilson Esq. <ahmedesq@justice.com>
To: karolbreen@yahoo.co.uk; annie.denver@yahoo.co.uk
Sent: Tuesday, 9 September, 2008 1:05 PM
Subject: Re: Re: Re: Re: ACCOUNT INFORMATION.

How dare you sent £1 (One pounds) and sent a slip of £10000 to me? Do you
realise that its a crime? Kindly go and collect it back and do not contact me
again.

From: Karol Breen <karolbreen@yahoo.co.uk>
To: ahmedesq@justice.com
Sent: Tuesday, 9 September, 2008 2:16 PM
Subject: Re: Re: Re: Re: ACCOUNT INFORMATION.

What are you talking about Alyson? I am confused.

From: Annie Denver <annie.denver@yahoo.co.uk>
To: dbent2net@yahoo.co.uk
Sent: Tuesday, 9 September, 2008 2:23 PM
Subject: Fw: Re: Karol JW Breen - Next of Kin of Andreas Schranner - Transfer of Funds

Dennis
What is happening? Is Mr Wilson trustworthy? I sent £10,000 and he is saying I only sent £1. Please reassure me that this is a bad joke. Karol is telling me that it is the same curse that afflicted his father all those years ago and that I should have listened to him.
Annie

From: Alyson Wilson Esq. <ahmedesq@justice.com>
To: annie.denver@yahoo.co.uk
Cc: karolbreen@yahoo.co.uk
Sent: Tuesday, 9 September, 2008 5:19 PM
Subject: Re: Re: Re: Karol JW Breen - Next of Kin of Andreas Schranner - Transfer of Funds

Your £1 (One pounds) is there. Go and take it back and do not write to me any more..

From: Mr. Dennis Bent <dbent2net@yahoo.co.uk>
To: Annie Denver <annie.denver@yahoo.co.uk>
Sent: Tuesday, 9 September, 2008 5:21 PM
Subject: Re: Fw: Re: Karol JW Breen - Next of Kin of Andreas Schranner - Transfer of Funds

What a smart man!
    It's not possible to send 10000 pounds at a go.
    It's not possible to pay 12 pounds for transfer of 10000 pounds.
    Its not possible to pay since 2nd September and hide the information till now.
All is not well. You have had a nice ride with me.
Bye

From: Annie Denver <annie.denver@yahoo.co.uk>
To: ahmedesq@justice.com
Sent: Tuesday, 9 September, 2008 8:21 PM
Subject: Re: Re: Re: Karol JW Breen - Next of Kin of Andreas Schranner - Transfer of Funds

Dear Sir or Madam (Alison Wilson?)
Be aware that your illegal activities are being monitored and all information you shared during these email exchanges is currently being scrutinised. You won't be hearing from me again, but you will be hearing from US!
Karol Breen (alias Annie Denver)
Fraud Detection Unit

From: Karol Breen <karolbreen@yahoo.co.uk>
To: ahmedesq@justice.com
Sent: Tuesday, 9 September, 2008 8:41 PM
Subject: Re: Re: Re: Karol JW Breen - Next of Kin of Andreas Schranner - Transfer of Funds

Dear dear Alyson
You sound so upset and petty. Remember, the next time someone replies to your grubby little scam, it might be Karol, or Annie, or Dennis, or Alison, or ME!
Karol Breen (alias Annie Denver)
Fraud Detection Unit

From: Karol Breen <karolbreen@yahoo.co.uk>
To: dbent2net@yahoo.co.uk
Sent: Tuesday, 9 September, 2008 8:45 PM
Subject: Fw: Re: Re: Karol JW Breen - Next of Kin of Andreas Schranner - Transfer of Funds

And so it comes to an end dear Dennis . . . There are better ways to live than taking advantage of vulnerable, gullible and sometimes stupid and greedy people.

Naomi Raaff Scam

29 October 2008
From: "naomiraaff@thecricket.co.za" <naomiraaff@thecricket.co.za>
To: ABCD
Sent: Wednesday, 29 October, 2008 16:28:12
Subject: Letter of mutual business corporation (Strictly Private)
Re: Letter of business corporation

Sir,
I received your private information from your the chamber of commerce of your country. I it my greatest wish to invite you to participate in a risk free, highly rewarding mutual business venture.

My name is Naomi Raaff. I am writting to request you to utilize your facilities to actualize the transfer of the total sum of 11 million dollars which is willed to me by my late husband. I have attached with this message detailed information including the origin of the funds and a memorandum of agreement which shall strenghten my business relationship with you.

My late husband, Terry Ford executed a contract with Zisco which he was paid 11 million dollars. This funds were secured in Standard bank South Africa. His demise (death) gave me the right of ownership of this fund. I intend to transfer this fund to your country for investment purposes.

Please contact me on this email naomiraaff@thecricket.co.za for detailed discussion regarding this business and our meeting.

Additionally, download these documents attached to this email. Go through the whole documents and revert back to me for further information. I shall also have the bank email you the recent statement of account of this funds from their corperate address.

I need someone who can receive this money in an oversea account and make it available for investment when needed. If you can guarantee me that you can be trused in such a matter then nothing limits us in doing this business. I await your urgent response in pursuant of this matter.

In your reply please provide me your mobile phone number. (Download the files now)

Thanks,

Naomi Raaff

The following documents were sent with this email and are available to view on the Paperbooks website (www.paperbooks.co.uk) (i) Zimbabwe Reserve Bank, Analysis of Fund Transfer Scheule; (ii) Office of the Minister of Finance and Economic Planning 'Recommendation Letter of Guarantee; (iii) Federal Board of Inland Revenue, Harare, Customer Receipt for US$96,000; (iv) Memorandum of Agreement, dated 7th July 2000 between Zambabwe Iron and Steel Company ZISCO and Mr. Terry Ford; (v) Ministry of Foreign Affairs, Zimbabwe, Foreign Exchange Allocation Authority, Remittance Certificate for the sum of USD11,000,000.00 to Terry Ford, Beneficiary, dated 2002/01/04; (vi) Business Agreement (Part I) between Ms. Naomi Raaff and "The Administrator"; (vii) Department of Geological Survey, Site Inspection Certificate, authorising payment of Eleven Million US dollars to Mr Terry Ford, dated 3/12/2001; (viii) First National Bank, multi-currency current account agreement with Mr. Terry Ford, dated 10/10/2000; (ix) Ministry of Finance and Economic Planning, Harare, Capital Gain Tax certificate.

From: Karol Breen <karolbreen@yahoo.co.uk>
To: naomiraaff@thecricket.co.za
Sent: Wednesday, 29 October, 2008 18:36:14
Subject: Re: Letter of mutual business corporation (Strictly Private)

Dear Naomi

Thank you for offering me this wonderful opportunity. I am not saying 'no' but I need to offer you advice regarding the $11 million you have inherited due to the untimely passing of your husband. Please accept my condolences.

My advice is that you should not transfer this money to a bank in the northern hemisphere. An horrendous credit crunch due to the irresponsible activities of the banking system has brought the US and most major European economies to the point of collapse. Gold is set to increase in value and I believe it is the best investment you can make during this global downturn.

Should you wish to pursue the conversation regarding transferring your money to Europe, then I am willing to consider your proposal, providing, of course, that you make it worth my while. I am a professional and honest person but I do not do charity. I have reviewed the documentation that accompanied

your email and I must admit to being impressed.
Yours respectfully
Karol Breen, Esq.

From: "naomiraaff@thecricket.co.za" <naomiraaff@thecricket.co.za>
To: Karol Breen <karolbreen@yahoo.co.uk>
Sent: Wednesday, 29 October, 2008 18:59:10
Subject: THANKS FOR YOUR REPLY

Good day,
My concern is to safeguard this funds and also to secure same into a profitable venture overseas. Let me know your detailed plan of action and be informed also that a meeting will be very important to actualize this deal.
    Let me have your contact details (mobile phone number) for a discussion.
Awaiting,
Naomi

30 October 2008
From: Karol Breen <karolbreen@yahoo.co.uk>
To: naomiraaff@thecricket.co.za
Sent: Thursday, 30 October, 2008 12:03:24
Subject: Re: THANKS FOR YOUR REPLY

Dear Naomi
Before we can proceed we need to discuss fees. I am a professional and trustworthy person and my fees will be:

Monthly Retainer: US$500
Legal Fees: US$5,000 (approximately)
Percentage of transactions: 12.5%

The $500 monthly retainer and all legal fees will be deductible from the 12.5% transaction fee. Please confirm that these costs are acceptable. You will appreciate that I am not in a position to discuss my ideas until we have agreed a professional relationship that will, apart from my own fees, have your best interests at heart.
Yours respectfully
Karol Breen, Esq.

31 October 2008
From: "naomiraaff@thecricket.co.za" <naomiraaff@thecricket.co.za>
To: Karol Breen <karolbreen@yahoo.co.uk>

Sent: Friday, 31 October, 2008 14:43:41
Subject: INFORMATION

I want to work with you but you seem not to understand the state I am and the state the fund is. I have no problem with 12.5 % for you but are you sure you understand this business. I am in a situation and my fund is held somewhere. calling you for help and you are asking me for money, where do I start from. This matter is serious hence tell me if you want to proceed so that we do not waste each other's time.

I am sorry if I am rude.
Naomi

From: Karol Breen <karolbreen@yahoo.co.uk>
To: naomiraaff@thecricket.co.za
Sent: Friday, 31 October, 2008 20:39:26
Subject: Re: INFORMATION

Naomi
You are not rude. We are in the process of establishing professional boundaries. If you do not have money to pay for my professional services at this time, please state exactly how you wish to proceed. I like your directness and honesty. That's exactly how I am too. So, we have the possibility of a good working relationship that can benefit both our interests.
With respect
Karol

1 November 2008
From: "naomiraaff@thecricket.co.za" <naomiraaff@thecricket.co.za>
To: Karol Breen <karolbreen@yahoo.co.uk>
Sent: Saturday, 1 November, 2008 8:19:46
Subject: THANKS

You sound like a very good person whom I can tell everything. I have nothing to hide from you if and only if you would listen to me and corperate with me without prejudice. The money is in Standard bank. But it is stuck because I was only his fiancee. We were not married yet before he passed away. But he has no other beneficiary and I am the only one who can claim the money. The banker who is helping me is ready to make this possible so if you are willing to corperate then nothing stops us.

Let me break it down:
1. We did not get married fully before he passed away

2. I know all the transactions and the bank knows me
3. His account officer knows me very well and he is the one who wants to make sure the money is paid to me
4. There is no person as next of kin or beneficiary in his account database
5. This matter is simple and if you want us to do it then we can do it. I await your urgent response so that we can proceed.
6. I love people who are straight forward. I can see you are because you did not even mind about the money but you went ahead to make your professional stand clear and you declared a non-charity status attitude in this business. This made me open up to you . Infact I want to work with you.
7. If you reply me then I shall provide you the email and phone number of the banker then he will tell you everything. He will email you from the bank's official website, a copy of the account statement. The money is more than 11million dollars becauser there is interest.
8. I like a person like you so please send me more details. If you do not want to reveal personal details, just activate a mobile phone and send us the number. I shall tell you without hiding anything to you that this money is available but we need corperation and transparency. I will not hide anything from you. I do not have money. When my fiance was murdered, I left the country and I am seeking asylum in South Africa. I shall send you my political asylum papers/ Identity issued by the UN.
There is no risk in this matter but we need confidentiality for my personal safety.

Answer me these questions:
1. Are you married ?
2. What is your profession ?
3. Do you have a passport ?
4. Have you done a business handling more than 1million pounds before ?
5. If yes what was the success ?
6. How old are you ?
7. Do you have a company one can buy shares in ?
8. How many people are you employing ?
9. Can you keep this matter strictly confidential ?

Please provide me brief answers and you will get more impressive and surprising details.
Naomi Raaff

From: Karol Breen <karolbreen@yahoo.co.uk>
To: naomiraaff@thecricket.co.za
Sent: Saturday, 1 November, 2008 18:45:14
Subject: Re: THANKS

Dear Naomi

I really like the tone and openness of this email. Yes, we have a deal. Let's move forward in partnership. It must be horrendous for you to have lost your fiancé. I am truly sorry but I am sure his good spirit will protect us as we navigate the various challenges ahead. I am currently in Paris on business and won't return to the UK until this day week. When I do, I shall activate a confidential mobile telephone.

In answer to your questions:

1. I am not married. I have had many opportunities but I haven't found my soul mate, yet.
2. I am an engineer by profession but I now operate as a freelance entrepreneur and consultant.
3. I have a European Union passport, issued in London.
4. My business has an annual turnover of £6 million.
5. I grew the business in three years from a £2 million to a £6 million turnover.
6. I am 45. (How old are you?)
7. I act as a consultant for several companies that may be worth investing in. We can discuss this later when we have secured your funds.
8. The companies I deal with, combined, employ over 20,000 people.
9. Confidentiality is essential for us both. Remember, I will be required to take risks on your behalf.

I look forward to getting your promised impressive and surprising details. You are an intriguing woman and I like the sound of you!

With respect

Karol

3 November 2008
From: "naomiraaff@thecricket.co.za" <naomiraaff@thecricket.co.za>
To: Karol Breen <karolbreen@yahoo.co.uk>
Sent: Monday, 3 November, 2008 5:32:43
Subject: GOD BLESS YOU

What you have to do for me now is to get a phone please. We need to speak and urgently.

You have inspired me and you have brough a ray of hopes in my life again.

I am glad also that you know the whole truth now. There is no risk in this business except that you just have to go along with the proceedures.

I shall start making change of beneficiary in your name so download the confidentiality agreement. You can sign it and send back to me via scanned email. Please just sign the confidentiality agreement so that the bank will

contact you from their corperate email address with the account statement. I am proud of you. Also send me your photo please.
I await an urgent response.
Meanwhile tell me how pari is.
Naomi

From: Karol Breen <karolbreen@yahoo.co.uk>
To: naomiraaff@thecricket.co.za
Sent: Monday, 3 November, 2008 8:18:17
Subject: Re: GOD BLESS YOU

Dear Naomi
Yes, I'll do all that you request as soon as I get back from Paris. Please, send me a photograph of yourself too. I would love to see you.
You did not send me an attachment. When you send it, I will do exactly as you have instructed.
With much love and kindness from gay Paris!
Karol

From: "naomiraaff@thecricket.co.za" <naomiraaff@thecricket.co.za>
To: Karol Breen <karolbreen@yahoo.co.uk>
Sent: Monday, 3 November, 2008 16:08:14
Subject: MY PHOTO/AGREEMENT ATTACHED

Sir,
Thank you for your kindness. I shall also pray for you.
The fact is that I need you to come to South Africa for the transaction and wire transfer. I have included a copy of the agreement and also my picture. Please sign the contract and send back to me by email attachment.

Also tell me more about yourself. I would like us to be communicating more frequently at least two emails perday and I would also like to know when you are returning from Pari. Johannesburg is only 8 hours flight from UK.

I can see that you are a Godly person and in that spirit we would succeed. In as much as we are doing business, you are rendering me a help and God will reward you for that. I beleive that it is destiny.

Meanwhile have a look at my photo and send me yours.
Thanks,
Naomi

'Naomi' sent me three photographs of a drop dead goegeous supermodel harvested from the internet.

From: Karol Breen <karolbreen@yahoo.co.uk>
To: naomiraaff@thecricket.co.za
Sent: Monday, 3 November, 2008 23:51:59
Subject: Re: MY PHOTO/AGREEMENT ATTACHED

Naomi

WOW! What more can I say? You are an angelic vision of heavenly beauty. I cannot believe how unbelievably beautiful you are. I've just called one of my colleagues across to look at you and he too is stunned. Lady, you and me are gonna rock and roll! This is a match made in heaven.

I'll happily sign the Business Agreement when I get home from Paris and have access to my own PC. I will get you a signed copy.

OMG! I am still in shock to discover that I am teaming up with not only a very wealthy young woman with some needs, but a sure fire cracker as well. I won't sleep tonight thinking about you. I really won't.

With much kindness and respect
Karol

4 November 2008
From: "naomiraaff@thecricket.co.za" <naomiraaff@thecricket.co.za>
To: Karol Breen <karolbreen@yahoo.co.uk>
Sent: Tuesday, 4 November, 2008 8:53:27
Subject: GREAT

Hi,
You sound like a philospher.

How old are you and when are you arriving in London.

What specifically do you do.

You can sign the contract and send to me and please do email me a copy of your photo also.

Thanks for your kindness.
I hope your friends would not get to know about our business.
Naomi

From: "naomiraaff@thecricket.co.za" <naomiraaff@thecricket.co.za>
To: Karol Breen <karolbreen@yahoo.co.uk>
Sent: Tuesday, 4 November, 2008 19:28:26
Subject: no message from you !!!

SIR,
I have not received any message from you.

Can you please email me urgently.

Naomi

From: Karol Breen <karolbreen@yahoo.co.uk>
To: naomiraaff@thecricket.co.za
Sent: Wednesday, 5 November, 2008 0:40:31
Subject: Re: no message from you !!!

Naomi,
Why the formal 'Sir'? I am disappointed by this.

I am very sorry for the delay. These past two days have been hectic. I have been in the Louvre Museum, Paris, installing highly advanced laser technology for Leonardo da Vinci's *Mona Lisa*. It interacts with the brain of the viewers and allows them to view a two-dimensional piece of art as three dimensional. The viewers can then have a virtual interaction with the subject of the art. At present it is installed as part of only one exhibition but we believe it will be the envy of museums across the globe.

It's hard to explain the experience. Have you ever smoked a joint? Apparently the experience is a bit like that. The laser causes lightness in the head and the admirer has the sensation of weightlessness, like an astronaut in space. Eventually, those viewers (mostly men) who are fascinated by the wry smile of the beautiful subject will be able to engage in a virtual kissing session and have virtual conversations with the lady in the frame. It's amazing.

The scientist who has developed the technology predicts that, within five years, viewers who are so inclined will be able to do a lot more. If I was on the Board of the Museum, I would petition the government to advance civil rights to the persons in the paintings. What do you think Naomi? After all, under Mugabe, you know what it means to suffer the loss of your rights. I am deeply traumatised by the thought of your suffering.

Tomorrow, unexpectedly, I must travel to Belgium. It is only an overnight trip and I will be returning on Thursday evening.

Take care my dear friend. I would love to see some more pictures of you. I have printed out a copy of your picture and you are now neatly snuggled within my wallet.
With much love and kindness
Karol

From: "naomiraaff@thecricket.co.za" <naomiraaff@thecricket.co.za>
To: Karol Breen <karolbreen@yahoo.co.uk>
Sent: Wednesday, 5 November, 2008 1:50:23
Subject: I like when you say love

Good day my precious friend and partner.

I am glad to read your email as I was so worried may be something happened to you so I could not just wait to read to know that you are fine and safe. Mugabe would soon die because his days are numbered but I want to migrate finally to UK because though I have lived there briefly in the past, my situation now would only warrant me to come when I have dealth with foundamental issues here. I would need us to expedite the transaction and carry out the transfer so that I can have funds to process my travel papers and also for other things that matter to me. I kind of think you are a very good and caring man. How old are you and has your life been since you are still a barchelor.

While in Belgium please make sure that you take good care of yourself and do not be deceived by those belgian women. (Just kidding)

I have been waiting for your picture so can you send it to me also.
Awaiting,
Naomi

From: Karol Breen <karolbreen@yahoo.co.uk>
To: naomiraaff@thecricket.co.za
Sent: Wednesday, 5 November, 2008 6:33:21
Subject: Re: I like when you say love

Dearest Naomi
I like you more each time I read your beautiful words. I am at the airport about to catch my flight to Belgium. As soon as I get home, I will send you my picture. I am 45 years old. Not exactly a bachelor – I was married but my wife passed away 10 years ago. I have two teenage daughters whom I love very much. But, after 10 years, I am ready for a new relationship. I hope you and I might have a future together dear Naomi.

I am feeling very happy. I awoke to the news that Barack Obama has been elected to be the next President of the United States. He is a breath of fresh air. I hope Barack will put the continent of Africa high up on his agenda. I have never been more hopeful!

Take care my dearest Naomi. God bless you! God bless Africa! God bless America!
With much love
Karol

From: "naomiraaff@thecricket.co.za" <naomiraaff@thecricket.co.za>
To: Karol Breen <karolbreen@yahoo.co.uk>
Sent: Wednesday, 5 November, 2008 16:27:27
Subject: I AM HAPPY FOR YOU

Dearest Karol Breen,

I cannot wait to see your photo. You write in a very passionate manner and from my understanding you are involved in a lot of travelling and you do great things for the world. I am excited at your being part of that installation. I shall also be delighted to see your daughters photos.

I am of the opinion and do strongly believe that your kind of person is a perfect match for both business and other things. The way and manner you approached my explanation to you made me feel so relaxed and happy and I am prepared to do a lot of things with you. Let me see your photo first and also that of your daughters and I would also like that at the preliminary stage we keep our dealings confidential.

Keep strong and email me as soon as you can.
God bless you too.
Naomi

7 November 2008
From: "naomiraaff@thecricket.co.za" <naomiraaff@thecricket.co.za>
To: Karol Breen <karolbreen@yahoo.co.uk>
Sent: Friday, 7 November, 2008 2:47:38
Subject: WHAT IS GOING ON !!!

HI
You almost ignited a fire in my mind with your wonderful messages. I knew that Obama could be the American President because he is a genuine person and people could trust those who have the brain power he has. I had some doubts though his greatness became a reality but I was wondering how a man could build a Rome in A day but it happened. I used to think that being a realist that some people could prove me otherwise that impossibility could become possible sometimes but they always fail because they prime the engine but when the motion starts they begin to look for another engine to prime. You nearly worn my heart but how come you could no longer write; may be all men are the same. My late fiancée delayed our wedding because he wanted women who were more beautiful than me; he continued to seek and wasted my time. I had patience but got no where. My life and destiny is in the fate of God because my late husband did not want the real thing which I could have given him rather he wanted to experiment with life and women.

He did not want to settle down and face the reality that a bird at hand is worth more than a million birds in the air. If the love is real then I think it should have been proven. I expected multiple emails and I can see you are more interested in your private businesses.

If I may ask, what happened between you and your previous wife? Did she divorce you because you cared most about the world than her ?

I want to hear the truth.

Can we focus on the business now as I do not want to lose focus? Have you signed the contract? I want us to expedite this transfer.

(PLEASE LET US DEAL WITH THE TRANSFER OF THE FUNDS TO UK AND URGENTLY)

I await your response.

Naomi

8 November 2008

From: Karol Breen <karolbreen@yahoo.co.uk>

To: naomiraaff@thecricket.co.za

Sent: Saturday, 8 November, 2008 12:28:24

Subject: Re: WHAT IS GOING ON !!!

Naomi

I am confused by the hot and cold tone of your email. I got home late last night – you knew I was away and I told you that as soon as I got back I would deal with the business matter.

You state that your late fiancé delayed your wedding because he wanted women who were more beautiful than you. I cannot believe this. Based on the photographs you sent me, it would be near impossible. You also talk about your late husband. Were you married as well? As for my wife, I can see you are a very poor listener. Read my previous email to you and you will learn what happened to my wife.

I thought Terry, your murdered fiancé, was a caring and conscientious man. I feel you dishonour his memory by writing what you have. I do not like it. It suggests to me that you are a shallow person, trying to guilt trip me into finalising the business proposition you have sent me. Is that all you are interested in? I will not help you under duress. I only want you to reply to me if you meet me as an equal.

Respectfully

Karol

9 November 2008

From: "naomiraaff@thecricket.co.za" <naomiraaff@thecricket.co.za>

To: Karol Breen <karolbreen@yahoo.co.uk>

Sent: Sunday, 9 November, 2008 6:27:58

Subject: INFO

Sir,

I am glad that you wrote.

Now it is impossible for us to mix business and relationship.

I want to work with you. I also want to be your a partner but I could see that non of those would work. I was not married to Terry Ford rather we were going to get married but the wedding did not take place until he died. You make me emotional and please I would not write you again. This is my last email. Let us forget everything.

Thanks and God be with you as you move on in life.

Naomi

From: Karol Breen <karolbreen@yahoo.co.uk>
To: naomiraaff@thecricket.co.za
Sent: Sunday, 9 November, 2008 9:00:42
Subject: Re: INFO

Dearest Naomi

I am sorry I upset you. I like you very much. I like your fiery and short temper. So, can we begin again? Do you still want me to send the signed contract?

I showed your photographs to my eldest daughter. She thinks you are one of the most beautiful women in the world. She said, 'She has one of those ageless complexions. She is one of those lucky woman who seem to get younger, even as they get older.' She wants to know how you look so young and beautiful. I would really appreciate it, Naomi, if you could advise her.

I'm glad to be back home in the UK. It's a bit overcast with some rain and winds, but it is fresh and I love that. Please write again. Everyone deserves a second chance.

With much love
Karol

10 November 2008
From: "naomiraaff@thecricket.co.za" <naomiraaff@thecricket.co.za>
To: Karol Breen <karolbreen@yahoo.co.uk>
Sent: Monday, 10 November, 2008 10:04:33
Subject: I AM FALLING FOR YOU NOT EVEN SEEING YOU

Sir,

I was falling in love with you when I have not even met you. That is the problem. Your words are so powerful and you melted my soul. I want to be with you. I want to be with your family as my own. I am falling for you.

Send me the signed contract let us do the transfer and I will come to you.

I am really falling for you. I need your photo and other information about you. Give me your number please.

Thanks,
Naomi

From: Karol Breen <karolbreen@yahoo.co.uk>
To: naomiraaff@thecricket.co.za
Sent: Monday, 10 November, 2008 15:12:45
Subject: Re: I AM FALLING FOR YOU NOT EVEN SEEING YOU

Dearest Naomi
Your words have also touched me greatly. I can tell you are a truly magical person. You have a magic that I want. You have the gift of transfiguration. Do you understand what I mean? The ability to change from a very beautiful and deeply hurt middle-aged woman into a stunningly hot babe! Amazing. Have a look at this link and you'll see what I mean:

http://news.bbc.co.uk/2/hi/programmes/breakfast_with_frost/past_programmes/2186686.stm

Can I take you on a roadshow? We could become fabulously wealthy together. But, there again, you are nothing but a scammer. A disgrace to your people. Preying on the suffering of others. Yuck!
I too am falling for you, sir!
Love
Karol

12 November 2008
From: "naomiraaff@thecricket.co.za" <naomiraaff@thecricket.co.za>
To: Karol Breen <karolbreen@yahoo.co.uk>
Sent: Wednesday, 12 November, 2008 4:01:32
Subject: I WANT TO COME TO UK

Sir,
Could you please send me the sum of 1000 pounds so that I can make my way to the UK. You need to see me face to face and not by email photo.
Awaiting,
Naomi

14 November 2008
From: Karol Breen <karolbreen@yahoo.co.uk>
To: naomiraaff@thecricket.co.za
Sent: Friday, 14 November, 2008 19:50:59
Subject: Re: I WANT TO COME TO UK

If you wish to come to the UK, then I will help you. You intrigue me.
Karol

15 November 2008
From: "naomiraaff@thecricket.co.za" <naomiraaff@thecricket.co.za>
To: Karol Breen <karolbreen@yahoo.co.uk>
Sent: Saturday, 15 November, 2008 16:15:17
Subject: I WANT TO COME TO UK

I KNOW YOU LIKE ME.
    CAN YOU PLEASE JUST SEND ME 1000 DOLLARS TO ARRANGE
MY TRAVEL DOCUMENTS.
TELL ME IF YOU CAN.
NAOMI

18 November 2008
From: Karol Breen <karolbreen@yahoo.co.uk>
To: naomiraaff@thecricket.co.za
Sent: Tuesday, 18 November, 2008 2:25:14
Subject: Re: I WANT TO COME TO UK

Let me have the details of your travel agent and I will arrange your flight.
Karol

21 November 2008
From: "naomiraaff@thecricket.co.za" <naomiraaff@thecricket.co.za>
To: Karol Breen <karolbreen@yahoo.co.uk>
Sent: Friday, 21 November, 2008 6:06:02
Subject: PLEASE

Sir,
If you really want to help me just send the sum of 1000 dollars to naomi raaff
76 de glen street, [Google Maps is not showing this address] johannesburg,
south africa
    send this money by moneygram.
    Please do this and I will confirm my travel plans.
    I know you love me and I know that there are some truth you want to know,
    I will tell you when we meet.
Send the money and send me the ref number.
Naomi

From: Karol Breen <karolbreen@yahoo.co.uk>
To: naomiraaff@thecricket.co.za
Sent: Friday, 21 November, 2008 22:21:41
Subject: Re: PLEASE

Naomi
I don't do moneygrams. Let me have the details of your bank account and I will forward the amount to you. I cannot wait to meet you. I'm not sure if I really love you. Perhaps it was an infatuation.
With kindest regards
Karol

22 November 2008
From: "naomiraaff@thecricket.co.za" <naomiraaff@thecricket.co.za>
To: Karol Breen <karolbreen@yahoo.co.uk>
Sent: Saturday, 22 November, 2008 10:15:59
Subject: USE THE ACCOUNT

Sir,
I am staying with a friend here and I haven't got an account. Please wire the money to the account below:

BANK: ABSA BANK
SWIFT CODE: ABSAZAJJ
ACCOUNT NUMBER: 9197763168
BENEFICIARY: BASIMISI BETTY PHAKATHI

PLEASE EMAIL ME ALSO A SCAN COPY OF THE WIRE SLIP.
THANKS,
Naomi

From: Karol Breen <karolbreen@yahoo.co.uk>
To: naomiraaff@thecricket.co.za
Sent: Saturday, 22 November, 2008 20:32:30
Subject: Re: USE THE ACCOUNT

Thank you my dear for the account details. I will take appropriate action on Monday.
Karol

23 November 2008
From: "naomiraaff@thecricket.co.za" <naomiraaff@thecricket.co.za>
To: Karol Breen <karolbreen@yahoo.co.uk>
Sent: Sunday, 23 November, 2008 8:43:20
Subject: I BELIEVE YOU

Sir,

I will tell you a lot of things that will make you happy. I will also reveal some other secrets to you. I know how you feel but just do the transfer so that I can come and see you then tell you all that you need to know because I did not disclose all to you. But everything is fine except a few .... here and there which I will tell you. I like you and I will be completely transparent to you. you are not infatuating because you are a real man and you are going to meet someone that will ignite happiness in your life but first of all we shall start from absolute hornesty. Let me come to UK then we shall take it from there. Please as soon as you do the transfer tomorrow, kindly email me a scan copy of the transfer. I await same

Thanks and have a wonderful weekend.
Naomi

From: Karol Breen <karolbreen@yahoo.co.uk>
To: naomiraaff@thecricket.co.za
Sent: Sunday, 23 November, 2008 9:14:51
Subject: Re: I BELIEVE YOU

Dear Naomi
To prevent the transfer of money to terrorist organisations abroad, banks now require proof of identity of the recipient. Would you mind, Naomi, sending me a copy of your passport so that I can assure the bank that you are a legitimate friend who is coming to spend time with me in the UK? I would also love to see another picture of you. I have missed your attachments. I still carry the first photo you sent me in my wallet.
Take care my dear Naomi. Soon we will be together.
Karol

From: "naomiraaff@thecricket.co.za" <naomiraaff@thecricket.co.za>
To: Karol Breen <karolbreen@yahoo.co.uk>
Sent: Sunday, 23 November, 2008 12:14:02
Subject: I can understand

Hi
Find attached the passport and other things.
Have fun
Naomi

With this email 'Naomi' sent a copy of a South African passport allegedly issued on 21/7/2008 to Naomi Raaph, Refugee, born in Zimbabwe 6/11/1972. The photograph is similar to the drop dead gorgeous female but not the same person. Furthermore, the photograph used is a side view

173

**perspective, which would not be acceptable for a passport image. 'Naomi'
also sent a reverse image of a previously sent picture of the supermodel.**

25 November 2008
From: Karol Breen <karolbreen@yahoo.co.uk>
To: naomiraaff@thecricket.co.za
Sent: Tuesday, 25 November, 2008 0:38:42
Subject: Re: I can understand

Dear Naomi
To surprise you, I sent a courier to deliver you $500 cash and your air tickets
to London but the courier was unable to find the address. Is 76 de glen street,
Johannesburg your correct address? Is it in a particular district? Let me know
what to do and I will give the courier company new instructions tomorrow.
Good night dear Naomi.
With much love
Karol

From: "naomiraaff@thecricket.co.za" <naomiraaff@thecricket.co.za>
To: Karol Breen <karolbreen@yahoo.co.uk>
Sent: Tuesday, 25 November, 2008 14:41:41
Subject: information

SIR,
Please send me the money to the address by moneygram or you use wire
transfer.
    I told you that I will tell you a lot of things with time when we meet but you
keep changing from one thing to the other. Let me know your mind because
you are changing a lot of things all the time and it makes me to think that you
are not serious with anything. When you tell me something, I beleive but the
next day you do your own thing and that confuses me. I will tell you what is
happening and full details when we meet. I know what you want to know but
do not keep taking me by surprises. Straighten up. I need the money to arrange
my travel issues..Courier people are not allowed to carry cash. It is against the
law and it is money laundering. Just keep straight and do as I instructed you
then you will hear the truth you want to hear. Send the money by moneygram
to naomi raaff ata the addresws and i will pick it up and when you ask the
moneygram officers they will tell you i picked it up/ otherwise send by wire.
    I await your comments.
    Send the money by moneygram with the name but please send 1000 dollars.
Thanks,
Naomi

From: Karol Breen <karolbreen@yahoo.co.uk>
To: naomiraaff@thecricket.co.za
Sent: Tuesday, 25 November, 2008 19:37:33
Subject: Re: information

Naomi
I already have $500 dollars in cash in Johannesburg along with your ticket to
fly to the UK. The air ticket is for one week to begin with and we can either
extend it, if we like each other, or you can return to South Africa to make your
arrangements. I thought I was giving you a great surprise by bringing you to
the UK for a holiday. Don't you want that?
   The money and ticket are there. Tell me where to deliver them.
Kind regards
Karol

From: "naomiraaff@thecricket.co.za" <naomiraaff@thecricket.co.za>
To: Karol Breen <karolbreen@yahoo.co.uk>
Sent: Tuesday, 25 November, 2008 19:52:06
Subject: THE OTHER WAY ROUND

HI,
On the other way round, tell me where the office of the courier people is so
that I can go there and fetch the money with my id. This is better so that we can
trust each other without ...
   Meanwhile tomorrow I shall send you my necked picture, may be that will
make you change your mind. you seem so facinating though.
Naomi

26 November 2008
From: Karol Breen <karolbreen@yahoo.co.uk>
To: naomiraaff@thecricket.co.za
Sent: Wednesday, 26 November, 2008 19:41:19
Subject: Re: THE OTHER WAY ROUND

My dear Naomi
Why would I want to see your naked picture? Do you think that is my motivation
for communicating with you? Your poor judgement makes me wonder about
you.
   What is the problem with the address you sent me? Is it a real address? Are
you lying to me? I truly hope you are not. I am at home now and the details of the
courier service I engaged are at work. All I know is that they are FedEx. I shall
get you the full details when I get back to the office tomorrow evening or Friday.

Naked? Is that the kind of person you are? I am not impressed. Indeed, I am quite disappointed.
Truly
Karol

27 November 2008
From: Karol Breen <karolbreen@yahoo.co.uk>
To: naomiraaff@thecricket.co.za
Sent: Thursday, 27 November, 2008 23:31:46
Subject: Re: THE OTHER WAY ROUND

Naomi
I must leave in the morning for Cape Town on urgent business. I have been asked to go there to negotiate a contract regarding the 2010 World Cup. Would you like us to meet while I am there? Please let me know. I won't have access to my email until late tomorrow as my flight will be almost twelve hours from London.
Kindest regards
Karol

29 November 2008
From: Karol Breen <karolbreen@yahoo.co.uk>
To: naomiraaff@thecricket.co.za
Sent: Saturday, 29 November, 2008 14:32:10
Subject: Re: THE OTHER WAY ROUND

Hi Naomi
I'm in Cape Town. I'm disappointed that it is raining and a bit cold. Would you like to come and meet me? I'll be here until next Saturday. I travelled first class yesterday with KLM. It was a real pleasure and I slept for most of the flight.
    Did you go to FedEx to collect the tickets and dollars? I'm sure you will love spending Christmas with us in London.
Take care my friend
Karol

4 December 2008
From: Karol Breen <karolbreen@yahoo.co.uk>
To: naomiraaff@thecricket.co.za
Sent: Thursday, 4 December, 2008 9:05:46
Subject: Re: THE OTHER WAY ROUND

Naomi

Where are you? I'm missing our communications. Cape Town is beautiful. It would be lovely to see you before I go home on Saturday.
Much love
Karol

11 December 2008
From: Karol Breen <karolbreen@yahoo.co.uk>
To: naomiraaff@thecricket.co.za
Sent: Thursday, 11 December, 2008 20:28:12
Subject: Re: THE OTHER WAY ROUND

I miss you. Why didn't you contact me when I was in Cape Town? I am at a loss. Your flight to London is booked for December 21st. I hope you will come.
Much love,
Karol

4 January 2009
From: "naomiraaff@thecricket.co.za" <naomiraaff@thecricket.co.za>
To: Karol Breen <karolbreen@yahoo.co.uk>
Sent: Sunday, 4 January, 2009 14:21:15
Subject: YOU ARE NOT SERIOUS

NO BODY SENDS MONEY BY FEDEX AND YOU DID NOT BUY ANY TICKET. THIS IS 2009 AND IF YOU WANT TO FLOW WITH ME THEN SEND ME SMALL MONEY AND STOP TURNING AROUND A CIRCLE.
NAOMI

From: Karol Breen <karolbreen@yahoo.co.uk>
To: naomiraaff@thecricket.co.za
Sent: Sunday, 4 January, 2009 15:06:36
Subject: Re: YOU ARE NOT SERIOUS

You've returned! Why didn't you communicate with me when I was in Cape Town? It would have been lovely to see you.

Yes, I did send you the money and ticket but the address you gave me was undeliverable. FedEx returned the package to me last week. The money was inside a small book and your air ticket was first class (I wanted to treat you well).

You crushed my hopes and my spirit by suddenly turning cold on me. I had looked forward so much to us having a wonderfully warm and intimate Christmas together.

It's your move now. And what about that picture you promised me?

Happy New Year my dear
Karol

6 January 2009
From: "naomiraaff@thecricket.co.za" <naomiraaff@thecricket.co.za>
To: Karol Breen <karolbreen@yahoo.co.uk>
Sent: Tuesday, 6 January, 2009 10:20:47
Subject: I WILL TELL YOU

THERE ARE SOME UNREVEALED SECRETS WHICH I WILL REVEAL
TO YOU. BUT PLEASE IN THE NAME OF GOD SEND ME JUST 700
POUNDS AND I WILL TELL YOU EVERYTHING ABOUT ME AND THIS
BUSINESS. I PROMISE YOU, YOU WILL BE VERY HAPPY.
    I HAVE MY PASSPORT SECURED SOMEWHERE SO SEND THE
MONEY TO A FRIEND OF MINE

MICHAEL OBI
88 CONSTANTIAL KLOOF
ROODERPORT
SOUTH AFRICA
PLEASE SEND BY MONEYGRAM.
go to www.moneygram.com

    click find us or locate us and get the nearest address to you and then go there.
Please do not let me down. I promse you that when I tell you everything you
will be happy this time around not bullshitting. I am real but there is something
about my identity which you do not know well enough. I shall reveal everything
to you. I have lied to you about my identity but the funds are real but not my
identity. My picture is real also. But not one jokes with the name of the lord
and I say send me just 700 pounds and I will be fine to travel and also i will
reveal everything to you. do not tell me about fedex and all those things as it is
unwise to send money through fedex. that is money laundering and what if they
discovered the money then i either get into trouble or you will so let us open up
now. Many things you will know as soon as you send this money.
    Just make the sacrifise. Naomir raaf fund is real but the identity i gave you
about me is not true though my picture is true. Just give it a try. I like you a lot
but i would not say that i am in love with you because you are not following
the instruction that I give you and in this world of equality women still have
rights so it cannot just go your way all the time. Let me see what you can do.

From: Karol Breen <karolbreen@yahoo.co.uk>
To: naomiraaff@thecricket.co.za

Sent: Tuesday, 6 January, 2009 16:10:27
Subject: Re: I WILL TELL YOU

Naomi
I can help you. I want to help you. But, truthfully, who are you? There's no use in feeding me a mystery. Why do I have to send the money first, before you tell me 'many things' about you? That doesn't make sense. If there is any possibility of us forming a partnership, and falling in love, it must grow from trust. Trust is the very foundation of friendship and love. I've been entirely truthful with you. You haven't been with me. I just wish you had met me in Cape Town, then we would have been beyond this stalemate.
Always
Karol

8 January 2009
From: "naomiraaff@thecricket.co.za" <naomiraaff@thecricket.co.za>
To: Karol Breen <karolbreen@yahoo.co.uk>
Sent: Thursday, 8 January, 2009 16:54:21
Subject: THIS IS STRANGE

JUST SEND ME A LITTLE BIT OF MONEY TO GET MY HEAD OFF THIS STRESS.
     WHAT KIND OF A FRIEND CAN YOU BE WHEN YOU ARE NOT A FRIEND IN NEED. JUST THE TOKEN TO RELIEVE ME PLEASE.
AWAITING,
NAOMI

From: Karol Breen <karolbreen@yahoo.co.uk>
To: naomiraaff@thecricket.co.za
Sent: Thursday, 8 January, 2009 22:50:54
Subject: Re: THIS IS STRANGE

Naomi
I want to help you, but I need to know who I am dealing with. So, tell me, truthfully, who are you?
Karol

10 January 2009
From: "naomiraaff@thecricket.co.za" <naomiraaff@thecricket.co.za>
To: Karol Breen <karolbreen@yahoo.co.uk>
Sent: Saturday, 10 January, 2009 3:05:01
Subject: THE TRUTH

Sir,

The deal of Naomi raaff is true. I am just a sister to Mr. Raaff. This is the truth..
My real name is Jennipher raaff.

Mrs. Raaff, my late brothers wife does not want to be actively involved
in this deal hence I was doing it on her behalf. I also have a personal email
address so let me know if we can divert to it and forget this business hence
discuss personal relationship. I want to hear from you.

Jennipher/Naomi

From: Karol Breen <karolbreen@yahoo.co.uk>
To: naomiraaff@thecricket.co.za
Sent: Saturday, 10 January, 2009 13:22:18
Subject: Re: THE TRUTH

Dear Jennipher/Naomi

Now we are making progress. Thank you for your honesty. Yes, I would very
much like to receive your personal email and to communicate with you on a
deeper and more intimate level. I cannot explain it, but from the beginning
you captured a corner of my heart and soul. Jennipher, what I told you about
sending you the money and also an air ticket was true. The courier was unable
to deliver them to the address you gave me. It is also true that I was in Cape
Town when I said I was.

I look forward to hearing from you, Jennipher. Please tell me all you can
about yourself and your family. And about dear Naomi. She has suffered too
much under that bully Mugabe. He was once my hero but he has presided over
the destruction of a wonderful country that now needs to be rescued and fixed.
I am also awaiting the additional photograph you promised me.

I feel elated that we are committing to an honest, no mystery, relationship.
Thank you!

Karol

14 January 2009
From: "jennipherraaff@thecricket.co.za" <jennipherraaff@thecricket.co.za>
To: karolbreen@yahoo.co.uk
Cc: karolbreen@yahoo.co.uk
Sent: Wednesday, 14 January, 2009 12:06:16
Subject: MY IDENTITY AND EMAIL

Hi Karol,

I am happy that you are a very understanding gentelman.

At this moment, there is no limit to what we can do. I am ready to be your
lover and someone to share your life with you.

You have been relentlessly writting me emails which shows that you care and I strongly appologise for what happened. It was a plan between naomi and I since she did not want to present herself for this matter. The money is real and the deal is real. My real name is Jennipher Raaf and in as much we may probably get into an intimate relationship we will also do this business but this time, I shall advise her that there is nothing to worry about rather she has to come out openly. I am the younger sister to Mr. Tony Raaf married to Naomy. Please I am sorry for everything but I think you are my kind of man . A man with so much compassion and spirit.,

How come you are like that because british people are kind of mean. I like you and I want to be with you.

In life it is difficult sometimes for the mind to express all that it harbors but I will not relent in expressing everything to you having known the kind of a person you are.

Please they say a hungry man is an angry man. Do me one favor with just a token sum of 600 pounds so that I can get myself together. I know it is strange but please do it for me.

There is moneygram here and also there is westernunion.

If you are ready let me know so that i can provide you receivers information.

We will discuss in details how we shall meet but for now please rescue me as it would be foolish if I do not alay my feelings to you.

I await comments.

Jennipher

15 January 2009
From: Karol Breen <karolbreen@yahoo.co.uk>
To: jennipherraaff@thecricket.co.za
Sent: Thursday, 15 January, 2009 1:15:47
Subject: Re: MY IDENTITY AND EMAIL

Dearest Jennipher
You are confusing me. You said that money wasn't an issue and that you wanted to start afresh. So, why are you still asking me for money? I cannot forget that you have already been duplicitous. Before I give you anything, here's what I want and need from you:

1. Your bank details – I will only transfer money into a legitimate bank account.
2. An explanation of why you now need this money.
3. Your confirmation that all the photographs you sent me are, indeed, of you.
4. A photo that shows you holding my name, so that I know you are telling the truth.

If you do this, I will make you very rich. How? You and I will become one!
Always, and with hope in you
Karol
PS. Please do not hurt me. Please do not betray me.

From: "jennipherraaff@thecricket.co.za" <jennipherraaff@thecricket.co.za>
To: Karol Breen <karolbreen@yahoo.co.uk>
Cc: Karol Breen <karolbreen@yahoo.co.uk>
Sent: Thursday, 15 January, 2009 7:09:30
Subject: Re: MY IDENTITY AND EMAIL

Hi Karol Breen,
I told you that Mr. Raaf is my brother. I and Mrs Naomi decided to do this business but she could not present herself hence she asked me to act as her. I was using her email to write you but when I sent you my photo and we began to connect I decided to open up to you because I do not know where this relationship will lead us because life is full of mysteries.

This business is legitimate but the only thing not legitimate about it is that I impersonated mrs raaf but that was our agreement please so do not take me for a negative person. We even wanted to let all matter known as we proceeded but thanks to this intimate relationship which overrided the business.

As I did tell you, the funds are held somewhere and needs some proceedures to get them out. We are not in possession of that funds now cash hence we are broke broke broke you cannot believe it and here is not a place where you go asking people for money. Also our status here is not citizens.

Before I send you any account information, I would like you to know that I want to be with you but in life you have to show concern to someone you want to be with. You have to come out and stand for someone you want to be in love with. I asked you for financial assistance and that does not mean the business we told you stopped.

I want to continue with you in this loving relationship may be we can find alternative means of carrying out that business so that it does not conflice with my relationship with you.

I do not want to be asked to raise a news paper, or stand on top of a mountain and take photos but I have taken photo of me holding your name saying that I think I love you.

Please do not ask me to do a lot of things. confirm to me if you are ready to help me and tell how much you want to send to me then I will provide you an account. I think I am beginning to love you and please I am who I said I am.

Download the photo to understand what I mean. I understand your kind of person. you are like an angel and I promise you if I am right, I will make you the happiest man on earth that you will live to fullfilled in your love life. But do not hurt me, do not betray me and do not brake my heart.

I sincerely need money to sort my accomodation issues, and we are owing a lot of people here and it is getting emarrassing. Tell me what you can be able to do then I will send you an account urgently.

thanks and have a wonderful day.

Sweet dreams,

With love from

Jennipher Raaf

'Jennipher', in response to my request for a photograph of her holding my name, sent a superimposed facial image on a picture of a woman with a white top and long black velvet gloves, holding a sign that reads 'I Think I Love You Karol Breen'

From: Karol Breen <karolbreen@yahoo.co.uk>
To: jennipherraaff@thecricket.co.za
Sent: Thursday, 15 January, 2009 19:37:37
Subject: Re: MY IDENTITY AND EMAIL

Dear Jennipher

Each time I see your picture my heart misses a beat and I love you more and more. You are my last thought at night and my first thought in the morning and, believe me, you have been the subject of my dreams. Some of them very passionate dreams.

I want to help you and Naomi. How much do you need? Is £700 enough? Tell me.

Thank you for doing as I ask. Thank you for letting me see my name beside your beautiful body. It is a connection that I hope will soon be an intimate union. I hope that one day there will be no hint of doubt in your declaration of love for me.

Always

Karol

17 January 2009
From: "jennipherraaff@thecricket.co.za" <jennipherraaff@thecricket.co.za>
To: Karol Breen <karolbreen@yahoo.co.uk>
Sent: Saturday, 17 January, 2009 12:08:13
Subject: PLEASE MY LOVE

Good day my love.

I am falling in love with you because from all indications you are a good man. I treasure such values. Goodness and integrity. I see that we are heading somewhere. Can you please send this money by moneygram because I do not know anyone here whom I can rely on in terms of using the account.

It is simple, go to the bank withdraw the money 700 pounds i okay then you visit www.moneygram.com click find us then type your details. You will receive listing of all the moneygram offices close to your house. Just go there with the money and send to:

PM
55 OBSERVATORY STREET [There is an Observatory Avenue, Johannesburg, but not Observatory Street, on the edge of Observatory Park, west of Bedfordview, Johannesburg]
JOHANNESBURG
SOUTH AFRICA

Moneygram is also wire transfer but if you insist on wire transfer, I shall ask Portia to open an account on monday then i will forward you the account information. You love me and I believe it so you can do anything for me. We have to agree in matters like this. Try moneygram please but if you insist on transfer then on monday you will get the account.
With love,
Jennipher

From: Karol Breen <karolbreen@yahoo.co.uk>
To: jennipherraaff@thecricket.co.za
Sent: Saturday, 17 January, 2009 15:26:27
Subject: Re: PLEASE MY LOVE

Dearest Jennipher
I need to be truthful with you, as you have been with me. The name 'Karol Breen' is a pseudonym. I have to be careful with my identity as to state openly who I am could be dangerous. For many years my family lived in fear of the IRA and now our biggest fear is Islamic fundamentalists who are at war with my country.

Before I reveal to you my true identity, I need you to swear to me, Jennipher, that I can trust you as a friend whom I would be willing to die for.

You'll understand why I can't use the moneygram system, so, please do send me a bank account and I'll transfer the money, as requested.
Always, and with deepening love
Karol

From: "jennipherraaff@thecricket.co.za" <jennipherraaff@thecricket.co.za>
To: Karol Breen <karolbreen@yahoo.co.uk>

Sent: Saturday, 17 January, 2009 17:48:36
Subject: Re: PLEASE MY LOVE

Sir,
Find below the wire instruction and I swear to you that I will not do anything
against our love. I love you so much now and I believe we will be together.
Please use the account details below

FIRST NATIONAL BANK
ADDRESS: SANDTON CITY COMPLEX, P.O. BOX 78086, SANDTON
2146
BRANCH: SANDTON CITY
BRANCH CODE: 254605
SWIFT CODE: FIRNZAJJ
ACCOUNT NUMBER: 62209832072
BENEFICIARY: JEARNETT MAGABANE

Thanks, Love from Jennipher

From: Karol Breen <karolbreen@yahoo.co.uk>
To: jennipherraaff@thecricket.co.za
Sent: Saturday, 17 January, 2009 23:24:03
Subject: Re: PLEASE MY LOVE

Dearest Jennipher
I want us to be entirely open and honest with each other and I am very happy to
get your honoured word. I am now about to shock you. I will continue to email
you under the pseudonym of Karol Breen, but I am, in fact, the 3rd Marquess
of Miserly-Scholes of Stoke-on-Trent, formerly of 'Brum', Birmingham,
England. I am a great great grandson of Queen Victoria and 98th in line to the
throne. I work in the Royal Household.

In 1984 the IRA tried to kidnap me knowing that I would be a big bargaining
chip in their terrorist campaign. The police told me that I could command
a ransom fee of £100 million! It's staggering, but true. It is because of the
sensitive position I hold and also because Her Majesty loves me dearly. While
the IRA are no longer a threat, a new and more terrifying threat has emerged in
the form of home-grown Islamic fundamentalists.

Jennipher, it is a small world. I know the bank you have given the details
of at Sandton City. In March 2004 I attended the unveiling of a bronze statue
of President Mandela at Nelson Mandela Square, close to the shopping centre.
I remember going to Absa Group Limited Bank and then to First National to
exchange £100,000 in cash, which I wanted to contribute to an AIDS project

run by Irish nuns. AIDS was and is misunderstood and I was amazed at the compassion of these courageous women.

Rather than me transferring the money to you on Monday, why don't I travel next week to Johannesburg to meet you? I would do this very discreetly. I have some ideas I'd like to discuss with you and Naomi about Mugabe. I would be willing to finance his removal.

I look forward to hearing from you, dearest Jennipher. Please send me another picture.

Always

Karol.

18 January 2009
From: "jennipherraaff@thecricket.co.za" <jennipherraaff@thecricket.co.za>
To: Karol Breen <karolbreen@yahoo.co.uk>
Sent: Sunday, 18 January, 2009 9:55:56
Subject: YOU SEE NOW !!!

Hi My love,
Let us prove our love for each other. I told you I need money and urgently please. Instead of you coming here, I think it is better if we make proper arrangements for me to come over there. The only problem I have no is that you made a promise and you changed. I ask you in the name of this young but growing relationship to send the money tomorrow. Just 700 pounds. I understood when you said that because of your identity you cannot do moneygram but why is it that you cannot ask someone to do it for you. It is simple to ask any person to send the money. I am beginning to fall in love with you but changing all the time is not a good way of doing things. I would want you to ask someone to send the money on your behalf by moneygram with the information I gave you before if you have a problem with wire transfer. Otherwise send the money by wire transfer. I will come there myself to see you..
I await your comments.
With love.
Jennipher

From: Karol Breen <karolbreen@yahoo.co.uk>
To: jennipherraaff@thecricket.co.za
Sent: Sunday, 18 January, 2009 14:02:08
Subject: Re: YOU SEE NOW !!!

Dear Ms Raaff
Why do you not make any reference to the important information I gave you about myself? This was a huge risk for me to take and I am wondering if I've

done the right thing.

All you are interested in is the damn £700. Is that all you care about? Am I seen as an easy touch? I don't like this. I am reconsidering my position with you. You didn't even send me a photograph of yourself – that was all I asked of you.

I will have my PA contact you tomorrow. Her name is Lady Sarah Macbeth. I will leave her instructions about what I have promised. Lady Sarah will have the measure of you.

I'm not sure if I ever want to hear from you again.

Karol

From: "jennipherraaff@thecricket.co.za" <jennipherraaff@thecricket.co.za>
To: Karol Breen <karolbreen@yahoo.co.uk>
Sent: Sunday, 18 January, 2009 14:28:11
Subject: THAT IS WHAT I AM SAYING

Hi ,
You also confuse me deeply.
I took you by your words and you are the one who changed so what do you want me to do in that instance. Additionally the secret you told me scared me and I preferred meeting you in person because such information cannot be exchanged via email. I saw what you said about yourself and i deeply respect that but the problem is that I do not want to feel intimidated by such as issues of love knows no bounds. Even if you are the son of the queen herself, it does not mean that we cannot be in love because I am less of a royal. You want someone to contact me but I do not know about the person and such things scare me too. I do not want to be scared of someone I shall be getting intimate with and also consistency is important. We cannot say something now and change tomorrow and when I say something about it you get angry. You scare and surprise me the more. I want to be with you but I need to understand you also. I also want to see your picture. If I told you that I have a personal problem which I need to solve, I see it not being a problem if I lay emphasies on it. We need money to pay our rent and other things and I asked you . You agreed and now you are making it look as if I am only interested in the money. I want to know you more and be with you but I want consistency. If you make a promise to your beloved and turn around not fullfilling it then what impression are you creating in her mind about you. Let us not divert from the subject matter. We will work out this relationship irrespective of your status and I think it is better if I come to UK. Let us not complicate this matter, I am in a financial crisis and need your help. If you do not want to hear from me again just because of this 'damn' 700 pounds then so be it.

I still think my heart and yours are meant for each other but if that is the way you want to end our relationship merely because I asked you for help then I will only feel the pain for a couple of days but I will be fine and I will move on with my life.

thanks for the email you sent to me.

Jennipher

From: Karol Breen <karolbreen@yahoo.co.uk>
To: ladysarahmacbeth@yahoo.co.uk
Cc: jennipherraaff@thecricket.co.za
Sent: Sunday, 18 January, 2009 16:18:41
Subject: Fw: YOU SEE NOW !!!

Dear Lady Macbeth,

Below is my email to a Ms Jennipher Raaff. I have promised to her that I would give some help. I should be happy if you would do this for me. I am feeling quite low and will take a few days off. You will know where to get me should there be an urgent development in the Royal Household.

God Save the Queen.

Affectionately,

Karol

3rd Marquess of Miserly-Scholes of Stoke-on-Trent

19 January 2009
From: Sarah Macbeth <ladysarahmacbeth@yahoo.co.uk>
To: jennipherraaff@thecricket.co.za
Sent: Monday, 19 January, 2009 9:27:51
Subject: His Grace, The 3rd Marquess of Miserly-Scholes of Stoke-on-Trent

Dear Ms Raaff,

His Grace, The 3rd Marquess of Miserly-Scholes of Stoke-on-Trent, Lord Karol, has copied you into an email he sent to me over the weekend, with instructions that I should contact you and arrange to have money transferred to you.

His Grace has departed to his hunting lodge in the Highlands of Scotland for a week. It seems that you have had a very profound effect on him. The last time I saw him descend into a depression like this was when his dear wife, Lady Victoria, passed away three years ago. It is clear that you have found a special place in his heart. Are you the beautiful young lady whose photographs he has taken to hanging on his wall and ceiling?

His Grace is a good man and within the Royal Household he is deeply loved and respected. We hate to see him so sad. His sadness is always so tangible and we cannot help but mirror his emotions in our own.

I am not aware of the arrangements His Grace has made with you, so please give me all the necessary details. All I know is that I must transfer funds to you.

I look forward to receiving your advice. I shall endeavour to respond with due diligence.

In the service of Her Majesty,

God Save the Queen!

Always,

Lady Sarah Macbeth

Personal Assistant

His Grace, The 3rd Marquess of Miserly-Scholes of Stoke-on-Trent

From: "jennipherraaff@thecricket.co.za" <jennipherraaff@thecricket.co.za>
To: <ladysarahmacbeth@yahoo.co.uk>
Cc: <karolbreen@yahoo.co.uk>
Sent: Monday, 19 January, 2009 17:54:16
Subject: Re: Fw: YOU SEE NOW !!!

Good day Lady Sarah Macbeth

I must confess that I am truly in love with him but the problem is that he does not understand me and also he does not understand that we are in a third world nation where things are terribly harsh and economic situation unbearable.

Tell him that I do truly love him but he has to understand me also. I am not of the royal but I have a royal heart and I am capable of being in love with any one who truly has genuine love in his heart.

I was only being hornest by telling him that I was in a situation and needed his help and I could not hide away from the truth.

I shall forward this email to him also and please tell him to read this email and he should not be angry. A man of his status and one that I want to be with should live beyond anger and some kinds of emotions. As one who is of the royalty, he should of course live beyond emotions. I want to be with him and he should kindly represent the kind of man I would want to spend the rest of my life with.

To cut the matter short, If you cold please visit a moneygram office and make a tranfer of 700 pounds as he promised, I would have be spared of a lot of distress around me. Please send the money to :

PM

Address: Johannesburg =-South AFrica

Moneygram is easier for me. And if you have a problem doing it yourself you can also delegate anyone to just go to the moneygram office and make the transfer.

Please in the name of the love I have for him, let him not ignore the little person that he fell in love with. I am not as big as him but he has to realize also that he fell in love with me so that has to be respected as much as I am also in love with him.

I await positive comments.

I shall also send him more photos as soon as I receive the transfer information.

Jenniher

21 January 2009
From: Sarah Macbeth <ladysarahmacbeth@yahoo.co.uk>
To: jennipherraaff@thecricket.co.za
Sent: Wednesday, 21 January, 2009 9:39:28
Subject: Money-Gram Transfer

Dear Ms Raaff

Greetings from the Royal Household. My apologies for the delay in replying to you. I am currently in Washington DC.

What do you think of President Obama? I realise you are white, living in Africa (an interesting experience, no doubt!), but do you think he will be good for Africa, given that his father was born in Kenya? I must confess that I worry. I'm not sure if the great USA is ready for an African-American President, even if he is up to the job. I can only imagine what it must have been like for you, Jennipher, trying to cope in darkest Africa. God bless you and keep you safe.

His Grace is currently at his hunting lodge in the Highlands of Scotland and, as such, he must not be disturbed unless there is a true emergency. He will receive the email you have copied to him upon his return, which, we expect, will be early next week.

Ms Raaff, you must understand that the Royal Family would create a scandal if they were to deal with a MoneyGram establishment. Furthermore, in order to do what you are suggesting, I would be required to withdraw money from the account of His Grace and either personally, or with the assistance of another, take it to a MoneyGram office for transfer. This is simply not possible – the very idea is abhorrent and quite demeaning. I can see we will have much to teach you once you come and join us.

I am entitled to instruct the bank to transfer money with the sanction of His Grace, which I have been given in this case. Please send me your bank details and I will endeavour to have this matter settled as quickly as possible.

In the service of Her Majesty

I remain

Yours sincerely

Lady Sarah

From: "jennipherraaff@thecricket.co.za" <jennipherraaff@thecricket.co.za>
To: Karol Breen <karolbreen@yahoo.co.uk>
Cc: ladysarahmacbeth@yahoo.co.uk
Sent: Wednesday, 21 January, 2009 23:45:04
Subject: Please communicate frequently

Hi my dear,
I was wondering if you could stay for a week without writting me email. I have known you to be a man with deep touch of love and feelings so I was kind of scared. I shall send you another photo tomorrow and please it would please me to have your photo also.. To the email you PA sent to me, I would also say that Obama only opened doors for Africans and his presence there is mysterious even if it is an arangement. Look at his achievements and other things he did. He is truly a greatman. I love you so much now with this email you sent to me. Meanwhile read about Obama:
[There followed a 900-word list of key events in Obama's life and career. I'll spare you the details, which are available on Wikipedia and other sites.]
Awaiting,
Jennipher

26 January 2009
From: "jennipherraaff@thecricket.co.za" <jennipherraaff@thecricket.co.za>
To: karolbreen@yahoo.co.uk
Cc: ladysarahmacbeth@yahoo.co.uk
Sent: Monday, 26 January, 2009 11:36:22
Subject: MY SITUATION/WIRE INSTRUCTION

Good day My sweet heart,
I have been sick all along.
    The day Mr. Obama was inaugurated as the 44th American president, we got carried away by the excitement. Two days after a party was hosted in my friends house, I went there but on my way back I was attacked by thugs. I go beaten up and my bag and phone taken from me by thugs. I was hospitalized but I am out now. I got your email nad decided to respond.
Please you can send me the sum of 1000 pounds to pull myself together again. Do send the money by wire transfer to:

FIRST NATIONAL BANK
ADDRESS: SANDTON CITY COMPLEX, P.O. BOX 78086, SANDTON 2146
BRANCH: SANDTON CITY
BRANCH CODE: 254605

SWIFT CODE: FIRNZAJJ
ACCOUNT NUMBER: 6220*******
BENEFICIARY: JM

As for the issue of Obama, he is both white and black so he is for everyone. We only need someone who will heal the world as the spate of terrorism and anger is high. We need a change in the world now so that there will be peace and stability. The bomings and terrorism is scary.

What if nuclear weapons gets into the hands of terrorists then we are doomed. The world needs a change now.

Please send the wire and email me a copy of the wire slip.

I await your urgent response.

Find my photo attached.

Jennipher

'Jennipher' sent me another picture of the supermodel, with the image reversed.

27 January 2009
From: Sarah Macbeth <ladysarahmacbeth@yahoo.co.uk>
To: karolbreen@yahoo.co.uk
Cc: Jennipher Raafe <jennipherraaff@thecricket.co.za>
Sent: Tuesday, 27 January, 2009 0:30:40
Subject: Re: MY SITUATION/WIRE INSTRUCTION

Your Grace

I am working late this evening in preparation for Lady Jessica's birthday. We will have 349 guests and I have been assisting security with the new vetting procedures we have in place following 7/7. I will stay in the staff quarters tonight as we still have quite a lot of work to get through tomorrow.

I must confess to having a niggling doubt about Ms Raaff. It is about the picture she sent you. As you know I am a great enthusiast of boating so I was interested in the beautiful picture of Ms Raaff, with its backdrop of warm inviting waters and several ships with their bow or stern in line with her beautiful eyes and forehead. The picture looked familiar, so I printed it off and walked to your bedroom to compare it with the picture you have framed and hanging next to Queen Vic. Your Grace, it is not a new picture. It is, in fact, the same picture Ms Raaff sent you on November 23rd, only reversed and cropped to give the impression that it is different. This appears to be duplicity for, I assure you, if I loved you as Ms Raaff confesses to do, I should wish to delight you with many beautiful pictures to keep alive your interest and fan your love for me. I am left wondering what game, if any, Ms Raaff might be playing with you.

Your Grace, I advise you to proceed with the utmost caution. I am not convinced that Ms Raaff is genuine. I do not wish to see you hurt again. Please understand that this communication is motivated by nothing less than the purist of intentions.

We anxiously await your return on Wednesday in time for Lady Jessica's birthday celebrations. The house seems so cold and lifeless without you.
Your humble servant
Lady Sarah

From: "jennipherraaff@thecricket.co.za" <jennipherraaff@thecricket.co.za>
To: <ladysarahmacbeth@yahoo.co.uk>
Cc: <karolbreen@yahoo.co.uk>
Sent: Tuesday, 27 January, 2009 7:35:47
Subject: Re: Fw: Money-Gram Transfer

Hi
I am not a begger so please you and Mr. Karol can keep your money. I am no longer interested in this drama. If you find it difficult to assist someone in need with your billions then there is no place for love in your heart. I do not have enough pictures here rather I have only three photos of mine and I have sent them to you. Please in the name of God, do not write me again and do not send any money to me. I am tired of this shakepare and macbeth drama.
Bye.
Jennipher

From: Sarah Macbeth <ladysarahmacbeth@yahoo.co.uk>
To: jennipherraaff@thecricket.co.za
Cc: karolbreen@yahoo.co.uk
Sent: Tuesday, 27 January, 2009 20:59:54
Subject: Re: INFORMATION

Dear Ms Raaff
How dare you make fun of my name! And, more importantly, how dare you abuse the goodness and kindness of His Grace. I am not going to stand idly by and see a phoney like you destroy him. Furthermore, you are a commoner. This is not the place for you. Don't write to us again.
God Save the Queen
Lady Sarah Macbeth

28 January 2009
From: Karol Breen <karolbreen@yahoo.co.uk>
To: Sarah Macbeth <ladysarahmacbeth@yahoo.co.uk>

Cc: Jennipher Raaff <jennipherraaff@thecricket.co.za>
Sent: Wednesday, 28 January, 2009 2:28:24
Subject: Re: INFORMATION

Dear Lady Sarah
I am, quite frankly, appalled at the arrogance of your email in response to what
I consider a very genuine and dignified letter from Jennipher. Once again you
have failed to exercise appropriate professional decorum. I consider this to be
a disciplinary matter, which I will deal with when I return to London.
God Save the Queen!
Karol

From: Karol Breen <karolbreen@yahoo.co.uk>
To: jennipherraaff@thecricket.co.za
Sent: Wednesday, 28 January, 2009 2:51:34
Subject: Re: Fw: Money-Gram Transfer

Dearest Jennipher
I must apologise for the hurtful email you have received from Lady Sarah. I
am incensed at her tone. Her unbecoming snobbery has no place in the Royal
Family. We may speak with posh accents, but I assure you, when we fart, we
smell.

The only connection she has with royalty is her name, yet she has never
been able to show me an authenticated genealogical chart that proves her
lineage back to the murderous impostor and his ambitious and malicious
wife.

Lady Sarah is jealous of you. She and I had an affair for three years, during
which she became pregnant. I do not accept her assertion that I am the father
of her seven-year-old son. I have told her several times that I would be willing
to submit, quietly, to a paternity test but she will not agree to this, preferring, I
believe, to exert some kind of emotional blackmail over me.

I cannot tolerate her jealousy. It is not the first time she has tried to drive a
wedge between me and a lover. When we meet, I will tell you about a night the
calculating bitch came knocking on my bedroom door just at the moment my
spirit was about to soar during a tantric encounter with my Indian Devi. It was
terribly disconcerting.

Please, don't give up on me. You did annoy me and you were the cause
of my departure to Scotland. But I like the way we can also reunite. It is a
sign that we have something special. I'll contact you tomorrow. Meantime,
please accept my humble apologies for the entirely inappropriate comments of
a Royal Lady who is, in truth, a tramp.

With deep affection and love.

In the service of Her Majesty
Karol

From: "jennipherraaff@thecricket.co.za" <jennipherraaff@thecricket.co.za>
To: Karol Breen <karolbreen@yahoo.co.uk>
Sent: Wednesday, 28 January, 2009 8:10:42
Subject: URGENT INFORMATION

Sir,
I can take a fresh picture sometimes over the weekend and send to you but how come of all the affections that I am developing towards you, you undermine the fact that I asked you to send me 1000 pounds to get my self together.

Additionally when I talk about it, you stop writting me or you get angry as if all I think about is money. I need money to pull myself together.

Going to the internet cafe, paying our rent and other things. We need this money please. I have provided an account for the transfer and instead of getting a warm response, I got anger and humiliation. I am so terrified with the situation. Let me know what is in your mind and please let us not run around circles. I am getting emotionally attached to you but you seem to break off and on at intervals. Let me see if you truly would take care of me. Just send the money. If you do not have it within your disposal, let me know and not make me promises and promises and promises and nothing happens. Make the sacrifise and see what happens next. I crave your understanding. As for more photos, you will get them but please I do not even have your own photo and I have sent all the few that I have. Most of my things are held in zimbabwe and not here. I have not considered taking photos because i did not need them until you asked me to hold your picture and take one. Please let us not ignore this assistace in the name of our love. I will make you happy and I understand the kind of a man you are and I will fullfill your dreams but prove to me that I will not be played around because when someone makes a promise and does not fullfill it and when one complains he gets angry then something is wrong.

I need convincing and practical actions.
With love
Jennipher

From: Karol Breen <karolbreen@yahoo.co.uk>
To: jennipherraaff@thecricket.co.za
Sent: Wednesday, 28 January, 2009 20:35:27
Subject: Re: URGENT INFORMATION

Dear Jennipher

I arrived home late this afternoon for Lady Jessica's party. The Royal Garden was packed with adults and children enjoying clowns, fire jugglers and magicians. I caught sight of Lady Sarah and her boy (Little Lord Fauntleroy I call him as he is such a spoilt brat). She came strutting across to me. 'Your Grace,' she said, with an air of arrogance and anger, 'we must speak NOW!' Her raised voice drew attention as she walked towards the palace. We entered the Lord Nelson Room, where Her Majesty was enjoying the company of our extended family.

Jennipher, I was greatly horrified and humiliated when she took hold of a silver fork and began to tap loudly upon a Wedgwood teapot. The room immediately fell silent. 'Your Majesty,' she declared, 'I wish to introduce you to a child you already know as the child of a servant to the Royal Household but who, in truth, is a child of royal descent.' She pointed to her son and then continued, 'And I am very happy to inform you that his father is your beloved cousin, the 3rd Marquess of Miserly-Scholes of Stoke-on-Trent.'

All eyes were firmly focused on my burning face. I spluttered and stuttered but I could not get words to come out. My heart began to pound and I felt faint. After what seemed like an eternity, I managed to walk out of the room.

This couldn't have happened at a worse time for me as a news story broke today while I was travelling back from Scotland about an unsuccessful assassination attempt carried out 40 years ago in Australia by suspected IRA bastards. I should be handling the security response to this matter but I can't for fear that word may have leaked out about Lady Sarah's accusations. Hopefully not, for I know both she and her nanny will have been taken aside to be debriefed by security after my hasty retreat.

This is a potentially seismic embarrassment for the Royal Household. An illegitimate child in the family is unthinkable! I have already received a note from Her Majesty requesting that I visit her at 10 a.m. tomorrow at Buckingham Palace. In order to legitimise the boy, she will insist that I marry Lady Sarah should a paternity test establish my genetic fingerprint in his cells.

Jennipher, I appeal for your help. I promise you, I will take care of you beyond your wildest imagination if you can respond caringly.

I detest the sight of Lady Sarah. Our affair meant nothing to me, other than nights of raucous passion. The memory of those nights leaves me breathless for she was rampant. And, in truth, even over the seven years since we ended the affair, she has come to my room two or three nights a year and I can't resist her. She is not as beautiful as you, but stunning nonetheless. I know she loves me. But it is a jealous and possessive love. The thought of being forced by the powers that rule my royal heritage into an arranged marriage with her is simply too much to bear.

I can hear you wondering whether I am the father of her boy. The truth is, I don't know. I have denied it for all these years, but intuition tells me the boy is mine.

Jennipher, I must run away until this storm passes and all becomes tranquil again. I simply cannot face this now. Tomorrow I will meet Her Majesty as arranged and I will agree to all that she asks. But in my heart I will be plotting my escape. My plan is to enter South Africa via Lesotho no later than Monday next.

I have just over five million US dollars deposited in gold shares in a secret account at AngloGold Ashanti, Newtown, Johannesburg 2001. I need to find a safe haven where the British Secret Service and their spies cannot find me. Believe me, Jennipher, within 24 hours of my disappearance, every hotel reservation database will be electronically searched. After about a month they will begin to wind down their search, at which point I will find it easier to begin moving about and creating a temporary life.

I would like to return to the UK in about six months' time with you, hopefully as my legitimate wife. By that time the Royal Household will have found a way of minimising any embarrassment that Lady Sarah might cause Her Majesty and she will be gone to a place where she will not cause us heartache again. I know, for I have had to deal with one such scenario in the past.

I have promised you £700. If you and Naomi look after me for 4 to 6 weeks. I will pay you both $1,000 each per week. We will also be able to talk about your own terrible situation and we can figure out a way of helping you and co-operating in your business plan.

I love you, Jennipher. More than any other human being in the world, I need you now.
Passionately
Karol

29 January 2009
From: Karol Breen <karolbreen@yahoo.co.uk>
To: jennipherraaff@thecricket.co.za
Sent: Thursday, 29 January, 2009 14:12:01
Subject: Re: URGENT INFORMATION

Oh Jennipher
What a morning. I was collected at 9 a.m. and brought to meet Her Majesty. She questioned me on my relationship with Lady Sarah and whether I had had unprotected sexual relations with her. She doesn't pull any punches. She sympathised with my embarrassment but said that the truth was necessary to establish how best to progress.

I told her that while I didn't know for certain, there was a possibility I could be the biological father of the boy. 'You won't mind then,' she said, 'if I call in a Royal Physician to assist us on that issue.' A few minutes later my shirtsleeve was rolled up and blood samples were being taken by a doddery old doc called

Nigel. Her Majesty told me that samples from the boy had already been taken. So, now it is wait and see time. I have a foreboding. My instincts are telling me we will match. I must return by 5pm this evening for the results.

Oh dear Jennipher, I feel horribly trapped. I just want to, and need to, get away. Have you spoken to Naomi about me staying with you? May I? I promise you, I will repay your kindness tenfold. Just tell me what you need and I will help you. Please reply to me. I need, more than any time since we began to communicate, to hear from you. I need someone I can trust.

With love and affection

Karol

From: Karol Breen <karolbreen@yahoo.co.uk>
To: jennipherraaff@thecricket.co.za
Sent: Thursday, 29 January, 2009 23:38:16
Subject: Re: URGENT INFORMATION

Jennipher

I am on an emotional roller coaster. The results have come back. And yes, I am the boy's father. When I heard this I broke down and wept. An enormous sense of guilt descended upon me. I've always known the boy was mine but I denied him and I've been unfair to Lady Sarah. After I had pulled myself together, Her Majesty sent for Lady Sarah and my son. I embraced them both with a loving tenderness that I did not know I was capable of. They are my family. I must be a father to my son.

Jennipher, I missed you today. It was a day when I needed to hear from you but you were not there. I was deeply hurt and disappointed for I thought you would, at least, send me a kind and encouraging word. I will not be coming to South Africa. This is my home.

Lady Sarah and I will be married in a private ceremony in St Margaret's Chapel in Edinburgh Castle on February 14th next, St Valentine's Day. If you and Naomi would like to attend, I would be honoured and I know I can get Lady Sarah's approval too.

Please forgive me, dear Jennipher. This was totally unforeseen. I want you to know that I still want to help you. I know I must send you £700 and I will do this tomorrow. Meantime, as a wedding gift that I would like to give to you and dear Naomi, please tell me what would your wildest dream be if I was to stand before you with a magic wand? Perhaps I can make dreams come true for you my dearest friend.

Always

Karol

30 January 2009

From: Karol Breen <karolbreen@yahoo.co.uk>
To: jennipherraaff@thecricket.co.za
Sent: Friday, 30 January, 2009 11:26:54
Subject: Bank Detail Required

Dear Jennipher
I apologise for any unintended hurt I may have caused you. I must honour my commitments to you and I have given my bank manager the following details:

First National Bank, Sandton City Complex, PO Box 78086, Sandton 214
Branch Code: 254605
Swift Code: Firnzajj
Account Number: 62209832072
Beneficiary: Jearnett Magabane

He asked me to enquire if you can get an IBAN reference as this will ensure that the money is transferred instantly to the account. The money will be sent from HSBC Private Bank (UK) Limited, 78 St James's Street, London SW1A 1JB, UK.

I have decided, given the trauma of the past few days and also your heartfelt appeals to my sometimes deaf ears, to transfer, in the first instance, £2,500 into the account. Forgive me for the delay. I am often suspicious of people's motives. And you bore the brunt of those angry thoughts. I am truly sorry. Later, after the wedding, I would like to talk to you and Naomi about your business proposal.

If you can write to me before 3 p.m. today, I should be able to get the money transferred immediately. Otherwise it will be Monday before I can transfer the money to you.
With much love and affection, in the service of Her Majesty
Karol
PS: My invitation to the wedding is genuine. Should you wish to come, I assure you, we would be delighted.

5 February 2009
From: Karol Breen <karolbreen@yahoo.co.uk>
To: jennipherraaff@thecricket.co.za
Sent: Thursday, 5 February, 2009 13:17:35
Subject: Re: URGENT INFORMATION

Dear 'Ms Raaff'
My bank manager called this morning to enquire whether I had received the IBAN number from you. I told him that you had gone quiet. He believes our

communication is one of hundreds of such scams across the Internet with people, mainly Africans, masquerading as rich people in distress who need help to free up their money. He told me of many people who have been badly hurt and some who have committed suicide because their trust was betrayed. He believes you are one such hoax.

Sadly, I am of the opinion now that you are a FRAUDSTER, a SCAMMER, a HOAXER and an utter disgrace to the noble people of Africa. I never want to hear from you again. You will reap what you sow. Your harvest will be a great curse on you and your family.
MAY GOD FORGIVE YOU!
Karol

From: "jennipherraaff@thecricket.co.za" <jennipherraaff@thecricket.co.za>
To: Karol Breen <karolbreen@yahoo.co.uk>
Cc: Karol Breen <karolbreen@yahoo.co.uk>
Sent: Thursday, 5 February, 2009 18:26:46
Subject: UNBELIEVEABLE

SIR,
STRANGELY ENOUGH YOU WROTE ME EMAIL TO HARRASS ME AGAIN. I BEGGED YOU FOR MONEY AND YOU PROMISED TO HELP. NOT ONLY THAT YOU BROKE OUR RELATIONSHIP BUT ALSO THAT YOU ASKED FOR A BANK ACCOUNT DETAIL AND I DID PROVIDE IT TO YOU. HOW COME YOU SAY SUCH A THING TO ME. YOU WERE THE ONE WHO WROTE AN EMAIL AND SAID THAT YOU WILL NOT WRITE ME AGAIN BECAUSE YOU ARE GETTING MARRIED TO YOUR WIFE. IN AS MUCH AS I NEED HELP FROM YOU, I MUST TELL YOU THAT YOU MAY AS WELL KEEP YOUR MONEY. IT HAS TAKEN TWO MONTHS NOW SINCE YOU MADE A PROMISE TO ME BUT YOU NEVER KEPT IT. YOUR WIFE CAME ON BOARD AND REIGNED INSULTS ON ME. WHAT HAVE I DONE TO BOTH OF YOU.

I AM REAL THOUGH I WAS NOT WHEN I WAS USING NAOMI TO COMMUNICATE YOU. THIS MATTER IS REAL BUT AS YOU SAID, I DO NOT WANT TO DISCUSS IT FURTHER. HERE IN SOUTH AFRICA THEY DO NOT USE IBAN NUMBER. I ASKED YOU BEFORE TO MAKE TRANSFER BY MONEYGRAM AND YOU ASKED FOR A WIRE DETAIL WHICH I PROVIDED YOU AND NOW YOU ASK FOR IBAN NUMBER. YOUR BANK MANAGER WOULD HAVE TOLD YOU THAT IBAN NUMBER DO NOT EXIST IN SOUTH AFRICA.

JUST DO A SIMPLE SWIFT TRANSFER OR YOU CAN SEND THE MONEY BY MONEYGRAM. I CARE A LOT ABOUT YOU BUT YOUR MIND SEEMS TO BE DISTURBED AND NOW YOU DO NOT BELIEVE

ANYONE AGAIN. I STILL LOVE AND CARE ABOUT YOU BUT IF YOU DO NOT WANT TO SEND MONEY TO ME, YOU DO NOT HAVE TO INSULT ME IN ANY MANNER AT LEAST FOR THE SAKE OF THE PAST AND ALL THE EMOTIONS WE SHARED BEFORE YOU TOLD ME THAT YOU NOW HAVE A SON AND A WIFE.

AT LEAST YOU ALSO COULD LIE SOMETIME. YOU CANNOT BLAME PEOPLE ALL THE TIME WHILE YOU STILL HAVE YOUR OWN FLAWS. I TOLD YOU WHAT HAPPENED AND WHY I HAD TO CONTACT YOU AS NAOMI. THAT WE THE ONLY LIE I DID TELL YOU AND GOD KNOWS AND INFACT IF YOU BELIEVE IN GOD YOU WILL KNOW THAT NO ONE CALLS THE NAME OF GOD IN VAIN.

GOD KNOWS THAT I WAS REAL TO YOU AT LAST BUT WHEN YOU AND YOUR WIFE STARTED ASKING FOR PHOTOS AND PHOTOS AND PHOTOS THEN I WAS WONDERING HOW AND WHY YOU KEPT ASKING FOR MORE WHEN YOU NEVER EVEN SENT ME ANY OF YOUR PHOTOS.

I AM NOT GOING TO COMPELL YOU BUT I SWEAR IN THE NAME CHRIST, I AM REAL TO YOU NOW BUT IF YOU ARE NOT SENDING ME MONEY, THEN DO NOT INSULT ME BECAUSE I FEEL TERRIBLY HUMILIATED. YOU TOLD ME YOU WERE NOT GOING TO WRITE ME AGAIN AND YOU WROTE ME ALL SORTS OF HURTFUL EMAILS THEN I THOUGHT THAT SINCE YOU ARE NO LONGER INTERESTED IN ME THEN I HAD TO MOVE ON. I DID NOT CHECK THE EMAIL AGAIN BECAUSE I WAS HURT AND HEART BROKEN. I EXPECTED YOU TO REALIZE THE PAIN YOU CAUSED ME AND NOW YOU CALL ME A SCAMMER AND YOU SAY THAT GOD SHOULD PURNISH ME. THAT IS TERRIBLY UNBELIEVEABLE FROM SOMEONE LIKE YOU.

TELL YOUR BANK MANAGER THAT HE IS NARROW MINDED AND ALSO PREJUDICED WHICH IS WHY HE CANNOT SEE BEYOND THE PEGION HOLE. WHAT MAKES HIM THINK THAT SUCH THINGS ARE NOT HAPPENING. FUNDS ARE BEING MOVED ACROSS THE WORLD EVERYDAY AND THAT IS WHY SOME FOOLS TAKE ADVANTEGE BUT TELL HIM THAT WE ARE REAL 100%.

IF YOU WANT TO RESUME COMMUNIATION WITH ME THEN DO NOT INSULT ME BECAUSE I ALMOST FELL IN LOVE WITH YOU AND ALSO I ASKED YOU FOR MONEY. I EXPECT A MORE FRIENDLY EMAIL FROM YOU.

HERE THERE IS NO IBAN NUMBER RATHER THE DETAILS I GAVE YOU. YOUR BANK MANAGER IF HE IS REAL WILL KNOW THAT SOUTH AFRICANS DO NOT USE IBAN NUMBERS.

YOU CAN SEND THAT MONEY BY WESTERNUNION/MONEYGRAM OR THE WIRE INFORMATION I GAVE YOU BUT I AM NOT COMPELLING

YOU.IF YOU DO NOT WANT TO DO IT, DO NOT WORRY.

GOD WILL BLESS YOU AND YOUR MARRIAGE AND PLEASE TELL LADY SARAH THAT I AM NOT ANGRY WITH HERE THAT I AM PRAYING FOR YOUR MARRIAGE WITH HER TO BE A SUCCESS. IF I HAVE MONEY I WILL ATTEND TO YOUR THINGS WHEN EVER I AM CALLED.

THANKS AND HAVE A LOVELY DAY.
JENNIPHER

From: Karol Breen <karolbreen@yahoo.co.uk>
To: jennipherraaff@thecricket.co.za
Sent: Thursday, 5 February, 2009 19:25:51
Subject: Re: UNBELIEVEABLE

Okay. There is no His Grace, the 3rd Marquess of Miserly-Scholes of Stoke-on-Trent in line to the British Throne. There is no Lady Sarah Macbeth. There is only me, Karol Breen.

For the last two months I have been scamming you. I know you sometimes wondered what was going on and if I was for real or not. Your instincts were telling you to doubt, but you didn't want to give up, just in case I was for real and was ready to send you money. It was a pleasure to turn the table on you.

Now, here's what I'm hoping. I'd really like to get to know the real you. Who is behind this Naomi and Jennipher Raaff scam and the downloaded model pictures you found on the Internet and doctored-up. I'm investigating the whole dark world of 419 scams. I need someone on the 'inside' to help me understand what is really going on, how they got involved and how successful the job of scamming is.

In my last email I deliberately tried to provoke you to break your silence. It worked. Now that you have come back to me, can we try and develop a different relationship? One that is more honest. Will you help me? I'm really looking forward to hearing back from you. This might, just might, be the beginning of a genuine relationship.
Kind regards
Karol

6 February 2009
From: "jennipherraaff@thecricket.co.za" <jennipherraaff@thecricket.co.za>
To: Karol Breen <karolbreen@yahoo.co.uk>
Sent: Friday, 6 February, 2009 1:06:10
Subject: I KNOW YOU WERE NOT ...

Hi,

I knew you were not whom you said you were. I also knew you were not sending me any money. I am in need of some cash now and if you want us to get into any relationship then borrow me some cash and please let us not run around a circle. Can you just lend me 1000 pounds then we will take it from there. At least since you were not being hornest in the first place it means now you will not have a problem sending money by moneygram.

Send me 1000 pounds and we will take it from there. I promise you that you will be satisfied. The account I provided you was not real because I knew also you were not going to send any money. you made the promises and failed many times so common sense told me that you were playing also. It goes not take a rocket scientist to read between the line and know that you were also a fluke when you were sending those email.

I can only do anything with you if you can borrow me 1000 pounds. You may be surprised. If u are ready let me know so that i can provide you information for the moneygram transfer but if now please do not border writting because I am not ready to run around a circle.

thanks,

Jennipher

From: "jennipherraaff@thecricket.co.za" <jennipherraaff@thecricket.co.za>
To: Karol Breen <karolbreen@yahoo.co.uk>
Sent: Friday, 6 February, 2009 1:29:56
Subject: ADDITIONAL EMAIL

HI KAROL,

I do not want us to run around a circle. Iam ready to corperate with you but something important is that I need 1000 pounds. If you can help me with this money then you will know that the british people are the greatest crooks on earth when they started running around African nations looking for minerals to steal and in return brainwashed everyone in the name of civilization and also slaved them metally with the bible and numerous churches. Who does not know that the roman chatholic church steals billions of dollars every year from poor african nations and promise them heaven and send the ones who do not believe in them to hell.

Who does not know that your queen elizabeth is the head of the Anglican church, and all they do is sell dreams in the glofied name of salvation and collect poor peoples money. Who does not know that aids is man's creation just to gain wealth or better say, population control. The problem with the british is that they never will remove the speck on their own eyes but they are always looking for specks in peoples eyes. Who does not know that Zimbabweans suffer today because a man wants to know how a visitor will own a land and the true owners will be slaved to work in the same land. Who does not know that George Bush went to iraq to steal oil and staged Bin laden just becuase they want to get saddam. ALL THESE ARE THE 419 TRICKS YOU ARE LOOKING FOR. Who does not know that the free masen is just an organization setup by a group of mafia to control the world and they are just playing tricks on peoples minds. Who does not know that most African leaders are pupets of british neo colonialist who ... Brother, I shall be of help to you but if you are ready to send me 1000 pounds (by moneygram please) then let us not waste each others time. You will be glad at the information I shall provide you my friend.

I must put it again to you that I am used to british people thinking that they are smart and that every one is a fool. When you asked for iban number, i knew there was no money to be sent. When so called 'lady sarah' asked for account and it was provided, i already knew there was no money to be sent so i cooked up a bogus account. When you asked for an account and in your next email you did not talk about it rather another issue and in next next email lady sarah came up to talk about white house, i knew there was no money. When you said that if this and that happens, you will make me rich and you came back to tell me that 700 pounds is what you can offer then I knew that either did not have any money or you were buying time.

I must tell you that I have an IQ close to that of Eistein and if you want us to work then I a ready to work with you. I do not do 419 but I know everything about it and if you want to stop that shit. I know the tricks to stop it and I will help you to achieve same. Just for 1000 pounds or better say for a loan of 1000 pounds. I can see you are always on the computer. Please do not waste my time so that I will not waste yours.

Have a great day .

Jennipher

From: Karol Breen <karolbreen@yahoo.co.uk>
To: jennipherraaff@thecricket.co.za
Sent: Friday, 6 February, 2009 10:43:12
Subject: Re: ADDITIONAL EMAIL

Dear Sir

Your 419 scamming is well documented on various scamming websites across the Internet. So please don't be in denial.

I concur with your comments about the historical and colonial abuse of Africa by political, religious and economic self-interest groups. As a European, I believe it was a shameful period in our collective past. Indeed, I believe that history should motivate us to work closely with many good and decent African leaders, at all levels of society, to build a better world and a more stable African continent where the security of its people is of paramount concern. And by security I am not talking about armed security. I am talking about the security that is enshrined in the Universal Declaration of Human Rights.

I don't have any money to send you my friend. So this may be the last communication we have. I have enjoyed our exchange of emails. Given the fact that I know of many good people who have been hurt by the actions of 419 scammers (some being driven to suicide) I have relished playing you at your own game.

While 419 scammers may justify their fleecing of 'gullible Westerners' on the basis of exacting revenge for past historical wrongs, the truth is you are doing enormous damage to the noble reputation of Mother Africa and feeding the prejudices of some who do, indeed, consider you to be inferior. I feel hurt for Africa for it has produced many great and inspiring leaders throughout history, Madiba being the paramount example. I have many wonderful African friends who are multilingual, cultured, enormously gifted and highly intelligent.

Apart from your 419 actions, I wish you well, whoever you are. And may God bless Africa – the cradle of humanity and civilisation.
With kindness
Karol

From: "jennipherraaff@thecricket.co.za" <jennipherraaff@thecricket.co.za>
To: Karol Breen <karolbreen@yahoo.co.uk>
Sent: Friday, 6 February, 2009 20:22:42
Subject: Because you know the truth now.

Sir,
This is my last email to you. Europeans must consider reparation because it is the only way to heal the wounds of the past. By nature europeans are greedy and their greed has plunged them together with the nation of zimbabwe into total collapse. Is it the creation of HIV while still asking Africans to forgive and forget. How can a man tell another to forget as if the brain is driven by a chip and a hard drive that can be formatted at will. How could a man come into another man's land with a gun and a bible.

If I may ask you one question my good friend, when God created Adam and took his ribs to make Eve, who saw that. Whe cain ran away and married whom did he marry since they said he and ebel were the first of adam and eve's kids and he killed abel. did christ work on waters. People like you should be mercineries in piloting the expedition of correcting the ills of the past which are being perpetuated as I am writting to you now. How many churches are being built in Africa every minute of the day. Why is it that your british and american brother cannot destroy mosquiteos rather they build pharmaceutical industries that manufacture treatment drugs when the cause can be destroyed. I ask God to forgive all of you for your wickedness against Mama Africa.

Sweet talks or trying to pretend as if you do not know how many people die everyday in Africa of poverty caused by mind diversion, hiv and malaria. The only way God will forgive all you euroepans is if you forgive yourself because as I am writting to you know, your brothers are injecting more hiv in the bodies of Africans just because they want to sell their AZT drug. But I must tell you today, it does not matter whether i ask you for money or not, forget those bullshit because I knew that you would not send a cent. "the justice of life is inescapeable, good begets good evil begets evil and a a man soweth on the phase of this plannet , that shall he reap. ". sum total of forces equals 0 and life is cyclical. No amount of pretense or ingratiating or asking God to forgive will eraze the wickedness done against the continent Africa.

Instead of developing the continent Africa your people prefer that we remain in perpertual paralysis and stagnation because here is a dumping ground for so many bullshit which enriches your people and if we wake up then your economy will crumple. Non of you deserve to even mention the name AFrica because if civilization truly began here in AFrica then for you to learn and advance only to use to conquer, kill and transform Africa in to a guinea pig continent and also transfer children of Africa into guinea pigs , I tell you, on the day of reckoning each and every one of you will pay the untimate prize. I never wanted your money because you would not give by your running around claimming to be smart style. Today a true African speaks to you from his heart and yo must relay this message to your brothers and sisters that their greed will plunge them into total collapse. At least marthin luther kind did say that a time will come when the slave will be come the master, the prophesy is almost getting completed. Very soon the ozone layer will finish from the creation of ccl.. gas which you and your brothers make and also the diseases which you are using to vanguish africans will start to ravage you all. Thank you for being a good email company.

Bye,

Mosato Dingi from Sudan

7 February 2009
From: Karol Breen <karolbreen@yahoo.co.uk>
To: jennipherraaff@thecricket.co.za
Sent: Saturday, 7 February, 2009 9:47:18
Subject: Re: Because you know the truth now.

There is truth in what you write Naomi/Jennipher/Mosato. Not the whole truth, but nuggets of truth. And I understand your cynicism and anger towards Europeans for the enormous damage we inflicted on your Mama Africa.

I too have enjoyed your email company. Our minds engaged in a fantasy and, at the end of the process, I feel a connection with a fellow human being that has not descended into hatred. I sense that you know I am not a racist and that I have enormous respect for all African people. I am not British, I am Irish. And we too suffered during a long and often very brutal colonial conquest. We have that in common. Our skin colour may be a different pigmentation, but underneath our blood runs red and our hearts are human.

I hope for Africa and all humanity in this wounded world.
Respectfully
Karol

From: "jennipherraaff@thecricket.co.za" <jennipherraaff@thecricket.co.za>
To: Karol Breen <karolbreen@yahoo.co.uk>
Sent: Saturday, 7 February, 2009 11:28:17
Subject: I SEE

I see why you could not release even a cent of your money. I know irish people are stingy. What do you want me to teach you and let me know if you can pay me 1000 pounds to teach you what you need to know. I know the irish were also slaved. But the passport of british now says great Britain and northern ireland so what is that all about. Can you raise 1000 pounds
for me.. Awaiting.

From: Karol Breen <karolbreen@yahoo.co.uk>
To: jennipherraaff@thecricket.co.za
Sent: Saturday, 7 February, 2009 11:41:29
Subject: Re: I SEE

Do you think that by insulting me you will open up my wallet?

In 1922 Ireland was partitioned by the British. They retained six of our 32 counties, as Northern Ireland, within the United Kingdom. I was born there. But I am very clear about my identity. I am Irish.

Who is the 'me' you refer to? All I know is that you are a liar. Why should I send £1,000 to a lying stranger? If I knew the real you, then perhaps.

From: "jennipherraaff@thecricket.co.za" <jennipherraaff@thecricket.co.za>
To: Karol Breen <karolbreen@yahoo.co.uk>
Sent: Saturday, 7 February, 2009 17:43:35
Subject: What guarantee !

Sir,
I promise to dislose my real real real identity to you even send you my personal I D for you to verify and you shall also send the money by moneygram to that personal Id of mine if you promise to send me this money. I need it for real.

Meanwhile be hornest to me too, who are you ?
From: Karol Breen <karolbreen@yahoo.co.uk>
To: jennipherraaff@thecricket.co.za
Sent: Saturday, 7 February, 2009 22:46:12
Subject: Re: What guarantee !

The only truth I can tell you at this moment is that I do not have £1,000 to send you. Perhaps I will have in the future. But I am a very long way from being in a position to believe you. How do I know that you will not create another identity and, again, attempt to hoodwink me into believing you are someone you truly are not?
Who am I? I am who I am.

10 February 2009
From: "jennipherraaff@thecricket.co.za" <jennipherraaff@thecricket.co.za>
To: Karol Breen <karolbreen@yahoo.co.uk>
Sent: Tuesday, 10 February, 2009 18:51:50
Subject: I AM ME

HI KAROL,
I AM ME.
    WHAT ABOUT 200 POUNDS.
    I NEED TO PAY MY RENT.
    YOU WILL SEND THE MONEY TO MY NAME OF COURSE.
    PLEASE CONSIDER SENDING ME THIS MONEY BY MONEYGRAM.
AWAITING.

Lessons Learned

What have I learned from my encounters with these email scammers?

The primary lesson is that scammers are amoral. Their sole objective is to defraud innocent and often vulnerable people. They will invoke the name of God and feign religious righteousness in order to gain your confidence and convince you of their genuine intentions. They will also feign care and concern in an attempt to build rapport and disarm their victim. They also seek to justify their actions on historical and political grounds, believing that greedy and exploitative Westerners deserve everything they get.

Their opening contact generally involves an appeal to human sympathy and the need for financial resources. Scammers' inventiveness in creating sympathy-arousing scenarios is fathomless and brazen. Two of the four scams featured here created a desperate situation: a dying man seeking to provide for the future of his adopted daughter, and a son wishing to access the wealth of his murdered father. In the other two, the scammer exploited real human tragedies: the Air France Concorde crash and the heart-breaking calamity of Zimbabwe. The financial reward on offer for showing compassion and reaching out to assist a brother or sister in need is the stuff of lottery dreams.

The scammers do not ask for money straight away. Like a good fisherman they will play you, sometimes for months, if they think you will eventually swallow their hook. There is a lead-in period during which they try to establish a relationship with their intended target. They wait until that relationship has taken root before they introduce the subject of advance fees. It should also be noted that the initial fees requested are always 'reasonable' amounts, especially when measured against the size of the promised reward. This strategy is all part of a clever psychological game. Once victims have committed some of their money, it is easier to entice further advance fees from them.

As the next chapter shows, having paid the initial advance fee, victims can be led to empty their bank account, sometimes with tragic consequences.

Unwilling to accept that they have been scammed and afraid of being branded naive or stupid, they continue to send money in the hope that their big payday will arrive. The virtual world of the Internet can very quickly become a real world for the victim and the pot of gold at the end of an illusionary rainbow can become a mesmerising and obsessive goal. The scammers know this and use it to manipulate their victims.

So, the cardinal lesson is simple:

If it seems too good to be true – it most definitely is!

The scammers always insist on confidentiality. They know that if a target speaks to family members and friends about the situation, someone will recognise that it is an Internet scam.

Do not be hoodwinked into believing that you are cleverer than the scammers. They know how to influence you. For example, scam emails are often written in poor English and littered with punctuation and spelling errors, which can be a deliberate ploy to make the reader feel superior to the scammer and, therefore, in control of the situation. The reality is, scammers are often highly intelligent and cunning, with lots of back-up support.

If you do decide to attempt to frustrate a scammer, it is imperative that you keep reminding yourself that you are dealing with people who will be very convincing in order to achieve their ultimate purpose and goal of getting some or all of your money. It is essential that you never supply your actual personal details.

Never, ever, send money. On one occasion I chose to ignore this fundamental rule and sent £1 via Western Union, which I then presented to the scammers, using a doctored receipt, as £10,000. In this instance I simply wanted to deliver a sting and make the scammers sample a bit of their own medicine. This is not something that I would advise others to copy.

Scammers love Western Union and MoneyGram. They prefer these methods of transferring money because they make it easy to present a false identity, collect the money and then disappear without trace. Both Western Union and MoneyGram are now warning their customers never to send money to someone they have not met in person. The Appendix reproduces advice from Western Union that is aimed at protecting customers and minimising the damage that scammers are causing to that company's reputation. The Appendix is worth reading for it has many useful tips and guidelines, amassed from the company's knowledge of how their system is being abused. But this is not enough and Western Union, MoneyGram and the banking sector in general can and must do more to make advance fee fraud more difficult.

I insisted on receiving details of a bank account into which I could transfer money because a bank account is traceable. In all cases I was, reluctantly, provided with bank details, and each time I immediately informed the relevant bank and/or the police. I have absolutely no idea what action, if any, they took.

In the case of the Lazar scam, I contacted HSBC and found myself on the wrong side of a rude and apparently disinterested official, who questioned my motives and, despite a verbal promise to do so, did not respond to any emails I sent. I would still like to have answers to the questions I posed in an email sent on 3 May 2007 to the HSBC official:

I am anxious to know what steps HSBC takes in the case of scams such as those I have alerted you to. Do you ask the police to investigate the matter? Do you pass on the information to your colleagues in the country from which the scam is emanating? Do they inform the local police to enable them to investigate? I have given you details of a bank account in London. This information should enable HSBC to trace the source of the scam and have the person prosecuted. Will you do this? In short, what is your policy for protecting innocent people from being hurt by a scam that is, in this instance, apparently using your banking facilities?

During the Lazar scam I also discovered details of a real Lazar Vukadinovic on www.cambridgewhoswho.com. I contacted him in Australia and told him that his identity had been stolen. He said that he knew the scammer personally and informed me that the Australian police were aware of his stolen identity. I passed the documents that Michael Smith had forwarded to me on to the Irish police, with a request that they be given to their Australian counterparts. I do not know if the matter was pursued.

I also made contact with the South African police about the Naomi Raaff scam, and, upon request, forwarded the various documents 'Naomi' had sent me, as well as bank details. I did not receive a response.

Scammers keep coming back in different guises, even reinventing scenarios aimed at confusing and convincing their target. Solicitor Michael Smith, for example, following the termination of the Lazar scam, re-appeared in my inbox as a diamond dealer. This suggests that scammers generally have several scams operating simultaneously. Michael Smith and Edward Hanegen, the alleged diplomatic courier in the Faustin scam, are well-known characters in the world of Internet scamming.

An important trick I learned was to cut and paste the scammer's email into an Internet search engine. The search results would lead me to various anti-scamming websites in which I found new or variants of the email letters I had received. For example, the following scam letter, in which Hanegen is named, was posted on the Internet as a warning to potential victims on 2 October 2008:

Good day to you,

My name is Mrs. Angela Wang of Angela Wang & Co. Solicitors based in Brussels. Our office sympathise with you on the death of one of our clients who mentioned you in his will as his next of kin. We have carefully delibrated on the instruction after enquiries and have decided to consult with you via email for security reasons. We have also notified our offshore agency and release office in France about this information and you will be required to consult with the agent in charge in France Dr. Edward Hanegen on phone +33 67 33 10 989 or email: hanegene@yahoo.com, he will guide you accordingly on the best and smooth way of receiving the inheritance, he will also let you know what inheritance you inherited. You are required to follow his instruction.

Regards

Angela Wang

Phone : +(32) 493375110

The scammers' tactics also continue to evolve. A new scamming method received widespread coverage in the British media when it involved Justice Secretary Jack Straw. The scam began on 19 February 2009, when Mr Straw's constituency office received an email stating that his Hotmail account would be suspended unless a reply, including passwords, was sent. This familiar tactic (often with the scammer masquerading as a bank and asking for account details) is used by scammers to gain access to people's personal details. Unfortunately for Mr Straw, a member of his staff replied to the email, believing it to be genuine and requiring immediate attention. The information imparted enabled the scammers to unlock a constituency email database and download hundreds of email addresses. Within days Mr Straw was inundated with telephone calls from concerned constituents, government officials and friends enquiring after his welfare. It transpired that an email had been circulated to a significant number of people on the Justice Secretary's database. The email claimed that, while on charity work in Africa, Mr Straw had lost his wallet and urgently required $3,500 to help him settle his hotel bills and pay for his flight home.

By coincidence, the same day that the news of this scam broke on British television, I was informed of another example of this type of scam, only in this instance it involved a nun, a member of the Franciscan Missionaries of Mary. The email, which was dated 26 February 2009 and labelled 'Really urgent!!', stated:

This has had to come in a hurry and it has left me in a devastating state. I am in some terrible situation and I'm really going to need your urgent help. Yesterday, unannounced, I came to visit a new researchers' complex in London, Imperial College London, Gallery Section, (South Kensington Campus, London SW7 2AZ), England. Well we actually got robbed in the Hotel I booked in and they made away with my wallet (which included my cash, diaries and credit cards). My cellphones were not brought along since I did not get to roam them before coming over. The phone cables have been burnt including the Hotel's database has been compromised as well. So all I can do now is pay cash and get out of here quickly. I do not want to make a scene of this which is why I did not call the office or my house, this is embarrassing enough. Please I want you to lend me a sum of $2,470, just to clear my Hotel bills and get the next plane home. Kindly help me send the Money via Western Union Money Transfer Below details:

Name – Leena XXXXX
ADDRESS – Harley Street
CITY – London

NB: . . . once you are done sending me the Money please help me scan a copy of the Western Union receipt or help me write out the Money transfer control number (MTCN). Thanks so much and waiting for ur soonest reply.

With lots of love,
Leena

Word circulated very quickly throughout the compromised database that Sr Leena's communication was a con. One email wondered, 'this is surely a big fraud. Perhaps others got it also!' Another stated, 'beware, it's a hoax. God bless you and protect us from scams.'

Amen to that!

The Bigger Picture

Spam is the bane of an email addressee's life. Unsolicited messages are sent to multiple email addresses and usually advertise a product or service in the hope of making a sale. They are an inconvenience to the receiver, but a cheap and easy form of global advertising for the sender. An industry has developed to harvest email addresses from the Internet and sell them to spammers. Criminals also use these databases. Their email scams attempt to dupe unsuspecting users into believing that a golden opportunity has fallen into their inbox. If all the emails I have received offering me a fortune in winnings or rewards were genuine, I would have joined that select group of billionaires who own an English Premier League soccer club.

Email scamming is a global phenomenon. It even has its own vocabulary. Scammers are known as guymen or yahoo millionaires. They work for an oga or chairman. The scammer who gets the victim to show interest is the catcher or owner of the job; another scammer may then take over and they share any money gained. The victim is called the mugu (which means fool) or one of many other insulting terms. Someone like me is known as a joker/jokeman or scambaiter.

Anything goes for email scammers and the range of ploys and intrigues used continues to widen. The formats vary too: foreign business offers from heads of corporations that promise you millions; influential government officials claiming they have the power to award you a lucrative contract; dream partners who offer you romance; notices that you've won a foreign lottery; opportunities to make easy money working from home. The list goes on. They all have one thing in common: you must forward processing fees or provide financial assistance in order to access a greater fortune in due course. If you do, you will not see your money again. This type of advance-fee scam is known as 419 fraud in reference to the relevant article of Nigerian law.

This chapter offers a brief glimpse into the world of scamming. Three scams

214

that have been investigated by the relevant authorities are discussed to illustrate the variety of forms scamming can take. This is followed by a closer look at the scammers and their victims.

John W. Worley

In an article in The New Yorker on 15 May 2006, Mitchell Zuckoff detailed how a 57-year-old psychologist, decorated Vietnam veteran and ordained minister, John W. Worley PhD, was drawn into a Nigerian 419 scam and subsequently ended up in jail. If the general perception is that only uneducated people fall for scams, Worley's extraordinary story gives pause for thought.

A happily married man with four daughters and seven grandchildren, Worley lived comfortably with his wife, Barbara, as caretaker of an historic estate in Groton, Massachusetts. In June 2001 he received an email from an alleged Captain Joshua Mbote, who explained that he had been chief of security for the President of the Democratic Republic of Congo, Laurent-Désiré Kabila, until the latter's assassination in January 2001. At the time of the assassination, the captain stated that he was in South Africa with $55 million in cash to buy weapons for a force of elite bodyguards to protect Kabila. Claiming that it was no longer safe for him to return to his homeland, the captain had now decided to end his secret mission and keep the money for himself.

Had Worley done some even cursory research, he would have discovered that Kabila was assassinated in a failed coup attempt and was succeeded ten days later by his son Joseph. The captain's loyalty and the $55 million should presumably have transferred to Joseph. Worley, however, accepted the contents of the email and began to swallow the hook, which had been made more palatable by a sugar-coating that pandered to his fundamentalist faith. Worley's most penetrating question concerned how he was identified as a potential partner. The captain replied that the South African Department of Home Affairs had supplied him with ten names and that, after seeking the guidance of the Almighty via a Pastor Mark, the Rev. Worley's name was pulled from a hat!

The proposition put to Worley was: 'With regard to your trustworthiness and reliability, I decided to seek your assistance in transferring some money out of South Africa into your country, for onward dispatch and investment.' In exchange for his confidential assistance, Worley was promised over $16 million. Worley replied, 'I can help and I am interested.' And so his journey to jail began.

Following several emails, faxes and telephone conversations, Worley received a cheque in August 2001 for $47,500. The cheque appeared to have been issued by an account owned by the Syms Corporation held at Fleet Bank, Portland, Maine. Worley was suspicious and when he called the bank he was informed that the cheque was a duplicate of one paid by the Syms Corporation to an international luggage manufacturer in Maryland. Worley requested a replacement cheque and when this did not materialise he informed the 'Captain Mbote' that their relationship was finished.

Sensing that their target was pliable and vulnerable for the taking, Worley's pursuers devised another scheme. They sent him emails that claimed to be from the eldest son of General Sani Abacha, the de facto President of Nigeria from 1993 until his death in 1998 in controversial circumstances. The correspondent, 'Mohammed Abacha', stated that Captain Joshua Mbote had, in fact, been operating covertly on behalf of the Abacha family. He told him that the story of Mbote buying weapons in South Africa was subterfuge, created purely to protect members of the Abacha family and their fortune, which was actually in Ghana. They had now decided to come forward and level with Worley in the hope of rescuing the partnership.

Again, basic research into Abacha's ruthless dictatorship should have pointed Worley's moral compass in the opposite direction. But no, before long Worley was communicating with a woman claiming to be Abacha's widow, Maryam. As an alleged widow in distress, her inventor soon had Worley convinced that he was on a mission of mercy, in accordance with the teachings of Jesus.

In November 2001 Worley consulted a US-based international tax attorney and was advised to end his contact with the alleged Abacha family. Despite having paid a considerable sum of money for this advice, Worley recklessly ignored it. Like a man under hypnosis, he believed he was dealing with the real widow Abacha and her son, concerning an amassed fortune from which he and his family would eventually benefit.

Worley investigated ways to ship money secretly and safely out of Ghana and researched countries with banks that would accept huge deposits without alerting authorities. He even deposited $4,300 to open an account in Bermuda. He also agreed to retain the services of a recommended Nigerian lawyer, to whom he wired over $8,000.

The 'widow' told Worley that her family had $45 million hidden in the Central Bank of Nigeria and asked him to help her claim it. Worley agreed to his Nigerian partners falsely registering him as a private aviation contractor, who was owed $45 million by the Nigerian government. Worley noticed that the spelling of Maryam Abacha's name kept changing. 'I would think,' he wrote caustically, 'that everyone would know how to spell their own real name. Obviously, someone does not.' Nevertheless, he continued to ignore his instincts and pursue the money.

Additional legal and filing fees were required and, when Worley eventually ran out of money, his lines of engagement began to blur his own professional boundaries. During a counselling session, Worley informed a client of his Nigerian project and asked her for a loan of $15,000. The client agreed and soon afterwards Worley wired the money to Nigeria via Western Union at a nearby liquor store. The loan was subsequently repaid by Worley, borrowing on his credit card.

Later Worley made a futile attempt to appeal to the widow's conscience by claiming to have cancer. When this failed, he threatened to abandon the project. 'To date,' he wrote, 'I have lost nearly fifty thousand dollars chasing a rainbow with a pot of gold at the end of it. I cannot go any further. It will take me two years to recover from this, and I will probably be dead by then.' The widow reassured him that all was progressing according to plan and that soon he would get his money. However, further fees of $13,000 were required to help complete the task. Worley found the money and wired it to Nigeria.

In April 2002 Worley wrote, 'I must stop this financial torment and anguish and pray that God forgives me for my pursuit of money, simply put, greed.' Communications with the scammers ceased until an unsolicited fax arrived in his office in September 2002. It was in the name of Mercy Nduka, a 'confidential secretary' at the Central Bank of Nigeria. She claimed to be secretly working with the Abacha family and wished him to know that a fund of $45 million was waiting for him to facilitate its release. First, however, she needed $500,000 to bribe five Nigerian bank officials and an additional $85,000 to cover fees. Since Worley was not in a position to meet these demands, Nduka and her boss, Usman Bello, claimed that they would borrow the money from investors. Worley's job was to receive and bank the investors' money, before transferring it to Nigeria. In return, he would get a share of the loot.

Before long Worley was receiving phone calls from alleged investors in New York and Washington demanding that he provide credit references and collateral for the loans they were about to make to him. The question of collateral was never an issue since he had none to offer. However, such demands convinced him that the callers were genuine on the basis that they were wishing to secure their investments. Worley was being cleverly groomed. He followed instructions, apparently without any moral or critical analysis. He received and lodged dubious cheques, transferred huge amounts to Latvian and Swiss bank accounts, and even wired $3,800 to buy a Rolex watch to bribe a bank official.

Unknown to Worley, a fellow American was also being scammed by the same source(s). Marcia Cartwright received an email in October 2002 from a man stating that he was desperate to get his money out of Nigeria. In January 2003 she received a cheque for almost $109,000, drawn on a Texas advertising firm's account. She deposited the cheque and, on instruction from her Nigerian correspondents, she sent $106,000 to Worley. Worley then transferred $100,000 to a Swiss bank account and sent the balance to Nduka for the purpose of bribing telex operators.

Meanwhile, the President of the Farmers & Merchants Banks, Booneville, Mississippi had learned that Cartwright's cheque was fraudulent and alerted federal and state officials. As the recipient of a large transfer from Cartwright,

Worley's bank account was also examined. Informed that he was being investigated for potential fraud, Worley sent frantic emails and made desperate phone calls to Nigeria, pleading for a replacement cheque. Nduka responded with the news that the fund would be released that Friday. All that was required, she told him, was another $1,000 to bribe a final telex operator. When Worley resisted, Nduka, skilled in knowing what buttons to push, informed him that she was an ordinary woman who struggled to survive on $400 a month. Worley sent her $1,000.

As the fraud investigation widened, Worley unleashed a torrent at Nduka:

I hate being taken advantage of by you evil bastards. This is all lies? Your day will come that you will be judged by God, and so will I. And I am ashamed, and shamed, and an embarrassment to my family, who are so precious and Godly people. What a terrible model of a Christian that I am. Thoughts of suicide are filling my mind, and I am full of rage at you despicable people. I hate living right now, and I want to die. My whole life is falling apart, my family, my ministry, my reputation and all that I have worked for all my life. Dear God, help me. I am so frightened.

It took four days for Nduka to respond. 'I am quite sympathetic about all your predicaments,' she wrote, 'but the truth is that we are at the final step and I am not willing to let go, especially with all these amounts of money that you say that you have to pay back.' All that she required was another $3,000, and the money would be theirs. 'You have to trust somebody at times like this,' she advised. 'I am waiting your response.'

Worley, however, was waiting to face charges of bank fraud, money laundering and possession of counterfeit cheques. He was tried in the US District Court in May 2005. All his correspondents disappeared without trace, having fleeced him for over $600,000. Their real identities and, indeed, their actual physical location outside cyberspace remain unknown.

State prosecutor Nadine Pellegrini scoffed at the suggestion that Worley had been simply scammed. She argued that he displayed 'wilful blindness' by ignoring clear warning signs of criminal intent. Defence lawyer Thomas Hoopes argued that Worley had shown 'blind trust' and described his client as a childlike man who had been tricked by sophisticated con artists. The jury found Worley guilty on all counts and US District Judge George O'Toole Jr sentenced him to two years in prison, plus restitution of nearly $600,000. Barbara Worley described the sentence as 'an atrocity', stating, 'My husband is the victim here.'

Zuckoff, interviewing Worley a week after the judgement, encountered a man who had not yet come to terms with reality. Worley told him, 'The communications that I had with those people were so convincing that I really believed that they were real, they were true. I would question them and they would come back with a response that was adequate to cover my concerns each and every time.' He still believed he had been communicating with the real Mohammed and Maryam Abacha, 'I think they were legitimately trying to use me and my resources to get their funds out of Nigeria into a safe place where they could have access to them.' However, he did suspect Nduka, 'Somehow there was a buyoff, a payoff, or something that went on there, and then it got switched to the point where I was then dealing with fraudsters.' He expressed the hope that the Abachas would get back in touch with him, primarily to help him make restitution for the $600,000 he owes.

On hearing these sentiments, Barbara asked her husband, 'If they sent you a cheque, would you put it in the bank to see if it cleared again?' He answered, 'Yeah.' In exasperation she exclaimed, 'John!' Sounding defeated, he eventually responded, 'I don't know. I have to have time to think about what I would do in that situation.' 'My husband is naive,' Barbara explained. 'He trusts people.'

Whatever the truth about Worley's motivation and character traits, his experience is insightful and his outburst at 'Mercy Nduka' in January 2003 was an eloquent summary of the intense gambit of emotions that scam victims can and do experience once they realise they have been swindled. Later in this chapter I summarise the distressing stories of four individuals who found those feelings too much to live with.

John Worley served 18 months. A Google search still gives his address as Groton, Massachusetts. However, having been released, he has relocated.

His case, however, has made Groton people alert to scams. On 14 June 2013, local newspaper, the GrotonHerald.com ran with the headline, "SCAM PATROL: Local, National & International Cheats Prey on Area Residents".

Recalling Worley's experience as "A Notorious Case in Groton", the article by Senior News Reporter, Connie Sartini, reports that Groton residents have been victimized recently "by telemarketing scam artists, especially targeting the financially strapped, lonely elderly."

Sartini reported Groton Police Chief, Donald Palma, who informed the newspaper that one elderly resident had repeatedly sent money order to scammers, believing money would be coming back to her. "It is estimated that she lost between US$12,000 and US$20,000 to the ruse".

The article did not specify the possible source of the scam nor does it give specifics as to what the scam was, but it has all the hallmarks of the Jamaican 'Montego Bay Scam'.

Montego Bay Scam
Jamaica's Montego Bay scam involves illicitly obtaining the personal data of US citizens and using it to con them into believing they have won a lottery. To

collect their supposed winnings, the victims are asked to pay a never-ending series of 'processing fees'. The lucrative nature of the scam came to light in 2005, when it became clear that several communities in the Montego Bay area of Jamaica were awash with cash. Investors in the area's information technology sector warned that the e-fraud aspect of the scam was having a negative impact on their business operations and could result in companies pulling out of Jamaica. Increased violence, including murder, was also associated with the scam network. The arrest of two police officers in late 2006 in connection with the scam further focused minds and galvanised an official response from the Jamaican authorities.

'Operation Kingfish' was launched in February 2007. Hundreds of police officers raided the Granville, Bogue Village and Westgate Hills communities in the Montego Bay area. A number of arrests were made and money, cars, phones, computers and documents were seized. Among the documents were lists of contact details for persons in the US. While Montego Bay remains the epicentre of the scam, investigations have extended to other parts of the island such as Kingston and Mandeville.

On 2 July 2008 The Kingston Chronicle reported that two people arrested by the Organised Crime Investigation Division had been charged under the Proceeds of Crime Act. Yowo Senhi Morle (27) and his mother, Hazel Clarke (48), faced charges of obtaining money by false pretences, conspiracy to defraud and engaging in transactions that involve criminal property. Morle, the newspaper reported, was one of the masterminds behind the lottery scam. He had significant assets and was found in possession of information indicating that several persons had fallen prey to his scams.

A new task force, which included US law-enforcement agents, was announced by the Jamaican authorities in 2008. It was hoped that its international composition would enable the police to bring people to justice in a much shorter time. Assistant Commissioner of Police, Les Green, stated, 'There are still many major players out there, but, hopefully, with this new task force, we will be able to bring them down. We have already several of these major players. Some are before the courts locally, while others have been extradited to the US and are facing the courts there.'

On 13 October 2008 the BBC reported that the lottery scam was contributing to rising crime and gang violence in Jamaica. Detectives informed the BBC that scammers particularly target US retirees, from whom they collect thousands of dollars per week via wire transfers to the island. Some of the money is used to buy high-calibre weapons and more than 1,200 people had already been murdered. Assistant Commissioner Green noted that the 'scammers won't go themselves to collect the money. They ask other people, and sometimes that doesn't come back so they order a robbery or hit.' Police admitted at the time that despite attempts to break it, the scamming ring remained active.

Indeed, a CBS News Special Report (March 12, 2013) on Jamaican Lottery scams" stated that complaints across the USA to the Federal Trade Commission about scams "jumped from 1,867 in 2007 to almost 29,229 in 2012." Federal Officials informed CBS News that the situation was actually worse as "far more are never even reported."

The CBS report confirmed BBC claims that the scammers were specifically targeting US retirees.

"It's one of the biggest scams targeting seniors in the U.S. right now", the CBS Special began. "Federal officials say "Jamaican lottery scams" are growing at an alarming rate, bilking the most vulnerable members of our population out of hundreds of millions of dollars a year."

A 79-year-old victim of the Jamacian scam, identified as "Dorothy", sent US$30,000 over a seven-month period. At the time she received her first phonecall Dorothy was struggling to help her family with medical bills. Her husband was preparing for a triple-bypass, her daughter had cancer, and a great-grandson was born three months premature.

Dorothy's is a classic case of how easy it is, at a vulnerable moment in life, to fall prey to such scams. As one looks at a deepening hole of debts and doubts the scam can appear like a desert mirage. "Eight point somethin' million dollars, plus I don't know how much in cash," she recalled being told by the caller heralding her big lottery win. "Maybe I wanted deep down to prove to my family that I could do something for them. I could help them. And he just sounded so convincing. So real."

And if the charm offensive begins to lose its effect, the scammers turn to vicious bullying. A recording left on Dorothy's answering machine in October 2012 agressively threatened: "Why you don't want to pick the fucking phone up. Pick the goddamn phone up and stop playing games with me. Want me to come over there and set your home on fire?"

Journalist Jeff Glor, onbehalf of CBS News, interviewed Doug Shadel, Senior State Director of Washington's American Association of Retired Persons. Shadel spoke of how relentless the scammers can be in their determination to make elderly people comply. "They will call 50 times a day, 300 times a week, until you give in. And the thing that's most worrisome to me," says Shadel, "is these are the most vulnerable people we have. They're 75- to 80-year-old seniors who are scared to death by these guys."

The horrendous sense of shame and loathing that victims often feel is demonstrated in Dorothy's concluding comment to CBS News, "I don't want nobody else hurt. He had guts enough to steal money from me. And I was foolish enough to do it. ... I pray that someday God will forgive me."

Nigerian 419 Fraud on a Massive Scale

Organisations as well as individuals are being defrauded. One of the biggest advance-fee scam carried out by a team led by Chief Emmanuel Nwude (a former director of Union Bank Nigeria), bilked a Brazilian bank, Banco Noroeste of Sao Paulo, of $242 million, causing it to collapse. Associated law suits were heard in Nigeria, Brazil, Hong Kong, Switzerland, the UK and the US, providing an insight into the global reach and complexity of this scam.

During a business trip to Nigeria, Brazilian banker Nelson Sakaguchi was introduced to Nwude, who was masquerading as the Governor of the Central Bank of Nigeria. Nwude claimed to have won a contract for the construction of Abuja International Airport and convinced Sakaguchi that it would be profitable for his bank to invest in the project, promising him a sweetener of $13 million in commission. Sakaguchi arranged for the transfer of funds from his bank to several corporate accounts controlled by Nwude and his accomplices. This was the first of many such transfers.

Eighty-six charges were brought against Nwude and his co-accused by Nigeria's Economic and Financial Crimes Commission (EFCC) in 2005. The figures involved are staggering. For example, one of the charges was that 'between the 2nd of April, 1995 and 20th of January, 1998 at Abuja [you obtained] the sum of $190,294,401.01 (one hundred and ninety million, two hundred and ninety four thousand, four hundred and one dollars and one cent) by false pretence from one Nelson Sakaguchi and Stanton Development Corporation which money belonged to Banco Noroeste S.A. of Sao Paulo, Brazil . . . purporting same to represent payment due to the Federal Government of Nigeria on the alleged contract . . . for the construction of Abuja International Airport . . .'.

It was a huge case for Nigeria, whose reputation as one of the world's most corrupt countries has been copper-fastened by the global reach of the 419 scams. President Olusegun Obasanjo (1999–2007) had promised to clean up Nigeria's government and civil service and to 'wage war against those who systematically destroy our economy'. He claimed there would 'be no hiding place for these criminals who tarnish Nigeria's image'. Many of the scammers had been flaunting their ill-gotten wealth, which included luxurious Nigerian homes and cars, European villas and a seemingly endless reservoir of currency. Treated by some as national heroes, they appeared to be immune from the law.

The EFCC was launched to tackle 419 scams, money laundering, drug trafficking, credit card fraud, bribery, smuggling, tax evasion, counterfeiting and intellectual property theft. Through it, Nigeria was anxious to show the international community that it was confronting the scammers. In its first year the commission arrested almost 200 suspected 419 kingpins, froze their bank accounts and seized more than $100 million in cars, homes, cash and other assets. A member of Nigeria's National Assembly was among those arrested.

The Brazilian bank scandal was the EFCC's highest profile case up to that point. Unofficially, the country's reputation was on trial. To emphasise its determination, the EFCC paraded the suspects, shackled in handcuffs, before the television cameras and members of the press. 'It was a massive, huge thing to do,' said Nuhu Ribadu, Executive Director of the EFCC. 'We don't have a culture of bringing people to justice, especially the rich and powerful.' These powerful and dangerous criminals did their best to stall the trial. For example, the defendants repeatedly changed counsel, evidence was tampered with, a witness was abducted and a court session was interrupted by a bomb scare.

The defence began to fall apart when Indian businessman Naresh Asnani testified against Chief Nwude, giving evidence of how he had assisted him to launder $127 million through banks in Nigeria and abroad. This was compounded by the evidence of star witness Nelson Sakaguchi, who was brought to court in a five-vehicle convoy of bulletproof jeeps and heavily armed mobile policemen.

One of the accused, Amaka Anajemba, pleaded guilty in return for leniency and the forfeiture of $48 million, including houses in Nigeria, the US and Switzerland. She was sentenced to two and a half years in prison. This development substantially weakened the increasingly desperate attempts of Nwude and his co-accused to avoid justice. Realising the game was up, they agreed to plead guilty in return for a lighter prison sentence. Credit for this victory must be given to the integrity and tenacity of the EFCC.

Delivering his judgement on 18 November, Justice Oyewole said the court must ensure that 'the financial element, which induces and motivates this class of offence . . . imposes sanctions that would signpost to society that crime does not pay and that certain conduct is simply not acceptable'. Nwude was sentenced to 25 years in prison and agreed to surrender $110 million to the affected bank and forfeit all his known assets, including property, cars, shares and money in various bank accounts. His companies also forfeited $11.5 million to the federal government, after which they were to fold. A co-accused, Nzeribe Edeh Okoli, was sentenced to twelve years in prison and forfeited all his property and assets.

What happened to Banco Noroeste is also symptomatic of the fault lines that exist throughout the international banking system, which have brought many economies in the Western World to the point of collapse. A system that allows one official, or a few, to siphon off and hide gargantuan sums of money that his bank was holding in trust, without the bank's internal systems or, more surprisingly, its external auditors noticing, or knowingly ignore, is deeply unethical. What is staggering in the Banco Noroeste case is the fact that the money was transferred over a four-year period for the construction of an airport that was never built.

Ireland and the fall of the Celtic Tiger

At the time of writing, Ireland is convulsing with its own banking crisis for very similar reasons. During the so-called 'Celtic Tiger', cosy cartels of bankers, auditors, property developers, senior civil servants and politicians, engaged in what initially appeared to be a beautiful ballet of fiscal fortitude which has turned out to be every bit a scam as the unsavoury activities outlined above.

Huge fortunes were made and lost by the unethical behaviour of bankers who, for a period, appeared to be given free rein until, that is, the wheels began to come off their blazing chariots. Seeing the impending crash, many moved to protect personal fortunes by shifting them offshore, placing assets in the names of others and, no doubt, paying homage to the expression "cash is king". And the really big fish, who have most to answer, ran away, leaving present and future generations burdened by the consequences of their greed and arrogance. And the consequences of their actions on individuals is every bit as devastating as the Nigerian or Jamaican scammers had on poor old Dorothy and other victims I write about below.

David Drumm, former head of Anglo Irish Bank, and one of the chief offenders, reacted to the public release of tape recordings which demonstrated his and other bankers contempt towards the Irish banking system and, ultimately, towards the Irish nation as a whole. Transcripts of the tapes, published in the Sunday Independent, Ireland's largest Sunday broadsheet, in June and July 2013, record Drumm and a colleague, John Bowe, laughing contemptuously as they consider breaking liquidity rules in order to falsely boost their crumbling bank's balance sheet.

In an interview with Irish State broadcaster, RTE, on July 7, 2013, Drumm complained about the 'drip, drip, drip' release of phone recordings and transcripts made at his bank in the Autumn of 2008.

"I am being made a scapegoat by politicians and politically connected former bankers and politically protected senior public servants," Drumm said. "These people do not want to see their role in the crisiss highlighted. A campaign of misinformation about the bank guarantee has been going on for several years and it has to stop if the public are to finally understand what happened."

Why would Drumm, who is now resident in the USA – far removed from the many financial traumas he helped inflict on the Irish people and economy – want to give such an interview to a public broadcaster? Is it not a shot across the bows of other powerful people in Ireland not to push the boat out too far, otherwise he will bring them all down by revealing the inner workings of a golden circle? If Mr. Drumm is so high minded and wishing to serve the public good by facilitating latent transparency, why is he not in Ireland assisting an ongoing police investigation, knowing as he does, that he is a key witness whom the police wish to interview?

In the decade when the Republic of Ireland will commemorate the 100th anniversary of the 1916 Rising which lead to its Indepence from Britian in 1921, Ireland is now, effectively, owned by foreign capital interest. According to the Irish National Debt Clock (www.nationaldebtclocks.org/debtclock/ireland), based on Irish Goverment data, Ireland's debt is over 143 billion and rising at a rate of 260 euros per second. For a small nation of less than four-and-a-half million citizens, these are staggering figures. Broken down, it equates to every citizen of the nation burdened with a debt of some 32,000 euros, and rising. It is a debt that will haunt generations to come. A debt that Drumm and his cohorts – Ireland's nouveau riche – significantly contributed towards, blinded by power, greed, arrogance and contempt.

Their actions, and the actions and omissions of "politically connected former bankers and politically protected senior public servants" were nothing short of treason, yet they have managed thus far to escape the rule of law, many of them retiring with inflated pensions and packages.

Below the surface there is a seething anger amongst affected citizens that has not yet found full expression. Citizens faced with increasing austerity measures, new taxes, diminished earnings and, due to the collapse of the property market, negative equity for dwellings that were over priced and often bought with 100% mortgages and bank loans that ignored warnings and indicators that the bubble was going to burst. And like all bubbles, when it burst it burst spectacularly, revealing a void of emptiness and nothingness that was readily filled by fear, anguish and depression.

People are hurting and are being plunged deeper and deeper into despair. According to the Central Statistics Office, suicides rose in 2011 by 7% on the previous year. Reacting to the increase, the President of the Irish Association of Suicidology, Dan Neville, commented, "The recession has had a huge impact on people's wellbeing. Those who lose their jobs experience a drastic reduction in their income or are in danger of losing their home experience a lot of anxiety, despair and depression. Relationship difficulties and marriage breakdown can follow on from that." Mr Neville also stated that the true figure for suicides would be higher when "undetermined" deaths were taken into account.

If Drumm is so concerned about his reputation and the interests of the public good, why doesn't he fully and unequivocally cooperate with an ongoing police investigation? Why doesn't he return to Ireland?

Comments left on the Irish American website 'Irish Central' are insightful as to how Irish immigrants and non-nationals reacted to Drumm's protestations. On July 8, 2013, the following reactions were recorded:

"Why is this unacceptable human being trying to justify his actions from his safe haven in the US? He needs to return to Ireland where he will have every opportunity to explain how and why he scammed the Regulator, the Central Bank, the useless politicians and why he ran away." (Username: pmoyni)

And on the same day, Angry Paddy wrote:

"Break this bank mafia/ political cartel the way they broke the mafia here in the US – long prison terms & huge fines – then watch the rats sing on one another and freeze their bank A/C until they can prove where they got the money... OR we could take the law into our own hands we know where they live."

Perhaps Ireland needs to learn from Nigeria and set up its own Economic and Financial Crimes Commission and parade Drumm and his cohorts, shackled in handcuffs, before the television cameras and members of the press.

The Scammers

Fortune Magazine published an article on 1 June 2006 in which journalist Leonard Lawal claimed that email scams were creating 'Yahoo! Millionaires'. Lawal wrote about a 14-year-old Nigerian scammer using the alias 'Akin'. He lives in Lagos with his mother, who earns $30 a month as a cleaner, and his father, who earns the same as a hustler at bus stations. 'But Akin has made it big working long days at Internet cafes and is now the main provider for his family and legions of relatives . . . He is one of a new generation of entrepreneurs that has emerged in this city of 15 million.'

Akin spends up to ten hours a day, seven days a week, at an Internet café in the Ikeja area of Lagos. There, using stolen credit cards, he buys laptops, BlackBerries, cameras and flat-screen TVs and has them delivered to safe houses in Europe. From there they are shipped to Lagos to be sold on the black market. The café, housing some 50 computers, is crowded most of the time with other teenagers who, like Akin, are working for a 'chairman' who buys the computer time and hires them to extract email addresses and credit card information from cyberspace. 'Akin's chairman,' states Lawal, 'who is computer illiterate, gets a 60 percent cut and reserves another 20 percent to pay off law enforcement officials who come around or teachers who complain when the boys cut school. That still puts plenty of cash in Akin's pocket.' A sign at the door of the café reads, 'We do not tolerate scams in this place. Do not use e-mail extractors or send multiple mails or hack credit cards. You will be handed over to the police. No 419 activity in this café.' 'The sign,' writes Lawal, 'is a joke; 419 activity . . . is a national pastime. There are no coherent laws relating to e-scams, the police are mostly computer illiterate, and penalties for financial crimes are light.'

Akin and his colleagues are involved in many online scams. The plots are varied and include tales of dying relatives and large sums of money in search of a safe haven. One popular fraud involves separating lonely men from their cash, and is often practised by boys pretending to be women. Fraudulent activities include MoneyGram interceptions, Western Union hijackings, cheque laundering and identity theft. When asked about his illegal behaviour, Akin answered, 'What do you want me to do? It is my God-given talent. Our politicians, they do their own; me, I'm doing my own. I feed my family – my sister, my mother, my popsie. Man must survive.'

Lagos lawyer Thomas Oli told Lawal, 'The deterrent factor is not there at all.' He cited the case of a former police inspector general who was convicted of stealing more than $100 million but was sentenced to just six months in jail. Lawal found that attempts to speak with Nigerian government officials about Internet crime were futile, 'They all claimed ignorance of such scams; some laughed it off as Western propaganda.' Some officials, who asked not to be identified, said young people are drawn into Internet crime as a way of getting back at a society that has no plans for them. Others see it as a form of reparation for the sins of the West. The article gave the last word to Akin, 'White people are too gullible. They are rich, and whatever I gyp them out of is small change to them.'

As my correspondence illustrates, scammers have no compassion for their victims and justify their crimes on the grounds that Westerners are rich because their countries stole from their former colonies. They portray their activities as just revenge, righting the wrongs of the past. Do not be fooled by this argument. The scammers do not use their ill-gotten gains to ease the suffering of their fellow countrymen and women. Rather, the scammers add to their suffering by feeding the perception, real and imagined, that corruption in these countries is endemic. Scammers are motivated by opportunities for personal gain and they do it because they are unlikely to be caught. It is probable that much of the money victims send to scammers is used to fund, as well as lavish lifestyles, other criminal activities, from robberies and assaults to human trafficking and murder.

Scammers are rarely punished. There are many reasons for this. Police forces do not have sufficient resources or expertise to investigate the large volume of scams and their efforts are therefore concentrated on those involving substantial sums of money. The cross-border nature of the crimes demands international co-operation between law-enforcement agencies and this can be slow and hampered by bureaucracy. The use of modern telecommunications and systems of money transfer makes it difficult to gather sufficient evidence to prosecute a suspect. In addition, corruption may result in scammers bribing their way out of the charges against them. As a result, scamming operations continue to expand. The hard work and perseverance of some police forces has resulted in high-profile arrests and prosecutions, however, these are few and far between. And when there is a clampdown in one area, the scammers often relocate their operations elsewhere. In reality, therefore, the consequences for the victims remain much more severe.

The Victims

Most of us think we are above being caught by an email scam. Indeed, we tend to label people who fall for such frauds as stupid or gullible. But, if you are honest, there probably has been an occasion when something opened up on your desktop that, for however brief a moment, made you wonder. One fairly convincing South African email arrived in my inbox a few years ago telling me I had won the lottery. I'm not ashamed to admit that my heart was beginning to rock until my brain introduced a few doubts. In fact it took a phone call to a trusted friend in Cape Town to put me right.

Scammers are very good at what they do and, sadly, people do get taken in and lives get ruined. Life circumstances can leave people particularly open to scams, not because they are naive or greedy, but because a combination of factors, such as ill health, fear for the future or immediate financial pressures, blurs their ability to think straight. At a moment of distress, worry or depression, a seemingly plausible email might appear like a cloud's silver lining or the answer to a prayer. Hence the need to remain vigilant and to do all that we can to frustrate the scammers until they realise their game is up.

The victims are often good, caring and intelligent people. They are in some way vulnerable and the scammers astutely identify and capitalise on that vulnerability. Some are hoodwinked into believing that their run of bad luck has changed. Some respond with compassion to heart-wrenching stories of strangers who are apparently in dire need. Unfortunately, their engagement with the scam often ends in personal tragedy. In addition to financial losses and debt, some victims have come to physical harm, including instances of kidnapping and murder. Many more are emotionally traumatised and must learn to cope with their feelings of guilt and shame. The five harrowing examples below demonstrate the horrific consequences of being caught in one of the downsides of the mesmerising World Wide Web.

Patricia Christine Sowens

I spoke to Rebecca Woodworth about her sister Patricia Christine (Chris) Sowens, who ended her life in 2006 after she was conned into believing she had won a European lottery. Rebecca told me that Chris, a university graduate, was very bright and energetic, a lover of art and writing, and full of life. However, following the death of their mother in 2003, Chris suffered from severe stress from which she developed shingles in her right eye. The condition deteriorated over a period of eighteen months and she almost lost her eye. Medical costs were diminishing her resources, which, in July 2005, amounted to around $400,000. Aged 55, and facing the approach of retirement, Chris began to feel desperate. Then Chris received an email saying she had won the European Lottery. 'She thought she was lucky,' Rebecca told me. 'Having sent back the information requested by the fraudsters, she was soon receiving very warm and friendly phone calls from a Mr Howard, allegedly calling from the Netherlands.'

When Chris's home was damaged by Hurricane Katrina, she and her cats were invited to stay with Rebecca's family in the city of Hammond, about 70 miles northwest of New Orleans. Rebecca recalls answering the phone to Howard, who sometimes called on a daily basis to speak with Chris to enquire how she was doing and about her health. Through these phone calls Rebecca learned of her sister's 'business' relationship with him.

Chris received an initial cheque from Howard as part of her winnings. However, she had to return this to cover fees and 'bureaucratic difficulties' that needed immediate attention. Before long Howard convinced her to start sending her own money. Two days before she committed suicide, Chris's bank accounts were empty. Over $400,000 was gone. She realised that her life savings had been stolen by strangers who had feigned genuine care and affection but whose only real interest had been fleecing her. Theft and betrayal of trust, along with the growing sense of shame and guilt, were too heavy a burden to bear.

Rebecca shared her sister's 35-page suicide note with me. It is a harrowing farewell to family and loved ones, burdened with a sense of stolen hope. Howard, whoever and wherever he is, bears enormous responsibility for her death.

My dear family,

I love you all.

I'm writing now, while I'm at Becky's because I still have some money and I'm not living alone. The pain is blazing and along with the anxiety/ panic makes it difficult to function but I find I have periods without pain – an unbelievable blessing. I try to follow my daily routine . . .

The key is to avoid shame and guilt. This has not gone well. It has taken me a long time to get my mental health under control. In fact, I need more time. And it costs a lot to keep me in medications . . .

The worst thing is that now that I know I have almost no more time I'm lying to you all. But I have to not give in to guilt. Or shame.

Incidentally, I need to work on anger – as you all will when I die, I'm sorry. Anger can lead to depression and, right now, to despair . . .

I should get the shame part out of the way as quickly as possible. Right now it seems unreal. I fell for an email lottery 419 Fraud Scam – the advance fee scam. I know about it now because my bank recovered some money from an account that has been flagged for 419 Fraud. So I looked it up.

Why.

. . .

I could make a list of choices and give the reasons but that's for a later time. Slow painful work. I'll do it if I can, probably one at a time. I know I owe you guys that. And it may help with your anger.

The combination of good luck and bad choices is a deadly one. And I had hope. And I believed in people. And then my original contact had a good grasp of the use of unnecessary detail, like being happy they had a winner from the Fiji Islands . . .

The key is to do the next thing in front of you.

There's a Japanese (?) Buddhist (?) saying

"Before I was enlightened I chopped wood and carried water. Now that I'm enlightened I chop wood and carry water."

I realise that this does not yet address the concerns that will most interest you but I have to take it as it comes . . .

I love you Becky and I believe in you. I wish I could stick around to support and enjoy you for years. Instead, I fear the loss of your support. I fear leaving your house. I wish I could lean on your laughter until the last day. Instead, I silence your laughter . . .

Please don't be angry with me.

Please don't lose a job over me . . .

Don't let the family assume you'll clean up my mess after I'm gone. You can't afford the time or negative energy. The landlords can clear the house . . .

Referring again to her experience with the advance-fee scam, Chris wrote:

All of this second guessing ignores the horror of my actual state of mind – the fear, insecurity, panic, dullness and confusion. The key is to avoid shame and guilt. This has not gone well. I don't want to leave. I want to live.

A beautiful life had been ruined by ruthless gangsters for whom life has little value other than what they can wrench, literally, from innocents abroad. Unfortunately, Patricia Sowens' suicide is not an isolated incident.

Leslie Fountain

On 30 January 2004 BBC News reported the findings of the coroner's inquest at Shire Hall, Cambridge, England, into the death of Mr Leslie Fountain, a senior technician at Anglia Polytechnic University. Dr Colin Lattimore, Deputy Coroner, recorded a verdict of suicide and said, 'Mr Fountain killed himself while suffering from depression, caused by what would have been good news but turned out to be very bad news.'

Police informed the inquest that Fountain had fallen for an Internet lottery scam run from Amsterdam, and being investigated by Interpol. The scam involved targeting Internet users and informing them they had won the lottery. When the winners supplied their bank details to enable the transfer of funds, those details were instead used to launder money. Fountain was told he had won $1.2 million in the lottery. He had tried and failed to access his winnings through the Internet. Realising that he was the victim of a scam, his frustration turned to depression.

On the morning of his death, he bought a can of petrol and left a message for his wife, Roberta, stating he could no longer handle the situation. His badly burned corpse was found in a field in Fen Ditton, Cambridgeshire on 18 November 2003, his 48th birthday. Dr Lattimore concluded the inquest with the warning, 'Anyone who gets an email saying they have won lots of money like this should ignore it and never pass on their bank details. If it sounds too good to be true, it probably is.'

Jaiyue Wang

In May 2008 Nottingham Coroner, Dr Nigel Chapman, described the death of Jaiyue Wang, a 23-year-old student from Hainan, China, as a tragedy. He stated, 'A young university student who doesn't speak very much English, whose parents don't speak English, who travelled to one of the great Universities [of England], has taken her own life because of a scam from Nigeria.'

Ms Wang arrived in England in the summer of 2007 to study law at the University of Nottingham. Shortly after her arrival, she received an email informing her that she had won £500,000 in an Internet lottery. Having been persuaded to send more than £6,000 in fees to release her winnings, the student realised that she had been defrauded. The following April she was found hanged at her residence in Beeston, Nottingham. A spokesman for the university, Jonathan Ray, described it as 'a despicable exploitation of a vulnerable person'.

Ann Mowle

On 1 November 2007 the body of 72-year-old Ann Mowle, a grandmother from Monroe, New Jersey, was found by fishermen amongst rocks, close to a jetty at Spring Lake, New Jersey. Mowle had committed suicide after what her family described as a 'vicious year-long con'. The day before, having donated her clothes to charity and left her dog, Molly, with a groomer, she drove to the spot where her parents' ashes had, years earlier, been sprinkled with deep love and affection. It was there she chose to end her torment.

Mowle fell for a Montego Bay lottery scam that claimed she had won $2.5 million. She received an initial letter, delivering the good news, in October 2006. In order to collect the jackpot, she would have to pay $18,000 in fees. She duly sent the money to Jamaica. After this, she was the recipient of relentless phone calls from the scammers, who convinced her to send more money in order to have her winnings released. In total, she handed over her entire life savings of $248,000.

This outgoing and caring woman, described by relatives as alert and competent, was so embarrassed and distraught at her predicament that she became a virtual recluse in the final months of her life. She refused to leave her home for fear of missing the elusive phone call with the good news that her winnings had, at last, been released. 'You're not talking about a gullible person,' her daughter, JoAnn Trivisonno, told journalist Tom Haydon of The Star Ledger, New Jersey. 'You're talking about a fearless woman.' Trivisonno then offered a sober warning, 'If this could happen to her, it could happen to anyone.'

Mowle was a college graduate who majored in business and worked hard all her life to raise three children as a single parent. She was a bookkeeper at Princeton University and her professional training meant that she kept meticulous records of every transaction she entered into with her fraudsters. These documents recorded over 50 wire transfers, ranging from $158 to $4,750, to addresses in Jamaica between October 2006 and June 2007. Her records included names and telephone numbers.

By late 2006 Ann Mowle was becoming suspicious and contacted her local police department at Monroe, New Jersey. She also contacted the US postal service, which dispatched investigators to her home in early 2007. Her records show, however, that she continued to wire money to Jamaica. Unable to trace and prosecute Mowle's swindlers, the authorities advised her family to intervene in an effort to convince her that her stalkers were only interested in deception and theft. The family told her to forget about the money.

Mowle communicated her suspicions to the scammers, who were calling her on a daily basis, sometimes as often as twelve times a day. Fearful of losing her, they schemed to turn the tables on her. Soon she was receiving calls from fraudsters masquerading as police investigators, government officials, lawyers and 'better business bureau' representatives from Jamaica. Not surprisingly, these services required advance fees to help her regain her stolen money. In desperation, the pensioner responded to their demands. Eventually, her bank account ran out and with it her will to live.

On 7 November 2007 Trivisonno arrived at her mother's home to prepare for her funeral. The telephone rang and she allowed it to go to the answering machine. It was a call from Jamaica, one of many messages left by her mother's tormenters in the days after her death.

Philip Hunt
Philip Hunt was a 58-year-old divorcee from Grimsby, England, when he met what he thought was a beautiful young white brunnett on an Internet dating site who convinced him that she was rich and needed his help in transferring US$2.9 million from Nigeria to the UK. Once the transaction had been completed, they would start a new life together. For Philip, it seemed the answer to his prayers. Sadly, he was being drawn into a web of deceit that

would ultimately claim his life.

According to his ex-girlfriend of three years, Lesley Smith, Hunt, who worked as a cargo officer with a shipping company, was a quiet, reserved and intelligent man. "Which", she told the Inquest into his death, "makes it all the more unbelievable that he fell for this, but he was at a low ebb and they got him when he was most vulnerable.'

As the 'love' relationship developed with his illusionary girlfriend 'Rose', Hunt lost control of his critical faculties and became increasingly embroiled in a world of fantasy through an exchange of texts and emails.

To meet the demands of Rose, who feigned illness and all manner of challenges that needed his cash to resolve them, Philip Hunt remortgaged his home, borrowed from lenders, accumulated overdrafts and even asked his employer to advance him £25,000, later retracting the request and resigning from his job. He began wiring money in December 2008 and by the time he took his life, on August 13, 2009; he had transferred £82,000 to the scammers.

Lesley Smith warned Hunt that he was the subject of a scam but to no avail. On the day he ended his life by throwing himself in front of a train at Hassel, England, some 26 miles from his home, he wrote a text to 'Rose' but never sent it. It read, "I'm cold, lonely and depressed, I'm so lonely without you tonight. Going to meet my maker.."

Smith told the Inquest that in January 2009 he sent her a text saying, "There are amazing things happening in my life... He told me that this lady needed to come to England with this case of money to be able to convert it into usable money."

British Transport Police informed the Inquest that Philip Hunt, under instructions, retrieved a suitcase from London's City Airport and went to the nearby Travelogue where he met two 'agents' who appared to do magic before his eyes. Opening the case they showed him stacks of black and grey paper. One of the men sprayed a blank sheet of paper with a solution that appeared to turn the paper into a US$100 bill. They needed money to pay for the chemical solution which he supplied.

When police investigating Hunt's death went to his home they found a handwritten note which read: "I just can't take any more." He also left bundles of emails that outlined the scale of the fraud and another message that read: 'I have insurmountable debts and will take my own life.'

After the inquest, held at Hull, England, on February 1, 2010, Lesley Smith told reporters: 'These people are out to get people when they are very vulnerable, they are like vultures. I'd like to alert people to this so they can be aware and be cautious.'

A United Response

Internet scamming is ruining lives. It is also damaging the international reputations of countries such as Nigeria and Jamaica. And it is funding the other forms of criminal activity practised by those involved in scamming. Every effort, therefore, must be made to frustrate and ultimately stop the scammers. But how?

The three primary tools of Internet scammers are the Internet, mobile phones and money transfer companies. Action must begin with these three sectors.

Internet service providers, especially suppliers of free email accounts, must find more efficient ways of protecting their legitimate clients. They must make it easier to report scam emails and they must aggressively pinpoint the source of the offence and immediately shut it down.

Mobile phones are a critical resource for the scammers. They happily supply their mobile numbers, with no apparent fear of apprehension by the authorities. The days of purchasing mobile phones without linking them to a verifiable and legitimate address should be a thing of the past. Legislation must be tightened to ensure that every mobile phone purchased is traceable.

More can and must be done by companies engaged in the instant transfer of money around the world. Western Union, with over 510,000 agent locations globally, depends on consumer trust and confidence to maintain and develop its business. In an attempt to achieve this, its website has a dedicated section headed 'Consumer Protection', which seeks to inform readers about various types of scams that fraudsters use to relieve victims of their hard-earned cash (see Appendix 1). The latest Western Union Customer Protection advice is at the following link: http://www.westernunion.ie/ie/faq-consumer-protection.

The advice may be summarised as:
Never send money to a stranger using a money transfer service.
Beware of deals or opportunities that seem too good to be true.
Don't use money transfer services to pay for online auction purchases.
Never send money to pay for taxes or fees on foreign lottery winnings.
This advisory service is positive and good, but more is needed to frustrate and deter the scammers.

Perhaps money transfer companies could work closely with law enforcement agencies to bait scammers. In the Schranner scam, I orchestrated the transfer of £1 via Western Union, which the scammers went to collect. Tagging such a transfer to an established scammer would enable the authorities to very quickly identify the location of the scammers and their accomplices. Once transferred money has been collected and the correct information recorded, the location of the scammers will be known. A condition of granting, receiving or maintaining a Western Union or MoneyGram franchise might be the instalment of video surveillance equipment, which could assist local police to identify the culprits.

Banks also have a major role to play, particularly with advance-fee cheque frauds. Ordinary people have looked on, aghast, at recent revelations of malpractice and corruption in the insatiably greedy financial sector. Advance-fee frauds, such as the Brazilian bank scandal discussed in Chapter 7, also demonstrate the negligence of the banking system and the appalling failure of independent auditors. The banks appeared inept and irresponsible when I presented them with examples of email fraud involving one of their accounts. Whenever I got bank account details from the fraudsters I informed the relevant bank, but the response was far from satisfactory and, in the case of one major international bank, rude and dismissive. Banks must create a user-friendly system whereby scambaiters can pass on information about accounts being used for fraudulent purposes.

As the tragic John W. Worley case illustrated, banks accept and credit false cheques to the accounts of scam targets. With non-existent money temporarily added to their accounts, victims are then requested by the fraudsters to forward some or all of the money to a designated account in a foreign country. Victims have often asked their banks if it is okay to transfer the money and been told yes, simply because the money is appearing in their account. However, when eventually it is discovered that the cheque is fraudulent, banks are reluctant to accept responsibility, instead debiting the money from the account of the victim and perhaps leaving them in serious debt and facing interest fees. This represents a major flaw in the banking system. Banks have a responsibility to protect their customers and, in this electronic age of instant communications, they can and must be expected to do better. If necessary, a mandatory clearing period should be set.

Government officials and agencies also need to take action against scammers, including the enactment of tougher anti-fraud laws. Severe penalties should be levelled against Internet cafés and outlets that permit scamming to flourish.

The media, too, can play its part. For example, the scammers often want to create a relationship with their target via mobile phone. There is, therefore, ample room for radio talkshow hosts to develop that relationship on air, drawing out the scammer and allowing the public to hear how they wriggle, eel-like, in trying to sound plausible and deflect penetrating questions that might give their game away. Such exposés could be enormously entertaining as well as informative for the listenership.

Discovering the damage that fraudsters have done to innocent and vulnerable people filled me with a determination to fight back. I suggest that we should not automatically delete scam emails when we receive them. Each time we select 'delete' we act as valuable filters for the fraudsters. No doubt they have their scams down to a fine art and know, on average, what percentage of replies they can expect from every thousand or so emails they send out. Those who do respond, therefore, perhaps less than one per cent (accurate figures are not known), are the prime targets of the scam, and potential victims. What is clear is that scammers receive sufficient replies from the thousands of emails they flood the Internet with to make scamming a lucrative and, in some cases, full-time career.

Internet users might consider replying, as I have done, in order to frustrate the fraudsters by wasting their time. I seldom spent more than ten minutes on a reply to the various emails received (although I did get caught up in the fun of creative expression for longer spells on occasion). In many cases my responses took less than one minute to type and send. I was amazed at how long the scammers persevered with me. If thousands of other people start replying to such emails with the aim of scamming the scammers, the fraudulent system would collapse under the weight of the confusion it would create. The aim would be to protect the innocent, vulnerable and/or gullible target by making it impossible for the scammer to know who is a genuine target and who is a scambaiter.

If you decide to engage in scambaiting, set up a separate email account for that purpose only. Make sure you have good anti-virus software or use an Internet café. And, no matter how hard the scammers try to persuade you with their sad and often tragic tales, never forget that they are fraudsters. As you establish a connection or rapport with a scammer, there is a danger that your defences might weaken. Always remain alert to this possibility and never send money or supply any personal details. Do not be tempted to reveal your true identity when you reach the end of your chain of correspondence. And remember, the official advice is to simply delete and ignore the solicitations of the scammers who, least we forget, are criminals abusing the modern communications networks.

The memory of the tragic consequences of scamming on the vulnerable lives of Patricia Christine Sowens, Leslie Fountain, Jaiyue Wang, Anne Mowle and Peter Hunt should keep us focused and determined to destroy this abhorrent industry.

There is an active community on the Worldwide Web who energetically engage in working to frustrate the worldwide scamming network. Should you wish to become a 'scambaiter' you can learn a lot from these websites and others. A Google search will help you to find more but some sites worth consulting are the following:

www.fraudwatchers.org
www.thescambaiters.com
www.scamorama.com
www.419baiter.com

If you have received an email that you suspect to be a scam, the following website is worth consulting:
www.scamomatic.com

"Scam-O-Matic" collects scams emails from vigilant web users and logs them on its system so that potential victims can be alerted to the real intent of an unsolicited email that offers to brighten up your day with a rainbow and its illusory pot of gold. You simply cut and paste the contents of the email into the form provided on the site and it will instantly help you to determine if it is, or looks like, a known scam.

www.met.police.uk/docs/little_book_scam.pdf

This link will bring you to a 42-page book, produced by the UK's Metropolitian Police Service, entitled "The Little Book of Big Scams".
http://content.met.police.uk/Site/fraudalert

The Fraud Alert Site is a website maintained by the Metropolitian Police with up-to-date Fraud alerts for all manner of scams, "as a resource to assist in combating fraud and other economic crime, and to prevent you becoming a victim of crime".

And never forget the golden rule:

> If it sounds too good to be true, it probably is!

Appendix 1

Western Union Security Alerts to Customers (the following information is from Western Union, copied at the time of writing).

Consumer Fraud Awareness
Don't be a victim of a scam

Fraudsters are always coming up with new, creative ways to try to get your money. The best way to avoid being a victim is to be educated.

Learn more about these scams with these helpful articles, courtesy of Western Union.

- Watch Out for Lottery Fraud
- Buyer Beware
- It's No Accident
- Beware of Up-front Payments
- Millions Waiting to be Shared
- They've Found Your Dog
- "Dream" Job Only a Dream?
- When Easy Money Isn't Easy

SECURITY ALERT
Watch Out for Lottery Fraud

It sounds too good to be true. Out of the blue you receive a telephone call or e-mail message telling you that you are the lucky winner of a foreign lottery. It might be Canada. It could be Spain, or any of a host of other countries. You might have won hundreds-of-thousands, or even millions of dollars.

It sounds legitimate. The person on the other end of the line is a tax agent or a representative of some other government organization. The caller seems both reputable and sincere. He or she has answers to all your questions and is anxious to get the money to you as soon as possible. There's just one catch. In order for the caller to release the funds, you must first pay any taxes or fees associated with your winnings. Perhaps you hesitate at this point. But the caller is convincing. And after all, what is a few thousand dollars now, when you will receive millions in just days or weeks? The caller instructs you to send the taxes or fees using a money transfer service. It's fast, it's easy and it will enable them to get the money to you sooner. So you send the money. But wait. It seems that there are further fees that must be paid and you are instructed to send additional funds – again using a money transfer service. The calls continue until you are no longer able or willing to send the funds. Unfortunately, the lottery winnings are never received. You have been the victim of a scam.

Western Union takes the issue of consumer fraud very seriously. We value our consumers and know they work hard for their money. When our consumers lose by becoming the victim of fraud, we feel like we lose too. That's why we're working to create greater awareness of the various types of consumer fraud.

Lottery scams
Who falls victim to lottery scams? Sometimes it's the unsuspecting. Sometimes it's people down on their luck - people whose circumstances leave them willing to take a risk for a chance at a better life. Unfortunately, these risks seldom, if ever, pay off. Although law enforcement agencies work diligently to catch these criminals, consumers are rarely able to recoup their losses.

Here are a few tips to help prevent you from becoming the victim of a lottery scam:

- The Western Union Money Transfer service is a great way to send money to people you know and trust. We do not recommend using this service when sending money to a stranger or someone whose identity you can't verify.
- Legitimate organizations will not demand money before they award lottery winnings or other prizes.
- If you have a concern about a solicitation, talk to family members or an attorney or even local police before making the financial decision to send money for a lottery prize.
- Be aware that it is illegal for anyone from a foreign country to solicit lottery ticket sales in the United States.

Remember, if it sounds too good to be true, it probably is.

SECURITY ALERT
Buyer Beware

It's incredible. You've found an online auction seller who can offer you today's hottest item or that one-of-a-kind article you've been searching for at a bargain price. You are anxious to get the item right away and agree to send the payment in cash, using a money transfer service.

You think you are being cautious. You put the transaction in the name of your brother, intending to change the recipient's name to the auction seller's as soon as you receive your merchandise. Or perhaps you establish a test question believing that the recipient won't be able to pick up the transaction until you give the answer. The money is sent, but the item either doesn't arrive or is not what you were expecting. Unfortunately, the money has already been picked up. You've been a victim of online auction fraud.

Online auction fraud

Internet auctions are one of the hottest phenomena on the Web. They offer buyers a "virtual" flea market from which to choose an endless array of merchandise. No longer are you limited to shopping at your local mall. Now you can purchase goods and services from anywhere in the world, often at discounted prices. However, along with the benefits of online auctions, there is also risk.

Fraudulent sellers can disappear into cyberspace, leaving buyers with few remedies against
them. While Western Union isn't associated with these sellers, our consumers are sometimes the victims of their fraudulent activity. That's why we're sharing this important information with you.

Below are a few tips to prevent you from becoming a victim of online auction fraud:

- Remember, Western Union recommends against using the Western Union Money Transfer® service to pay for online auction purchases. It is important to note that Western Union does not offer any type of purchase protection or escrow service and is not responsible for the nonreceipt or quality of goods or services. Western Union is in the business of transferring funds from a sender to a receiver. We are not a collection or holding service.
- Be cautious if an online auction seller will only accept a money transfer. Most legitimate sellers will accept more than one form of payment.
- Be sure to check out any seller references or "feedback" before you make a purchase. Please remember, however, that seller references or "feedback" can be created and may be bogus.
- Remember that Western Union does not allow consumers to send money transfer transactions to fictitious names and doing so does not protect you. Criminals often have access to fraudulent identification, which can be very difficult to distinguish from legitimate IDs.
- Test questions are designed for use in an emergency situation when your receiver has lost his identification. They should never be used to delay payout of a transaction and are not intended as a form of protection when purchasing goods or services from a stranger.

Remember, if something sounds too good to be true, it probably is. Western Union takes the issue of consumer fraud very seriously. We value the consumers who use our services and know that they work hard for their money. When consumers lose by becoming victims of fraud, we feel like we lose too. That's why we're working to create greater awareness of the various types of consumer fraud.

SECURITY ALERT
It's No "Accident"

After failing to sell your bike through a local newspaper ad, you place an advertisement for your barely used, 1980 Harley-Davidson on a specialized web site. Just hours after placing the ad, you are contacted by a buyer claiming to specialize in purchasing quality used bikes to resell to collectors.

Everything appears legitimate. You even receive a cashier's check overnight. The only problem is that the check is written for $5,000 over the sale price. The buyer explains that there was some error and advises you to deposit the check and refund the overpayment using a money transfer service. In good faith, you transfer the overpayment and ship the merchandise.

Just over a week later, your bank informs you the check was fraudulent and, therefore, no funds have been deposited into your account. Unfortunately, the Harley-Davidson has already been sent, along with $5,000 in cash, leaving you without the bike, without the cash and without recourse.

Over-payment scam

This scam involves someone offering to buy an item you might be selling – usually a high-ticket item such as a motorcycle, a car or some type of specialized equipment. For some contrived reason, the buyer pays more than the asking price, often claiming that the over-payment was an accident or that it must be paid to a third party shipping agent. The scam is in the payment – typically a fraudulent cashier's check or money order.

The plan is to get you to send the difference before you realize that the check is a fraud. Because some banks will allow funds to be drawn before an item has cleared, you might not learn of the fraud until it is too late. When the payment is determined to be a fraud, the funds are withdrawn from your account. In this type of scam, you could possibly lose not only the amount of the "overpayment," but also the item you were selling.

If you suspect an over-payment scam, please review the following tips before sending a money transfer transaction:

- Remember, Western Union does not recommend using a money transfer service to send funds to someone you don't know.
- Be wary of a buyer who is anxious to complete a transaction immediately. Most buyers will spend time asking questions and negotiating a price.
- Check with your bank to find out how long it will take the check to clear. Remember, just because the bank has given you access to the funds, it does not mean the check has fully cleared.
- Wait until the check has cleared before sending the amount of the over-payment.

Remember the old adage: If a deal sounds too good to be true, it probably is. Western Union takes consumer fraud very seriously. We value our consumers and know that they work hard for their money. If they lose by becoming the victim of fraud, we feel like we lose too. That's why we're working to create greater awareness of the various types of consumer fraud. If you feel you have been the victim of fraud, please contact your Attorney General and/or local law enforcement.

SECURITY ALERT
Beware of Up-Front Payments

It's a sad situation. Maybe you are having a hard time financially. Perhaps you've lost your job or have been hit with unexpected expenses. But at least you've found a solution to the problem. You read an advertisement, either online or in the newspaper, offering loans to individuals regardless of current financial situation or credit history. Sure, the interest rates might be a bit high, but it will provide you with the help you need until you can get back on your feet again. You've spoken to the lender and provided all the information and you've been assured that your loan is approved. The only catch is that you have to provide the first two loan payments in advance as a show of good faith. You've been instructed to send the funds using a money transfer company. The lender promises that you will receive the full amount of the loan as soon as the payments are received.

Unfortunately, once you make the payments, you find that the telephone number to the lender has been disconnected. You are no longer able to reach anyone from the company and the promised loan never arrives. You've been the victim of the "Advanced Fee Loan" scam.

Advanced fee loan scam
"Bad credit? No credit? No problem." We've all seen the ads – offers of guaranteed loans regardless of financial history or credit problems. The offers are placed in reputable newspapers or online. They may appear to be from well-known and trustworthy companies. They appeal to hardworking people who have fallen on hard times and, unfortunately, they often take advantage of those who can least afford it.

While there are legitimate companies that specialize in loans to consumers with less than perfect credit, fraudulent loan scams are on the rise. Fraudulent lenders can appear very genuine. They know the right questions to ask and how to reassure suspicious consumers. However, fraudulent lenders will all have one thing in common – they will demand some form of payment or fee before the loan can be disbursed.

Below are a few ideas for avoiding advanced fee loan scams:

- Remember, Western Union does not recommend using a money transfer service to send money to someone you don't know or whose identity you can't verify.
- Be sure to research any potential lender carefully. One way to do this is to check with the local Better Business Bureau or Attorney General to see if there have been any complaints about the company.
- Remember that legitimate lenders will not require payment in advance for a loan you have not yet received. "You don't have to pay money to get money."
- Remember that sending money using a money transfer service is like handing over cash. Western Union is not associated with the lender or business in question and therefore can't guarantee the receipt or quality of the goods or services you are purchasing.

As always, if a deal sounds too good to be true, it probably is.
Western Union takes the issue of consumer fraud very seriously. We value our customers and know that they work hard for their money. When consumers lose by becoming the victim of fraud, we feel like we lose too. That's why we're working to create greater awareness of the various types of consumer fraud.

SECURITY ALERT
Millions Waiting to be Shared

It definitely seems odd. You receive an email from someone who claims to be a person of importance in a foreign country. They might claim to be the manager of a large bank, or perhaps a government official. They might even claim to be the wife of a deposed dictator. While the details vary, the basic message is this: somewhere in this foreign country there is a large sum of money just waiting to be shared.

The manager, official or wife is the only person who knows of the existence of this money – usually in the millions of dollars. However, for a variety of reasons he or she is not able to access it alone. What is needed is a decent, trustworthy person who is willing to provide information such as their name, address, passport number and bank account information. Once this information is received, the individual swears that he or she will deposit the full amount into your bank account and arrange to divide the money between the two of you. Your proposed take from this deal can be anything from 25 to 50 percent.Perhaps an official-looking check arrives and you are instructed to send a share back to your business partner through a money transfer service. Or you might be harassed for "Advance Fees" for lawyers or facilitators. Most likely, you will find that your bank account has been drained of funds or your identity stolen.

Scams such as this are at best fraudulent and at worst criminal. But it's important to remember that scam artists can be very creative and convincing. Consumers have been tricked into believing that these are legitimate transactions. They are, of course, another example of consumer fraud.

The "Nigeria scam"
Often referred to as the "Nigeria" scam - because the scam artists claim to reside there - this scam is actually perpetrated by unscrupulous individuals from all over the world. The important thing to remember is that there is no such thing as free money. If deals like this were legitimate, the individual would have no need to contact a stranger via the Internet. Certainly there would be thousands of people lining up for the opportunity to take part.

If you are contacted with an unsolicited financial "opportunity," you would do well to remember the following tips:

- Know with whom you are doing business with. Use extreme caution if approached by a stranger with a "once-in-a-lifetime" opportunity.
- Never provide confidential information such as your social security, credit card or bank account numbers to any person not affiliated with a legitimate business.
- Be wary of any "investment opportunity" that requires you to send money in advance via money transfer.
- If you believe a solicitation is fraudulent, contact your state Attorney General's office or local U.S. Secret Service Office.

As always, remember that if an offer sounds too good to be true, it probably is. Western Union takes the issue of consumer fraud very seriously. We value the consumers who use our services and know that they work hard for their money. When consumers lose by becoming victims of fraud, we feel like we lose too. That's why we're working to create greater awareness of the various types of consumer fraud.

SECURITY ALERT
They've Found Your Dog!

Recently, your beloved pet and best friend somehow managed to stray from home. Your dog (cat, bird or other family pet) has been missing for a few weeks and you've put up posters and placed advertisements seeking anyone who can help you locate your pet. Finally your perseverance has paid off. Your dog has been found!

It seems that the dog was wandering by the side of a highway and was picked up by a concerned truck driver. With a tight schedule to keep, the driver hadn't had time to search for the dog's owner and return him right away. So the dog is now with him on the other side of the country just waiting to come home. The driver describes the dog and provides enough information to be convincing.

The driver has offered to ship your pet home via an airline. He seems very caring and concerned. He isn't even looking for a reward. All he needs is the money to put the dog on the plane. Because he is on the road, he suggests that you send the money via a money transfer service. That way he can stay on schedule, receive the funds wherever he is and get the dog back home as soon as possible.

You send the money and wait anxiously at the airport. Unfortunately, your dog never arrives. In fact, the "concerned driver" was a con artist who never actually had the dog. You have been the victim of the Lost Pet scam.

Lost pet scam

As anyone with a four-legged friend can tell you, it's difficult when they are lost or injured. The Lost Pet scam is designed to prey on a consumer's emotions. Distraught over the loss of a beloved pet, consumers often post information including the pet's name, distinguishing marks and the area in which it was lost. Con artists use this information to convince a consumer that his pet has been found.

The scam may vary. Sometimes the individual may try to claim any reward offered as well as expenses to return the pet. He or she may claim that the animal has been injured and that they need money to pay for veterinary care before the pet can be returned. They may claim that someone they know has stolen the animal and that they can help you get it back – for a price.

The scammer may call back several times, inventing more and more expenses that must be paid to retrieve the animal.

As emotional as these situations are, it is important to use caution and common sense when dealing with anyone demanding money for the return of a pet. Below are a few ideas for avoiding lost pet scams:

- Ask yourself whether the information used to identify the pet was included in an advertisement or flyer. If so, use caution before sending funds to a stranger.
- Try to obtain information about the animal that was not posted publicly in order to be certain that the individual is, in fact, in possession of your pet.
- Contact local law enforcement to determine if other people in the area have been victims of a lost pet scam.

Remember, Western Union does not advise using money transfer services to send money to a stranger or someone whose identity you can't verify. Western Union takes the issue of consumer fraud very seriously. We value our consumers and know that they work hard for their money. When consumers lose by becoming the victim of fraud, we feel like we lose too. That's why we're working to create greater awareness of the many types of consumer fraud.

SECURITY ALERT
"Dream" Job Only a Dream?

It sounds like the perfect job. You've been job hunting for quite a while, but recently you came across an advertisement in your local newspaper for a great position aboard a cruise ship. You called the number provided and, after faxing your application or resume and participating in a brief telephone interview, you've been told you have the position.

You're sure that the offer is legitimate. After all, it was publicized in a reputable newspaper. The person on the phone sounded very professional and asked all the right questions. They even talked about pay and benefits. Surely this is the opportunity of a lifetime. All you have to do is wire a few hundred dollars to purchase your uniform and shoes.

Unfortunately, once the money has been wired, you find that the employment agency no longer returns your calls. You may even find that the phone number has been disconnected with no forwarding information left. When you contact the cruise line directly, you find that the company has never heard of the agency you spoke to and your dream job aboard the cruise ship does not exist. You've been the victim of a job scam.

Job scams
Anyone who has ever hunted for a job can tell you that it is often a long and frustrating process. Sometimes looking for work can seem to take more effort than working itself. That's why consumers are so likely to jump at the opportunity when the "perfect job" comes along.

Unfortunately, less than scrupulous individuals have come up with a way to take advantage of those seeking employment.

Job scams may vary. The "cruise ship" scam has appeared frequently, but this scam could apply to any type of job. The key is this; scam artists will always require some type of payment before employment can take place. It might be for uniforms or shoes. It could be an application fee or a fee for a security screening.

When the job of a lifetime comes along, it's only natural to want to take every possible step to quickly secure the position. But when asked to provide funds in advance, you should always take the time to do some homework and make sure the person or agency you are dealing with is legitimate. Below are a few ideas for avoiding a job scam:

• Always use caution when some type of payment is required in advance of employment. Most legitimate employers will not require advance payments for things like uniforms.

- Remember that Western Union advises against using money transfer when doing business with strangers or with someone whose identity you cannot absolutely verify.
- When dealing with an unfamiliar agency or company, take a moment to contact your Better Business Bureau to determine if the company is legitimate or if there have been recent complaints. A quick phone call may be all it takes to save your hard-earned money.
- If you have been the victim of a job scam, you should take a moment to advise both law enforcement and the newspaper that printed the employment advertisement. Doing so may not only help to catch a fraudster, but it may also prevent another unsuspecting individual from falling prey to such a scam.

Western Union takes the issue of consumer fraud very seriously. We value our consumers and know they work hard for their money. When consumers lose by becoming the victim of fraud, we feel like we lose too. That's why we're working to raise awareness of the various types of consumer fraud.

SECURITY ALERT
When Easy Money Isn't Easy

The offers sound tempting. "Work at home." "Just a few hours a day." "Earn up to ten percent commission." "No experience necessary."

Lured by these attractive promises, you might agree to work for a company transferring funds around the world. The process seems simple enough. You simply provide your bank account details so funds can be deposited into your account by the "employer." Then all you do is withdraw the funds, take a ten percent commission and transfer the balance to a third party via a money transfer service.

The company seems professional. They provide detailed information about the work to be performed and you might even be contacted by the company's human resources personnel. The money is to be transferred via a legitimate money transfer company, like Western Union, and you are provided with links to the Western Union® web site and details on how to send funds. You're instructed to tell anyone who asks that you are sending money to friends and family. The "employer" explains that this is simply to save the time and trouble of filling out extra forms that would be required if this was designated a corporate transaction.

Unfortunately, your "employer" is a criminal enterprise. By agreeing to send money for this "company," you are unknowingly participating in a money laundering crime and may be subject to prosecution by law enforcement.

Another version of the "job scam"
Unlike other job scams that require "employees" to pay for uniforms or processing fees in advance, this scam does not require you to invest any of your own money. Instead, you are unknowingly recruited to help move the proceeds of ill-gotten gain.

In order to cover their trail, these criminal organizations recruit unsuspecting individuals to act as "mules." As in the example above, these individuals receive money in their accounts and then transfer it to third parties using a money transfer service, making the culprits and the stolen funds more difficult to trace.

Here are a few tips for avoiding such a scenario:

- If you are asked to send money as part of your job or in response to a "work at home" advertisement, contact the Western Union Customer Service Center and ask for someone specializing in fraud (1-800-634-1311). Our fraud experts can often help you determine if a transaction is legitimate.
- Use caution when receiving an unsolicited offer that sounds too good to be true. While it's tempting to accept an offer that allows you to make good money for limited effort, such offers are usually fraudulent.
- Remember that Western Union advises consumers against using the money transfer service when doing business with strangers.
- If you are dealing with an unfamiliar agency or company, take a moment to contact your Better Business Bureau to determine if any complaints have been filed.
- Always be suspicious of an offer that instructs you on how to respond to questions by Western Union. Any time you are instructed to lie, chances are something is wrong.

Western Union takes the issue of consumer fraud very seriously. We value our consumers and know they work hard for their money. When consumers lose by becoming the victim of fraud, we feel like we lose too. That's why we're working to create greater awareness of the various types of consumer fraud.

Appendix 2

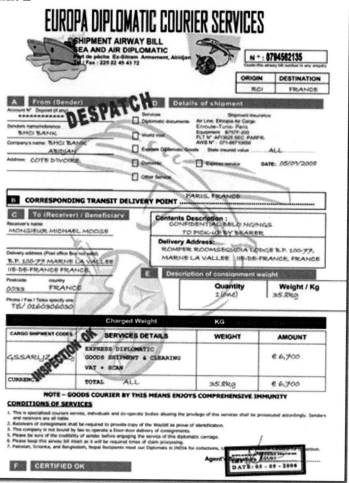

Appendix 3

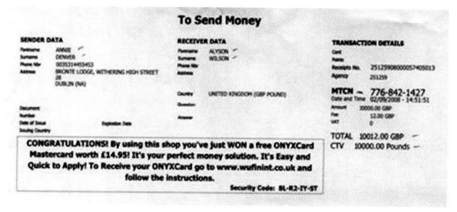

Lightning Source UK Ltd.
Milton Keynes UK
UKOW03f0359190314

228416UK00002B/2/P